Genres of Privacy in Postwar America

Post 45 Loren Glass and Kate Marshall, Editors
Post•45 Group, Editorial Committee

Genres of Privacy in Postwar America

Palmer Rampell

Stanford University Press
Stanford, California

Stanford University Press

Stanford, California

©2022 Palmer Rampell. All rights reserved.

An earlier version of chapter 2 first appeared in *ELH*, vol. 85, no. 1 (Spring 2018): 221–252, and is reprinted here with permission. Copyright © 2018 Johns Hopkins University Press.

Excerpts from chapter 4 appeared in a different form in *American Literature*, vol. 91, no. 1 (March 2019): 151–182. They are republished with the permission of Duke University Press.

Select quotes featured in chapter 1 are from Patricia Highsmith's unpublished Cahiers and her book manuscript "First-Person Novel" (1961), Patricia Highsmith Papers, Swiss Literary Archives, Bern, and are republished with the permission of Diogenes Verlag AG. Copyright © 1993 Diogenes Verlag AG Zürich, Switzerland. All rights reserved.

No part of this book may be reproduced or transmitted in any form or by any means, electronic or mechanical, including photocopying and recording, or in any information storage or retrieval system without the prior written permission of Stanford University Press.

Printed in the United States of America on acid-free, archival-quality paper

Library of Congress Cataloging-in-Publication Data
Names: Rampell, Palmer, author.
Title: Genres of privacy in postwar America / Palmer Rampell.
Other titles: Post 45.
Description: Stanford, California : Stanford University Press, 2022. | Series: Post·45 | Includes bibliographical references and index. |
Identifiers: LCCN 2021037161 (print) | LCCN 2021037162 (ebook) | ISBN 9781503629219 (cloth) | ISBN 9781503631892 (paperback) | ISBN 9781503631908 (ebook)
Subjects: LCSH: American fiction—20th century—History and criticism. | American fiction—20th century—Themes, motives. | Fiction genres—Themes, motives. | Privacy in literature.
Classification: LCC PS374.P647 R36 2022 (print) | LCC PS374.P647 (ebook) | DDC 813.009/353—dc23
LC record available at https://lccn.loc.gov/2021037161
LC ebook record available at https://lccn.loc.gov/2021037162

Cover design: Michel Vrana

Cover photo: iStock | cyano66

Typeset by Newgen North America in Minion Pro 10/15

For Kelly

Table of Contents

Introduction: Genres of Privacy   1

1 The Queer Art of Murder   18
2 Midcentury Black Cops   48
3 The Science Fiction of *Roe v. Wade*   75
4 Exorcising Child Abuse in the 1970s   101
5 Bury Me Not on the Lone Prairie   129
   Conclusion   163

Acknowledgments   173
Notes   175
Index   213

Genres of Privacy in Postwar America

INTRODUCTION
Genres of Privacy

A FLASH OF BLOOD on the balcony of the Capitol. A row of women in red cloaks and white hoods stood side by side. Armed police officers surrounded them. This was not a scene from a movie or book, though it may have seemed like one. In March 2017, pro-choice women began protesting laws restricting abortion by wearing the red gowns of *The Handmaid's Tale* to state capitols and in other public areas. In Washington, DC, and in Texas, Ohio, New Hampshire, Missouri, and even Ireland and Argentina, pro-choice women seized upon the red gowns as highly visible symbols of the way the new laws would collapse their individuality.[1] As Margaret Atwood's imagination come to life, the cloaks were blood-red, making the women all look like homogeneous uterine figures: "two-legged wombs" or "ambulatory chalices." The white hooded wings around their heads were designed to disguise their individuality: "to keep us from seeing but also from being seen."[2] The red cloaks worked especially well as symbols because their strong association with inherited generic forms threatened to flatten out the women's personhood. The costumes made the women look childlike—innocent Little Red Riding Hoods ("fairy-tale figures").[3] Or they could have been Scarlet Letter bearers (Atwood was inspired by Boston Puritans), their personality reduced beneath a sign of their gender. Or perhaps, fitting the title, they were transformed into types like the nameless Miller, Knight, Squire, and Nun's Priest in Chaucer's *Canterbury Tales*. As real-life women, they made the statement that they were stuck in yet another inherited genre—feminist dystopia.

Atwood did not want real-life women to be thought of as generic non-persons. She felt similarly about her fictional characters. As a writer, Atwood has been notoriously resistant to the category of science fiction, which she says is about "rockets, chemicals, and talking squids in outerspace."[4] She thinks of herself instead as writing "speculative fiction," which concerns real people in scenarios that could really happen.[5] But in spite of her dismissiveness toward genre, Atwood is far from the only genre writer in the period to imagine a productive tension between generic forms nominally populated by flattened characters and a political liberalism dedicated to protecting the distinctness (or roundness) of private individuals. In and out of the world of the text, characters in genre fiction—whether androids or criminals or Handmaids—are often thought of as less than people. As such, this book argues, genre fiction has been a particularly provocative place in which to consider the right to privacy, which, especially in the aftermath of *Roe v. Wade*, has often been understood as a right to define oneself as a person.[6] The red cloak of the Handmaid gave protesting women a readymade symbol to express the legal logic that tied privacy to abortion: without the right to control their own bodies, they were not being treated as people with distinct private lives and choices to make.

Genres of Privacy argues that Atwood's *The Handmaid's Tale* is only one of myriad instances of postwar genre fiction incisively engaging with the tensions surrounding the right to personal privacy. The constitutional right to privacy was legally enshrined in relationship to questions of sexual reproduction, as a right for a married couple to use contraception, in *Griswold v. Connecticut* (1965). But before and after its official legal establishment, legal scholars, judges, and everyday people thought about the right to privacy as the right to define oneself as a person, thereby encompassing other issues of personal autonomy and bodily freedom—like queer sexuality, police surveillance, abortion, child abuse, and euthanasia. This book shows how certain aesthetically ambitious genre writers—Patricia Highsmith, Chester Himes, Philip K. Dick, Octavia Butler, Stephen King, Cormac McCarthy, and many more—imagined each of these issues in their fiction, and in doing so, also reimagined their genres. Each chapter examines a different genre—villain-centered crime fiction, the police procedural, New Wave science fiction, mass-market horror, literary westerns—and shows how it developed through an engagement with an issue that fell under the penumbra of the right to privacy. Precisely because they did not write about people (or so their critics imagined), certain genre writers of the postwar era turned out to be particularly incisive in formulating ideas about the right to personal privacy.

To understand more fully why there should have been a deep relationship between the right to privacy and genre fiction, it is worth dilating on the two terms of my argument—first right to privacy, then genre fiction. The phrase "right to privacy" was coined by Samuel Warren and Louis Brandeis in their classic *Harvard Law Review* article, "The Right to Privacy" (1890), which was concerned with the invasive forces of "instantaneous photographs," a newly literate mass public, and yellow journalism. Brandeis and Warren claimed to have discovered the right to privacy within the common law, the collective body of cases reaching back hundreds of years in America and England, even though that right to privacy was never explicitly mentioned as such. But even Warren and Brandeis's original framing was inconsistent: their definition of the right to privacy oscillated between "the right to be let alone"—a freedom from interference—and "the right to an inviolate personality"—an ownership of the core aspects of one's very self.[7] By the early 1960s, most states recognized different types of privacy torts—like publicly disclosing embarrassing facts or appropriating a name or likeness—but privacy had not been established as a constitutional right.[8]

In fact, before the 1960s, even the legal concept of a "right" was comparatively limited in scope. Constitutional law was more concerned with federalism—the division of power between states and the federal government—than with civil liberties. While in 1933, only 9 percent of cases the Court heard dealt with civil rights and civil liberties, by 1971, that number had ballooned to 65 percent.[9] Over the course of the 1960s, society witnessed what constitutional scholars call a "rights revolution," a social movement that dramatically expanded the scope of civil liberties, leading to new freedoms for women, people of color, criminal defendants, prisoners, children, people with disabilities, the elderly, and other groups.[10] Rights became the lingua franca for argumentation about a just society (the Equal Rights Amendment, Miranda rights, the right to an abortion, the Civil Rights Act, etc.) and even spread throughout the broader culture so that people began to use the idea of a right to make extra-legal claims about private duties, obligations, and norms (i.e., what gives you the right?). Though the legal "rights revolution" was in practice composed of, and enabled by, many different movements and groups with diverse politics—civil rights activists, feminists, disability rights advocates, judges, nonprofits, foundations, a robust middle class with access to higher education—in retrospect, we can see that these different movements had a potent ideological vision at their core. First, the fundamental liberties enshrined in the Bill of Rights, and further developed in the 1965 Civil Rights Act, would be extended to as many groups as possible. Second, a right was not only a "trump" against government; it stood for a guarantee at the core of postwar American liberalism: the idea that people should, as much as possible, be allowed and empowered to pursue their own ends.

Because it was a right that was not explicitly written within the Constitution or Bill of Rights, the right to privacy stood, perhaps more than any other, for the way the idea of a "right" underwent a profound transformation in the postwar era. In 1965, the Court first established the right to privacy in *Griswold v. Connecticut,* in which the ACLU orchestrated a challenge to an old Connecticut law outlawing contraception that had not been enforced for many years. In deliberating, Chief Justice Earl Warren said that "basic rights are involved here—we are dealing with a confidential association, the most intimate in our life."[11] Justice Douglas, author of the opinion, had initially suggested that the case concerned freedom of assembly, but the Court ultimately chose privacy.[12] In Douglas's notoriously cryptic formulation, privacy could be found "emanat[ing]" out of the "penumbras" of the Bill of Rights.[13] There were aspects of the First Amendment (freedom of assembly), the Fourth Amendment (freedom from search and seizures), the Ninth Amendment (the possibility of unenumerated rights), and the Fourteenth Amendment (due process) that seemed to guarantee it, even if it wasn't explicitly enumerated as such. In that initial opinion, Justice Douglas, writing for the majority, described it as the right of a family, protecting "the intimate relation of husband and wife."[14] In *Katz v. United States* (1967), a landmark case that found warrantless federal eavesdropping in a phone booth unconstitutional under the Fourth Amendment, the Court ruled that the right to privacy was "left largely to the law of the individual States."[15] It was not until *Eisenstadt v. Baird* (1972), an abortion rights case preceding *Roe v. Wade,* that the Court spoke of the privacy right as the right of an individual "to be free from unwarranted governmental intrusion into matters so fundamentally affecting a person as the decision whether to bear or beget a child."[16]

When, in *Roe,* the Court protected early trimester abortion rights, its phrasing seemed designed to allow for ambiguity and expansion. "The right to privacy," the Court wrote, "is . . . broad enough to encompass a woman's decision whether or not to terminate her pregnancy."[17] It did not specifically enumerate the other activities that could be included under this "broad" right. As Mary Ziegler has shown, in the decades since *Roe,* different groups have cited it as providing precedent for claims about gay and lesbian rights, sex work, the treatment of mental illness, alternative medicine, and euthanasia.[18] The Court's rhetoric interpreting the decision in *Roe* has also grown more bombastic. In *Thornburgh v. American College of Obstetricians and Gynecologists* (1986), Justice John Paul Stevens described privacy not as a right to freedom from interference but as a right to "self-determination."[19] In *Planned Parenthood v. Casey* (1992), the Court explained privacy as "the right to define one's own concept of existence, of meaning, of the universe, and of the mystery of human life."[20] In the span of less than thirty years, the Court had gone from not recognizing a right to privacy to claiming it as a right to define not only oneself but also the meaning of the universe.[21]

Many have decried the right to privacy for being not only atextual and ahistorical but also contradictory or inadequate. The law professor Daniel Solove, who believes the term refers to several different types of violations, has chronicled a list of complaints lodged against privacy since *Griswold* as "exasperatingly vague and evanescent," "infected with pernicious ambiguities," and "engorged with various and distinct meanings," among others.[22] From the perspective of some on the Left, the focus on individual liberty cannot address systemic inequalities based on gender, race, or class. A woman's right to choose an abortion does not guarantee her access to one. The right to privacy has been used to shield marital rape and battery.[23] The imagination of privacy as heterosexual (and the corresponding regime of don't-ask-don't-tell) has denied queer people public legitimation.[24] The right to privacy has done little to protect people of color from a surveillance state, nor does it have much purchase on the poor who lack the privacy of the middle-class home.[25] For many on the Right, privacy is ahistorical and atextual, nowhere written in the Constitution. Conservatives frequently saw *Roe*'s right to privacy as celebrating working women over caregivers or homemakers and as shunting the unborn or those with disabilities to a place of lesser importance.[26] They viewed it as an anti-democratic, anti-familial attempt to impose a certain set of moral values on the rest of the population.[27]

Nonetheless, the idea that individuals should be empowered to pursue their own private idea of the good life was a powerful one, binding together groups with remarkably diverse political commitments: privacy could accommodate a midcentury liberal's commitment to political deliberation and reflection; the New Left anti-establishment emphasis on the realization of the authentic self; and the neoliberal sense of atomized individualism and personal responsibility in the 1970s and beyond. It was at the heart of the most celebrated text of postwar liberal political philosophy, John Rawls's *Theory of Justice*, which harked back to

Brandeis and Warren's peculiar notion of "inviolability" on the very first page: "Each person possesses an inviolability founded on justice that even the welfare of society as a whole cannot override."[28] For Rawls, the goal of a just society was not to maximize collective happiness, to foster civic debate, nor to ensure the spread of a given culture or religion, but to put fair procedures in place so that individuals could pursue their own visions of the good life—to enable private choice. The new right to privacy may have been atextual, inconsistent, even incoherent, but it also stood for the basic political promise of postwar liberalism: the freedom to make one's own choices, define one's own priorities, determine one's own affiliations, pursue one's own idea of the good. (This emphasis on individual choice was in contrast to the previous period's New Deal–era commitment to social solidarity.)

While classical liberals like Rawls were relatively inattentive to the distinctiveness of feminist, queer, or racial claims about justice, liberal activists and theorists imagined that privacy could be reformed to include women's claims to personal autonomy, LGBTQ rights, or rights for people of color.[29] Betty Friedan, for instance, adopted the autonomy argument implicit in *Roe* in speaking of a woman's right to an abortion as grounded in "the basic personhood and dignity of woman."[30] The National Organization for Women, ACLU's privacy project, and the Gay Liberation Front all drew on *Roe* to argue for recognition of women's and gay rights.[31] In arguing for aid to Black mothers addicted to drugs, the legal scholar Dorothy Roberts imagined that privacy could stand not merely for a right to be left alone, but for the "affirmative duty of government to protect the individual's personhood from degradation and to facilitate the processes of choice and self-determination."[32] To some, privacy was inadequate and inconsistent; to others, it was the fulcrum by which to obtain legal recognition for new groups and new types of claims to personal autonomy.

The protean right to privacy was thus central to what many in the period imagined as the just society, even as it was also incoherent, constitutionally atextual, and sustained by different groups with conflicting ideologies and priorities. As such, analyzing the explicit letter of the law will take us only so far in understanding the evolution of the idea of privacy. To comprehend how the Court could go from not recognizing a constitutional right to privacy in the early 1960s to claiming, in 1992, that the right to privacy entailed the right to define one's conception of the universe, we need to look not only at the texts of the

Court's decisions surrounding privacy, the legislation, and the legal arguments, but to the culture surrounding all of these—the powerful discourse surrounding the law that Mary Ann Glendon calls "rights talk."[33] Many scholars have shown how the culture of the Cold War framed American individualism against privacy-destroying communism and totalitarianism.[34] More recently, Sarah Igo has extended that logic beyond the Cold War framing, demonstrating that a bevy of new cultural artifacts, sociological structures, and media technologies—suburban architectures, personality testing, mass media, computer databanks, science fiction, and spy movies—gave rise to the overwhelming sense that a long-cherished right to privacy was disappearing.[35] Privacy can be found in legislative history or judicial opinions, but it can also be found on the news, in literature or film, in architecture and advertising. When faced with new issues of privacy, Supreme Court justices and legislators often find themselves referring to works like *Nineteen Eighty-Four*, *2001: A Space Odyssey*, or more recently, *The Hunger Games* to justify their claims.[36] Culture was the medium on which the right to privacy developed, the invisible ether through which it propagated.

Certain authors of postwar genre fiction turned out to be particularly insightful about privacy primarily because of a confluence of three factors: a semi-marginalized position in a literary field oriented around the private person, aesthetic ambition, and inherited anti-realist and illiberal forms. While the law of privacy expressed the evolving vision of postwar liberalism—that every person should be entitled to define their idea of the good life—literary critics and novelists imagined literature as playing a particular role in the definition of that vision. Literature, by which they most often meant realist literary fiction, enabled people to understand the multifariousness of the ways that people choose to live their lives. Literature encouraged private reflection and cultivated an appreciation for private choice. A long line of influential critics—Lionel Trilling, Ian Watt, Lynn Hunt, Jürgen Habermas, Martha Nussbaum—have connected the reading of novels with the development of the private individual in a tradition that stretches back to the birth of eighteenth-century liberalism.[37] Novel reading, the argument goes, helped people orient themselves to a new mode of life in which individuals had distinct personalities, private lives, and private selves. Personal identity was no longer subsumed in relationship to the church or the aristocracy; distinct individuals, nurtured into being by the private spaces of the home and the family, were positioned in contradistinction to the public spaces of the market, the government, or the town. Novel reading was not only designed to take place in these new private spaces, but it also provided models of individual character and private interiority that individuals could use to shape their newfound individualities. It taught people to imagine and understand the private lives of others different from them.

Authors of literary fiction took up the mantle of defending liberal privacy and personhood, announcing their project as rescuing the private person from the homogenizing forces of mass culture and the marketplace. The liberal political vision of the period—in which people were rational, deliberative citizens who determined their own priorities—was uneasily married to the commercial culture of the marketplace—in which people were desirous consumers. Literary writers saw themselves as protecting the deliberators from devolving into the consumers. In an article for *Harper's* entitled "On Privacy" (1955), William Faulkner wrote that without privacy a person would become one "identityless integer in that identityless anonymous unprivacied mass." Defining himself against the mass media of advertising, film, and radio, the true artist counteracts these forces; he represents "the private individual human spirit."[38] David Foster Wallace similarly imagined his fiction decades later as depicting the fundamental qualities of what it meant to be human. He said something similar to Faulkner but added an expletive: "Fiction's about what it is to be a fucking *human being*."[39] Like Faulkner, Wallace imagined "commercial art" culture as infantilizing, training a reader to be "childish" and lazy. In Wallace's view, while fiction writers were particularly and acutely conscious of the distinction between public and private life, television was most insidious when it provided the fantasy of unmediated voyeurism, that "we're transcending privacy."[40] In other essays, Jonathan Franzen waxed nostalgic for the "distinction between public and private," and Richard Powers missed the possibility of "a life lived off the record."[41]

For certain literary novelists as well as critics like Edmund Wilson and Dwight Macdonald, an individualized capacity for self-expression and reflection was the hallmark of the private person; genre fiction, by contrast, was "not about people at all," fucking or otherwise.[42] Mark McGurl described the literary fiction of the creative writing program as defining itself against "the machine-made quality of genre fiction."[43] Wilson claimed that neither the stock villain nor the stock hero of detective fiction was "a person like you or me."[44] Critics and theorists like Macdonald, Theodor Adorno, and Jürgen Habermas agreed that mass culture produces a slack-jawed mass subject, capable of neither thought nor action, but only of mindless consumption and enjoyment—as if neither its characters nor its consumers could properly be called persons.

Certain writers of postwar genre fiction—like Patricia Highsmith, Philip K. Dick, Stephen King, and Larry McMurtry—were particularly attuned to the fault lines in the liberal imagination of privacy, in part because they were perceived as inveterate creatures of the marketplace that allegedly threatened to destroy it. Even so, they longed to be lifted out of that indifferentiable miasma of genre fiction and into the pantheon of literary fiction that explored private life. The fact that genre was being published in paperback form, alongside reprints of literary classics, brought its writers ever closer to the ideal of prestige, which their characters also approach by alluding to works of literary fiction and high art. Dick's androids sing Mozart's opera and look at Edvard Munch's paintings, McMurtry's cowboys read Milton and Virgil on the plains, and Highsmith's Tom Ripley quotes from *Macbeth*. Through these allusions, their authors are staking their claims to be included in the tradition of literary fiction, showing their characters' capacity for distinctive self-expression by their relationship to works of high art. As Andrew Hoberek and Nicholas Brown have shown, aesthetically ambitious genre fiction often experiences a divided allegiance between artistic autonomy and fixed or commodity form.[45] That tension between the desire to express oneself and a dependence on inherited forms made these authors particularly incisive thinkers about the right to privacy, which was newly understood in the period as a right to self-express or self-define.

While they may have aspired to transcend their position in the literary field, genre authors' proximity to the marketplace nonetheless put them in touch with the anxieties, fears, and desires that percolated underneath the seemingly serene exteriors of postwar America—and which often pivoted around questions of privacy, questions like: Do I have full control of my own body? Are children in my neighborhood being abused? Will the police arrest me because of how I look to them on the street? If liberalism celebrated private, reflective individuals capable of distancing themselves from the market, certain creative genre writers figured out how to use those qualities that the marketplace demanded and that critics abhorred—flat characters, a desire to witness spectacle, repetitive plotlines—to comment on the ways the promises of liberalism were incoherent or else unfulfilled. They showed how certain types of people or behaviors deserved to be included in its schema; they revealed that emotions like fear could prove more powerful than rational deliberation; they grappled with privacy's adequacy to address economic inequality.

The particular forms genre writers inherited had, in fact, been conceived in skeptical or anxious response to the originary split in eighteenth- and nineteenth-century liberalism between public and private life. Many of genre's urtexts—like Mary Shelley's *Frankenstein*, Edgar Allan Poe's Dupin stories, James Fenimore Cooper's novels, Samuel Richardson's *Pamela*, Horace Walpole's *The Castle of Otranto*—were specifically designed to approach questions of privacy.[46] Shelley wondered who and what counted as a private person; Poe incited fears about people or creatures who refused to govern themselves in private according to Kantian moral law; Cooper nostalgically looked back to the private moral codes that existed before the existence of the public state; Richardson dramatized anxieties about the dangers of women exercising their choice in private bedrooms; Gothic novelists represented fears about violence in the privacy of the home. The lawlike qualities of genre fiction—its repetitive, reiterated plotlines—enabled its authors to adapt these old responses to liberalism to newly salient legal issues surrounding privacy. This book extends Theodore Martin's argument that genre writers renovate inherited forms to craft their own shrewd and canny responses to their period—in this case applying them to postwar debates about privacy.[47] Science fiction writers turned to *Frankenstein*, a created-monster story allegorizing pregnancy, to write about abortion; horror novelists recast the Gothic haunted house narrative to address the newly salient issue of child abuse.[48]

While liberalism was dedicated to the preservation and cultivation of individual distinctness (or roundness), the forms genre writers inherited were often populated with flat characters. By flatness, I partly refer to E. M. Forster's idea that a "flat" character is a "type" or "caricature"; it has "no pleasures, none of the private lusts and aches," "the incalculability of life" that we would typically associate with a "round" character.[49] Flat characters, as Forster noted, could appear in realist fiction, too, especially as scaffolding for the round ones, and not all genre characters (e.g. Tom Ripley) can adequately be described as flat. But whereas realist round characters and settings often reinforced the inexorability of middle-class private life, genre's flat characters—its monsters or androids or villains—threatened the consistency and stability of that way of life. They harked back to older, anti-realist modes of characterization—like allegory, melodrama, or romance—that inscribed the individual in explicit relationship to a larger social order.[50] Genre's characters were rarely used in the service of providing an ever-more accurate phenomenological depiction of one person's private experience. Genre authors instead used their tropes—villains, monsters, androids, and cowboys—to explore the social structures that produced them, both those within the narrative (e.g., the police state, heteronormative culture) and outside of it (a literary marketplace that demanded such characters).

A key finding of this book is thus that a good deal of sophisticated genre fiction can be read, like Atwood's *Handmaid's Tale*, as a double allegory, its tropes representing both political and literary personhood. At the same time that they allegorized an issue of privacy like child abuse or abortion, genre authors also commented on how their characters and fictions were perceived in the literary field. The urtext for this kind of allegory is *Frankenstein*: while the creation of Frankenstein's monster can represent what it feels like to give birth to an unwanted or miscarried child, it can also be read as a story of female literary production.[51] Haunted houses in Poe and Hawthorne express an anxiety both about titles to private property and about venturing into the publicity of the literary marketplace.[52] In the postwar era, Chester Himes imagined the ambivalence of his Black cops, charged with surveilling the population of Harlem, as mirroring the author's ambivalence about representing African American life in crime fiction. For Philip K. Dick and Octavia Butler, the android and the alien stood for fetuses or newborns; at the same time, these tropes could represent science fiction's marginalized position in the literary field. Stephen King saw the haunted house both as a figure for the literary marketplace and for the political and legal systems that exacerbated child abuse. All imagined the historical and cultural forces shaping the literary field as continuous with the issues of private personhood they cared about.

At the same time, genre writers' investments in privacy discourse were not solely theoretical. If writers of a certain strand of aesthetically ambitious genre fiction were among privacy's foremost theorists, acutely attuned to the contradictions and inadequacies implied by the idea, the reason was not always that they were explicitly invested in debates about the law, but often because they were especially adept at displacing private moments into public mythographies. Rather than aspire toward ever-more realistic narration of the details of everyday life, they reassembled their personal experiences into a collage that resonated with many dealing with the same issues in their own lives. They expressed the emotions and concepts at stake in issues of privacy like abortion or child abuse or queer sexuality—not by narrating, in ever more realistic fidelity, the minute details of lived experience, but by taking private moments and experiences and recasting them in a powerful, allegorical public form. Thus, as we will see, Philip K. Dick expressed his anger about his wife's abortion by writing a story about a humanoid robot being murdered by a heartless woman, while Octavia Butler used alien parasites to narrate the hardship and terror of pregnancy. Chester Himes transformed his encounters with cops into his police procedurals. Stephen King refracted his abandonment by his father into a story about child abuse in a haunted house. Patricia Highsmith took the stigmatization she faced as a queer woman engaging in what was regarded as immoral, sociopathic behavior and wrote stories about Tom Ripley, an immoral yet sympathetic sociopath. Those genre writers who belonged to what we might call the upper middlebrow took subjects that could be sensitive, difficult to talk about or think about, and displaced them into an evocative genre form that dramatized the emotions or concepts or social structures involved in demarcating the boundaries of public and private. Genre authors transmuted moments in their own lives into their inherited, illiberal forms.

In rethinking the relationship between genre and privacy, this book also builds on and modifies the longstanding idea that literature's central value is that it helps us understand (or respect the alterity of) the private life of another. Because genre frequently imagines morality and politics as part and parcel of the marketplace, it rebuts the argument that fiction is a market commodity able to create noncommercial emotional connections among readers, characters, and writers.[53] This argument is rooted in eighteenth-century liberal philosophy, particularly that of Adam Smith, who imagined a liberalism that would counterbalance the pursuit of self-interest he described in *The Wealth of Nations* with the altruistic affect he outlined in *Theory of Moral Sentiments*. The idea that literature, in particular, should generate market-independent empathetic connections gets refracted through various intellectual trends and modes of expression whose purported antagonism masks an underlying consensus. For postwar liberals and New Ethicists alike, the imaginative encounter with a character's interior life generates a destabilizing alterity, which can help a reader to a better ethics. And yet, studies of literary ethics rarely deal with the fiction of the postwar era or with generic texts. The fact that Henry James, the consummate art novelist, should appear so prominently in the writing of the New Ethicists suggests that their data set is skewed toward the art novel.[54]

The authors here often could not imagine themselves as apart from the marketplace, nor could they position reading as cultivating empathy and self-reflection. Instead, they saw reading to understand the private life of another as resembling stalking and identity theft, racist police surveillance, or titillating horror films. The familiar tools of the New Ethics—an appeal to alterity or empathy—seem fundamentally inadequate to account for the political issues they took up in their fictions.[55] Those who celebrate fiction for its alterity-producing powers need to reckon with the fact that Dick attempted to use his fiction to acknowledge the alterity of the fetus. By contrast, Octavia Butler found that fiction was more politically efficacious when it dehumanized; she turned the human fetus into a parasite in her story "Bloodchild." Arguing for euthanasia, Charlotte Perkins Gilman tried to reduce empathy in her writing, imagining an old man as "a gross baby, a huge, brainless baby lying like a log in an unclean bed."[56] Neither appeals to empathy nor alterity can give us much traction in theorizing the ethical value of these fictions.

Genre is not a place to hone one's sense of Otherness or empathy; it is rather the dynamic space in which unresolved and perhaps unresolvable social contradictions and tensions are explored in new, powerful, and conflicting registers. Restoring historical specificity to the generic imagination also corrects an older view that genre is either fundamentally reactionary, providing imagined resolution to liberalism's insuperable contradictions, or else fundamentally subversive, celebrating Marxist or posthuman collectives.[57] Though genre fiction, with its flat persons, has often been orthogonal to a liberalism centered around the deep private interiority of the individual, the precise politics of genre's limited illiberalism is never predetermined. From the perspective of the contemporary Left, sometimes genre's challenges to liberalism and empathy discourse can look welcome, aligned with feminism, Marxism, queer theory, and disability studies. Genre writers often took up subjects who did not fit neatly in the neutral schema of liberalism, for whom the right to privacy seemed inadequate or incomplete: queer people, fetuses, pregnant women, people of color, children, people with disabilities, and the elderly. But equally often, close examination of generic texts reveals that writers whose politics initially appear progressive were quite reactionary in other respects—and in ways that trouble familiar pieties about the left-liberal politics and ethics of reading.

In the chapters that follow, I will proceed roughly chronologically, pairing key moments in the postwar history of privacy with certain practitioners of genre fiction, writing in the decades surrounding those moments and turning to privacy issues to reframe their genres. Thus, I match the right of privacy for heterosexual marital sex (*Griswold v. Connecticut* [1965]) with 1950s queer and proto-feminist crime fiction; the War on Poverty/War on Crime (1964–1970s) with 1950s and 1960s Black crime fiction; *Roe v. Wade* (1973) with 1960s and 1970s science fiction; the Child Abuse and Prevention Act (1974) with 1960s and 1970s horror; and the right to die (*In re. Quinlan* [1976], Oregon's Death with Dignity Act [1997], *Vacco v. Quill* [1997]) with almost a century of fiction encircling it, placing special emphasis on the westerns from the 1960s to *No Country for Old Men* (2005). The arguments for this structure are twofold. On the law/cultural history side, pairing salient moments of legislative or judicial history with fictional texts slightly removed from them in time shows that privacy has a strong cultural basis. Generic texts often explore key issues of privacy many years before the law takes up the very same issues. On the genre side, we see how certain practitioners of genre fiction, those with aspirations to literary merit, draw on issues in their own lives to reformulate their genres in striking ways, and how the issues they choose become integral to the period's understanding of privacy. Reading various genres in relationship to the historical moments they sprang from, we can see privacy's cultural evolution from a right to protecting heterosexual marriage to a more generalized right to personal autonomy to a right with a more narrowed focus on the atomized individual.

The first chapter, "The Queer Art of Murder," focuses on female writers of crime fiction in the decade prior to the establishment of a constitutional right to privacy in *Griswold v. Connecticut* as a right protecting heterosexual marriage. In the years leading up to *Griswold*, the right to privacy existed only as a generalized sense of anxiety about something that was vanishing—the individual, the family, the home, or the hearth. Liberal midcentury literary critics celebrated the reading of literary fiction precisely for its capacity to restore privacy: it was read in private; it contained accounts of private life; and it cultivated deeper, more reflective individuals better able to participate in public discourse. Female crime novelists writing about villains during roughly the same period, the late 1940s and

1950s (many years before the "personal" became the "political")—Patricia Highsmith, Dorothy Hughes, and Margaret Millar—instead imagined the traditional heterosexual "zones" of privacy as spaces of oppression. They saw the reading for empathy celebrated by liberals as having a good deal in common with stalking or identity theft. But they also believed that their crime fiction—which focused on outrageous, sympathetic villains—could give them a different kind of privacy: it was the ideal place to conceal taboo ideas about sexuality within public view.

The second chapter, "Midcentury Black Cops," analyzes why Chester Himes decided to write crime fiction about Black police officers surveilling the working-class community of Harlem. One way of telling the story of privacy is as a right that expanded throughout the 1960s and 1970s with *Griswold*, *Katz*, and *Roe*, but it has looked quite different for African Americans. Many found little refuge in the right to privacy as the War on Poverty and the War on Crime placed them under heightened state surveillance. Beginning his series in the mid-1950s, Himes came early to a version of this narrative, with his description of two brutal but heroic Black cops who surveilled the African American neighborhood of Harlem. In this chapter, I recover the history of the man who inspired the novels—Jess Kimbrough, a Marxist playwright, memoirist, and one of the earliest Black police officers in Los Angeles—where mass incarceration began decades earlier than in other cities. Tasked by his publisher with writing crime fiction for an audience that wanted to behold sleazy depictions of African American life, Himes saw a doubling between the ambivalent positions of the Black crime writer and cops like Kimbrough, both tasked with surveilling working-class Black life for a predominantly white establishment.

The third chapter, "The Science Fiction of *Roe v. Wade*," uncovers the way science fiction authors of the 1960s and 1970s reshaped their genre to respond to abortion. After *Griswold* and *Roe*, legal scholars, activists, and many in the public came to understand "the right to personal privacy" as a more generalized right to define oneself as a person. But who or what counted as a person, and what did people need to define themselves? Philip K. Dick, Octavia Butler, Kurt Vonnegut, Harlan Ellison, Ursula K. Le Guin, and James Tiptree, Jr. took various analogies establishing legal personhood—comparing fetuses to parasites or to slaves—in law, morality, and popular culture and used them as the starting premise for fictional worlds. It is a critical truism that science fiction has been invested in the philosophical question of what it means to be human or posthuman, but this chapter reveals that, since around 1960, its investigations of that question have been rooted in the abortion debates.

The end of the Great Society and the resurgence of political conservatism brought a backlash against the idea of privacy as autonomy or self-definition. How much autonomy was too much autonomy? The fourth chapter, "Exorcising Child Abuse in the 1970s," shows how horror novelists and filmmakers like Stephen King, Ira Levin, and William Peter Blatty exploited popular fears about child abuse shielded by middle- and upper-class privacy. In order to pass legislation to protect abused children in an era of family values and austerity politics, Senator Walter Mondale discounted statistics linking child abuse to class, arguing that, for wealthier families, privacy shielded the rampant abuse transpiring behind closed doors. Horror novels and films of the period tapped into the social anxieties Mondale stoked, imagining, in their demonic children and satanic families, the specter of abuse that had hitherto been concealed by the privacy of the home.

In Chapter 5, "Bury Me Not on the Lone Prairie," I trace a cultural history of euthanasia from Edith Wharton's long-neglected euthanasia novel, *The Fruit of the Tree* (1907) to Jodi Picoult's *Mercy* (1996), touching briefly on a variety of genres—social realism, science fiction, westerns, and romance. I argue that the western interceded at a decisive moment in the cultural history of the right to die. When citizens of the frontier state of Oregon legalized the right to die in the 1990s, they imagined it as the prerogative of the self-determining cowboy on the range. It wasn't always imagined this way. In the early part of the century, euthanasia's critics condemned it as the effete and cowardly surrender of a person who could not endure pain. In response, Wharton imagined the figure of the female professional nurse as ideally suited to carry out euthanasia because of her sensitivity to pain. In the ensuing decades, euthanasia became seen as an instrument of fascistic social planning, and Charlotte Perkins Gilman framed both euthanasia and eugenics as part of a science fictional utopia. In the 1970s and 1980s, westerns reframed euthanasia as an act of masculine, individual agency. In works like Glendon Swarthout's *The Shootist* or Larry McMurtry's *Lonesome Dove*, authors of the western conceived of the right to die as the cowboy on the prairie, incorporating it into the concept of the right to privacy as a right to self-definition explored in previous chapters. Finally, drawing on the romance, Jodi Picoult sought instead to imagine euthanasia as the ultimate act of love.

All the authors I consider here depict various inadequacies in the period's framing of the right to privacy: it excluded queer people or people of color; it did not apply to fetuses or to women seeking an abortion; it could license child abuse in the home; it did not include a right to die. And yet, few, if any, gave up on the promise of the concept. They instead imagined ways of transmitting verboten private meanings in public view, or of expanding the right to privacy to encompass a group or procedure that had been excluded from it. Even as they proved some of its sharpest critics, they rarely forsook the idea of privacy altogether.

When juxtaposed against some of these authors' ideas, the public debate about privacy today can feel somewhat anemic.[58] There have been of late many outcries about the death of privacy: how digital corporations like Facebook and Google subject our private lives to unprecedented scrutiny.[59] But these most often imagine privacy as a matter of data and information—and not as a matter of personal (and embodied) self-definition or self-expression. Meanwhile, with the balance of the Supreme Court skewing originalist, the type of privacy guaranteed in *Roe* and other cases is likely to be increasingly under siege as fundamentally atextual. But to frame privacy solely as a matter of dataflow, or else as an ahistorical legal fiction is to lose sight of what the concept can mean. Privacy has been loaded with contradiction and ambiguity, yet it has also provided many people with a language to reason about the appropriate boundaries among people, governments, and corporations—and the personal decisions that most profoundly affect the course of their lives. To understand that language, we may look to what might seem an unlikely or unpromising place: the phantasmagoria of genre fiction.

 # The Queer Art of Murder

IN 1961, Patricia Highsmith tried to write something different than the pulp thrillers to which she was becoming accustomed: a realistic, confessional novel about gay life. She would never finish the book. It remains in her archives in Switzerland in a manila folder entitled "First-Person Novel." "First-Person Novel" was supposed to describe the life of a woman "who cannot stop herself from practicing homosexuality, even if for social reasons she would wish to."[1] It is composed as a letter from a forty-one-year-old woman named Juliette Tallifer Dorn to her husband Eric and her lover Edith. Juliette has been married for eighteen years to Eric, who tacitly acknowledges that Edith is her longtime romantic female companion. But Juliette has become smitten with a younger ballet dancer named Penny Quinn. Juliette writes a letter to Eric and Edith that defends herself by way of a memoir of her discovery of her own sexuality. In it, she argues that sexual desire is as uncontrollable and irresistible as the appreciation of beauty. Pressed by her lovers to give up Penny, she claims that the impulse to beauty is inescapable: "That is like saying to me, listen to a beautiful concerto, but show no indication that you think it's beautiful or have taken any pleasure from it."[2]

Though incomplete, "First-Person Novel" is nonetheless instructive as to how to read Highsmith's work, because her most famous creation, Tom Ripley, is a consummate appreciator of beauty. Tom's thinly veiled queer desire for Dickie Greenleaf, the young heir living in Europe whose parents have hired Tom to get Dickie to return to America, is surrogated in a variety of ways: first in Tom's dotage on Dickie, then in his murder of Dickie, and then in his desire to impersonate Dickie. The landscape of the novel also reflects Highsmith's own queer love story: Mongibello, where much of the novel is set, is based on the town of Positano, where Highsmith stayed with her lovers, Ellen Hill and Kathryn Cohen.[3] While

Ripley's sexuality is never explicitly discussed, throughout the novel he is repeatedly given to irresistible aesthetic impulses. He is attracted to inscriptions from Tasso, paintings from Van Gogh, and sketches by Reni. The perception of beauty in artwork—uncontrollable and unmistakable, independent of morality—for Highsmith could be a justification of the perception of beauty in humans. But her society nonetheless deemed queer sexuality immoral, even a form of psychopathy.[4] In writing *Ripley*, Highsmith slyly defended queer sexuality not only by representing a queer-seeming character's irresistible aesthetic impulses but also by rendering sympathetic a different psychopathic desire—that of murder.

We might understand "First-Person Novel" as a narrative strategy that Highsmith attempted and then abandoned—a realistic story told through several layers of remove. Her use of the confessional narrative was a way of making queer life public—albeit through the layer of fiction.[5] But she chose not to finish it or publish it. For most of her career (with the exception of *The Price of Salt*), Highsmith preferred a mode of representation of queer life that was far more oblique and less confessional, one with a more complex relationship between private life and the public audience: crime fiction. In Highsmith's diaries, she viewed her closeted existence as a queer person as irrevocably linked to the imaginative act of writing. "Writing," she once wrote, "is a substitute for the life I cannot live, am unable to live."[6] In another entry, she posited that closeted gay people have more active imaginations than straight ones, because they are forced to sublimate their passions into artwork. "The homosexual," she claimed, "partakes less of the physical and the biologic forces for his passions, his intellectual powers. Is his sexual love not within the highest faculty of humans, the imagination?"[7] Leaving "First-Person Novel" in a drawer was a symbolic decision to stay in the closet—it was a way of refusing the structure of the realistic, confessional narrative of coming out.[8] Rather than the narrative confession, which made the private public in a straightforward way, Highsmith preferred the free play of imagination and ambiguous signifiers she found in crime fiction.

The argument of this chapter is that Highsmith, like Dorothy Hughes and Margaret Millar, saw a productive tension between the period's emergent idea that privacy was the paramount virtue of American society and the relatively new genre of villain-centered crime fiction. Privacy was one of the most important, if overdetermined and contradictory, ideas at midcentury. It could refer to many things: inner thought, the flow of data or information, the home or the bedroom, heterosexuality, and the capacity to pursue one's individual choices. If there is a family resemblance between these disparate referents, it is that all were bound up in a vision of postwar liberalism—that, in contrast to communist and totalitarian collectivism, American society was organized around the idea that individuals should be left alone to pursue their own visions of the good life.

Highsmith, Hughes, and Millar saw midcentury privacy for what it was: a shifting, contradictory set of values that could be as confining as they could be salutary. They came to this position for two reasons. First, as three women, one queer, they keenly felt their exclusion from the growing clamors to protect heteronormative privacy; the vision of the good life they wanted to pursue was verboten. But the second and perhaps less obvious reason is that they were genre writers.[9] Critics of the period imagined literary fiction as expressing and cultivating the value of the private individual, while they often saw genre fiction as specializing in unfeeling, unrealistic flat characters. Of course, characters like Tom Ripley and Dix Steele were not altogether flat; in fact, as we will see, Ripley, in particular, was a remarkable experiment in the representation of consciousness. But genre's authors were not interested in depicting realistic personal depth. They were instead more concerned with how they could render a murderer sympathetic and in what achieving that sympathy might suggest about mass audiences' relationship to privacy.

Writing from the margins of the field, the three female crime novelists of this chapter showed that the traditional heterosexual "zones of privacy" (as the Supreme Court eventually called them) were not only riddled with contradiction, but they could be sites of confinement or danger, of horror and terror. Detective fiction had, since the days of Auguste Dupin and Sherlock Holmes, engaged with a central premise of liberalism: that individuals would discover and abide by the Kantian moral law in the private sphere. Poe and Doyle wrote stories about detectives who brought to heel those individuals or creatures who refused to give themselves the law in private (e.g., the Ourang-Outang, Professor Moriarty).[10] But, unlike many of their predecessors, Hughes, Highsmith, and Millar latched onto the perspective of the murderous villain rather than the righteous detective. They did so because they were interested in depicting transgressive sexuality. In their eyes, homing in on the sympathetic villains of crime fiction showed how the form itself testified to readers' desires to witness private and immoral acts they would otherwise claim to abhor. At the same time, these authors used the crime novel to achieve their own kind of privacy in public view—because the plots were so concerned with the outrageously immoral acts of violence and murder, the crime novel turned out to be an ideal medium in which to encode taboo queer and female private desire.

Postwar Privacy and the Novel

The idea that privacy was disappearing attained a new urgency in the aftermath of the Second World War, with the ever-present threat of totalitarianism or communism. For many Americans in the early years of the Cold War, the ability to freely cultivate one's private life was the virtue that distinguished American liberalism from the individual-destroying forces of competing forms of social organization. But privacy was vanishing. Many commentators viewed it as being obliterated by the development of mass society, the way an individual (by which they usually meant a white man) was enmeshed in surrounding institutions: the white-collar office, the mass media, the surveillance state, the suburb. David Riesman observed in *The Lonely Crowd* (1950) that "Home ... is no longer an area of solid privacy," because a new pattern of nuclear families living in smaller spaces (apartments, suburbs) meant that everyone was more closely watching everyone else.[11] In *The Organization Man* (1956), a tract about the ever-encroaching threat of corporate America, William Whyte observed that there was no real privacy in planned suburban communities, that both "doors inside houses" and "barriers against neighbors" were disappearing.[12] "Nowadays men often feel that their private lives are a series of traps," wrote C. Wright Mills in the first sentence of *The Sociological Imagination* (1959), testifying to the way that people (again mostly white men) felt themselves encircled by larger social forces.[13]

Alarms about privacy's death reached a crescendo toward the end of the 1950s and into the next decade. In *The Naked Society* (1964), a widely read jeremiad about the disappearance of privacy, Vance Packard identified a number of privacy-destroying trends that had all come to a head. Urban and suburban living had brought individuals into close contact, thereby increasing both the number of crimes and police surveillance. Wiretapping had become widespread during the two world wars, and the Red Scare heightened the government's tendency to surveil its citizens. Postwar economic prosperity fomented an advertising industry that became ever more aggressive, and new leisure time contributed to the growth of a mass media that was organized around conveying scandalous details of private lives to a broader public. The sheer number of private investigators exploded, enabling both businesses and jealous spouses to surveil others. Lie detectors, personality tests, concealed cameras and microphones, background checks, subliminal advertising, credit bureaus and credit checks, mass solicitation lists, aggressive policing tactics—all of these contributed to the overwhelming sense that the distinctive private individual and the family were being encircled and obliterated by the forces of "mass society"—the government, the corporation, the mass market.[14]

By the middle of the 1960s, anxieties about the need to protect privacy intensified enough to promote a change in the law. Though it had never been officially recognized, in 1965, the Supreme Court established that a right to privacy had existed in the Constitution all along. In *Griswold v. Connecticut* (1965), the Court overturned an outdated Connecticut law forbidding couples from using contraception. *Griswold* nominally protected the "sacred precincts of marital bedrooms." At the same time there was ambiguity about what exactly lay within *Griswold*'s "zone of privacy." The decision hinted at the possibility that privacy could be more than a familial right; it referred to rights like the "freedom of association," and Justice Goldberg's concurrence quoted from Louis Brandeis's dissent in *Olmstead v. United States* (1927) about "the significance of man's spiritual nature, of his feelings and of his intellect."[15] The Court continued along this trajectory over time. "If the right of privacy means anything," the Court wrote in 1972, "it is the right of the individual, married or single, to be free from unwarranted intrusion into matters . . . fundamentally affecting a person."[16] But years before there was an official right to privacy—in the decades in which Hughes, Millar, and Highsmith wrote—privacy was nonetheless so cathected as to be perhaps the most important value of a just society, even as it was not well defined or constitutionally established. It could refer to a great many things—the home, the family, sexuality, the individual, interior consciousness, the value of liberty. It was felt most acutely as a palpable anxiety, a slow-burning sense of unease about something fundamental to individual personhood that was vanishing.

Diatribes about the disappearance of privacy were often framed in universalist terms, but as the language of *Griswold* suggested, privacy protected "the marital bedroom," which was "a sacred precinct" most obviously for white men and heterosexual couples.[17] With the end of World War II and the beginning of the Cold War, a period of relative permissiveness with respect to gender roles gave way to an intense restrictiveness. Women were expected to become homemakers and mothers, premarital sex became a greater taboo, and couples were expected to achieve happiness through intercourse.[18] In 1948, the Kinsey Report brought the ubiquity of same-sex intimacy to the public eye, and as a result, homosexuality accrued more stigma than ever before. Stories of sex crimes sprung up in the newspapers, and fifteen states established commissions to study "sex deviation." The Miller Act, known as the sexual psychopath law, penalized sodomy with a fine of up to $1,000 or twenty years in prison; a recidivist whom psychologists found to be a "sexual psychopath" would be institutionalized. A fear that homosexuals would be more liable to blackmail led to queer individuals being fired from the federal government.[19]

The period's understanding of privacy reflected these heteronormative values. Even after the right to privacy's constitutional establishment in 1965, it protected spousal rape, and it failed to encompass queer sexuality until 2003. Finding privacy for women and queer people could be a constant struggle within daily life.[20] In *The Feminine Mystique*, Betty Friedan observed that a lack of privacy was part of life for many women at midcentury. A woman, she wrote, "does not have the privacy to follow real interests of her own"; she risks "becoming an ogre to her children in her impatient demands for privacy."[21] In his sociological study of midcentury queer encounters, *Tearoom Trade*, Laud Humphries noted that participants need to "maintain . . . privacy in public settings" by choosing spaces with separators—"walls, stalls, and opaque windows"—and "by being completely silent."[22] Queer life could subsist only in private spaces, and not within those recognized or protected by the law.

At midcentury, many literary critics believed that literary fiction had a crucial role to play in preserving the postwar vision of liberalism. "Privacy" was not a word that they used often, at least at first, but by "liberalism," they referred to the idea that society should be organized to allow each person to pursue their private vision of the good life. A good novel would force the reader to empathize with feelings that might have seemed abhorrent or alien and thus produce individual moral reflection—a private encounter that would make them better public citizens. We can see the ethical model in question most clearly in a passage from Trilling's "Manners, Morals, and the Novel":

> For our time the most effective agent of the moral imagination has been the novel of the last two hundred years.... [I]ts greatness and its practical usefulness lay in its unremitting work of involving the reader himself in the moral life, inviting him to put his own motives under examination, suggesting that reality is not as his conventional education has led him to see it. It taught us, as no other genre ever did, the extent of human variety and the value of this variety. It was the literary form to which the emotions of understanding and forgiveness were indigenous, as if by the definition of the form itself.[23]

For Trilling, reading is a dynamic process that begins with alterity: a reader encounters something that makes him realize that "reality is not as his conventional education has led him to see it." Through a process of reflective contemplation in private, he comes to understand "the extent of human variety" and its "value." The transcendent vantage point on society and social value that literature produces could help readers produce a better liberalism. In Trilling's view, the trouble with liberalism is that creating a society dedicated to the promotion of happiness and freedom is always fraught with danger because people do not necessarily understand one another's private values. Because those who attempt to create such a society would "select the emotions and qualities that are most susceptible of organization,"[24] liberalism might tend to generalize and oversimplify, forgetting the multiplicity of needs people have and the heterogeneous ways they can structure their lives. For Trilling, literature and literary criticism recall liberalism to its most fundamental values of "variousness, possibility, complexity, and difficulty."[25] The private scene of reading leads to better participation in public life, which, in turn, helps to ensure a society of individuals allowed to pursue their own private ideas of what counts as a good life.

Though not all called themselves "liberal," a remarkable number of critics of the period agreed that literature's value was that it provided readers with a destabilizing encounter with alterity—the opportunity to empathize with motives and impulses that might otherwise be quite foreign. In this, it strengthened their capacity for private reflection and thereby made them better able to participate in public life. For instance, W. K. Wimsatt argued that poetry reminded its readers of "a wide realm of motives which may be profoundly moving and sympathetic though falling short of the morally acceptable."[26] Wayne Booth wrote there is "immeasurable value in forcing us to see the human worth of a character whose actions, objectively considered, we would deplore," just so long as we are ultimately reminded that that character's actions are evil.[27] Harold C. Gardiner, the critic for the Catholic magazine *America*, praised Graham Greene's *The End of the Affair* precisely because it revealed "deep compassion and understanding" for sinful characters (even as it ultimately condemned sin as such).[28] They disagreed about how much alterity was permissible, with critics like Booth and Gardiner suggesting that a fiction writer still had a duty to illuminate the distinction between moral and immoral, but they nonetheless all looked to reading for its capacity to produce some degree of alterity. Henry James, in particular, figured prominently in many of these accounts. For Trilling, James's experiments in ambiguous points of view epitomized literature's capacity to produce moral contingency; for Booth, James's complex characters and plots represented the threshold case of how much a writer could confuse a reader in presenting literary alterity.[29]

The model of reading in which an empathetic encounter with alterity led to self-bettering moral reflection in private derived from eighteenth- and nineteenth-century classical liberalism. It stretched back to John Stuart Mill and Adam Smith and was perpetuated in E. M. Forster and Matthew Arnold. By the 1960s, scholars were explicitly claiming that this model of reading had been intertwined with the value of privacy from its origin. In 1962, Ian Watt wrote of the novel that "there had never before been such opportunities for unreserved participation in the inner lives of fictional characters." For Watt, the novel was "better suited to the communication of private feelings and fantasies" than any previous medium.[30] Jürgen Habermas argued that eighteenth-century novels had trafficked in "intimate mutual relationships between privatized individuals who were psychologically interested in what was 'human,' in self-knowledge, and in empathy." Reading novels became a "precondition" for a sense of one's participation in the public sphere; in order to enter into public life, one had first to cultivate a sense of private interiority and acquire empathetic knowledge of others through reading.[31] In later work, Trilling explained that "private and uniquely interesting individuality" emerged from novels and other eighteenth-century literature, out of "the newly available sense of an audience, of that public which society created."[32] Booth exhorted the artist to recultivate a sense of the public sphere, to transform his "private vision, made up as it often is of ego-ridden private symbols, into something that is essentially public."[33]

The smear against mass culture—genre fiction, dime novels, television, movies, comics, advertising, and so on—was that it would dissolve the private, self-defining individual so celebrated by postwar critics. In perhaps the most representative polemic from the postwar period, the left-leaning critic Dwight Macdonald wrote that a work of "High Culture" was "an expression of feelings, ideas, tastes, visions that are idiosyncratic and the audience similarly responds to them as individuals." By contrast, consumers of "Masscult" (Macdonald's preferred term for mass culture) "might as well be eating ice-cream sodas."[34] Literary fiction was aligned with privacy, individuality, and distinctive intellectual reflection; mass culture was characterized by the market, mass consumers, and a homogenized emotional response. This is another reason why literary ethicists since Trilling have taken Henry James as a touchstone; James was among the first to help usher the novel into the realm of high culture, providing the "axiom" that "no good novel will ever proceed from a superficial mind . . . cover[s] all needful moral ground." For James, at least in "The Art of Fiction," the novel needed to be responsible only to "beauty and truth," to the complexities of life.[35] His is a definition that would exclude the reiterative plotlines and the melodramatic characters of genre fiction, of putatively low culture.[36]

Even a cursory glance at polemics against genre fiction, like those gathered in the collected volume *Mass Culture: The Popular Arts in America*, suggests the extent to which critics believed genre fiction, and specifically crime fiction, did not cultivate an individual's capacity for reflection in private. Irving Howe complained that genre fiction contributed to "the depersonalization of the individual," who was reduced to "semi-robot status" or a "spiritless zombie." Howe described a film like *Double Indemnity* as appealing to "the least individualized and most anonymous aspects of ourselves" and "our role of social anonymity."[37] Edmund Wilson complained that the characters in crime fiction were "not, after all, a person like you or me."[38] Anxieties about "mass culture" were anxieties that individual private life and reflectiveness would be overwhelmed by the homogenizing delights of commercial culture.[39]

Literary critics, too, did not acknowledge queer life as fitting into their version of the private person. While Trilling and Leslie Fiedler celebrated books like *Lolita* for their capacity to produce moral contingency, they showed little such sensitivity to the lives of queer people.[40] Trilling wrote that literature's strength was that it made people sympathize with foreign, immoral urges, but he argued in *The Liberal Imagination* that the Kinsey Report's desire to treat homosexuality as innate was a sign of "intellectual weakness."[41] Fiedler identified homosexual desire as a major theme in American literature and yet treated it as a sign of immaturity to be outgrown.[42]

Even as they were ignored by literary critics who believed they would produce not private reflection but rather unreflective consumption, there can be little doubt that crime writers like Highsmith were the chroniclers of the macabre underside to postwar private life—the smoke-filled bars, telephone booths, private detectives, eerie suburbs. This was partly, as I suggested at the start of this chapter, because of the form they inherited: the detective novel had been dedicated to inspecting the boundaries between public and private since its inception. Detective fiction emerged when evil became a question not of divine privation but rather individual private psychology.[43] As Sean McCann argues, if nineteenth-century liberalism was organized around the idea that rational, self-governing individuals would come together to create a public order so as to protect their private lives, the villains of crime fiction represented the anxiety that certain people are not fundamentally capable of rational self-government. They were instead ruled by base or mercenary instincts, and their incapacity for self-government of their private moral urges poses an ever-present danger to the harmony of public life. The private detective is thus that unique figure capable of both discerning the deviant private urges of others while also carrying out Kantian self-legislation, bringing licentious criminals to heel while also restraining himself and thereby restoring the appropriate balance of public and private.[44]

The most unique feature of the crime fiction of midcentury—by authors like Highsmith, Hughes, and Millar, as well as Jim Thompson, Cornell Woolrich, and David Goodis (who also thematize alternative sexualities)—was that it followed villains, not private investigators. These novels exemplified the dictum of the postwar literary critics: in inducing sympathy with a murderer, they could lead a reader to question her own motives and impulses and therefore become a more reflective individual. This capacity to induce sympathy with a sociopath is partly why *Lolita*, which borrows so much from detective fiction, was so beloved by Trilling.[45] But rather than imagine themselves as producing a sense of moral contingency, writers of crime fiction imagined their fiction as a form of expression that could furtively disclose a story of illicit sexual desire within a narrative that engrossed most readers in spectacle and terror. This was a mode of expression that would be particularly powerful for queer and female authors.

As we will see throughout this chapter, Hughes, Millar, and Highsmith each imagined the villain-centered crime novel not as a site for producing moral self-betterment in private, but as a place in which they could secrete ideas that challenged the period's emphasis on heteronormative privacy as the overarching virtue of postwar American life. Writing about sympathetic villains with "perverse" tendencies provided Hughes, Millar, and Highsmith with a space in which they could surreptitiously question the reigning heterosexual ideas about privacy and even inscribe taboo private desires to be legible within a public setting. As the author with the greatest literary ambitions, it was Highsmith who perceived most acutely the contradiction in the way literary critics celebrated fiction for its capacity to depict a private life that produced a sense of moral contingency, while ignoring the villains of genre fiction. And she was also especially familiar with how queer people needed to find ways to express private meanings within public settings.

Lonely Places and Telephone Booths

Dorothy Hughes began writing about female sexual transgressions in her poetry, which often represented lone female figures in a mythic or fairy-tale setting who struggled with taboo desire. In one poem in her first book *Dark Certainty* (1931), Hughes sympathetically reimagines the mythological character Circe not as an enchantress but as a woman who loves differently from what society allows: "You hear her weeping all night long / Because her loving must be wrong."[46] Another, "Bewilderment," describes a woman abandoned by the man she loves, her "dreams an empty shell," while "Purity" narrates a supposedly chaste woman who with "her jeweled finger tips" is secretly "tallying each sin."[47] Later in life, Hughes claimed to be no feminist—she didn't think women faced obstacles preventing their success as writers. But she nonetheless abjured traditional ideas about female chastity and marriage: writing about her twenties, when the poems in question were under construction, she remembered: "I deliberately decided to have sex, I didn't do it out of love, romance or being tipsy. If anything else, I decided now it's high time that you grew up."[48] She initially did not want to get married and turned down at least one suitor; she eventually became pregnant out of wedlock and married the father a month into the pregnancy, planning to get a divorce as soon as the baby was born. (As luck would have it, they stayed together, and despite the emotional turmoil of her fiction, Hughes claims to have been quite happy.)[49]

In her crime fiction, Hughes figured out how to take the project that she began in her poetry—the vulnerability and transgression bound up in female sexuality—and narrate it in a contemporary setting for a mass audience. Written in third-person limited narration—with Dix Steele's murderous desires initially hidden from the reader—*In a Lonely Place* follows Dix, a returning veteran and aspiring detective novelist, who, visiting postwar Los Angeles, is haunted by memories of his first love Brucie. Dix becomes a serial strangler, preying on women in dark, lonely places. Dix socially reengages his old friend from the war—Brub Nicolai, now a detective—all the while concealing his secret identity as a murderer. Sylvia, Brub's wife, has lived in Santa Monica Canyon all her life, but Dix's appearance has made it a place of fear for her. "But the canyon at night, the way the fogs come in—it's a place for *him*," explains Brub, her husband. Dix, the serial murderer, is the *him* who takes safe public places (the canyon) and makes them into private, haunted ones beyond the view of the law.

Hughes's investigations of the dangers and ambiguities of privacy are most visible in the many permutations of the title phrase: "lonely place." Thus, the word "lonely" or its derivatives refer to the fog (which makes public spaces temporarily private), to Dix's bachelor's life ("lone wolf"), to his veteran's psyche (he fondly remembers the "loneness in the sky" as a pilot), to his conscience ("caught there in that lonely place"), to his resettlement in LA after the war ("You've been lonely . . . it takes time in a new place"), and to the scenes of his murders ("it would be lonely up here at night").[50] In these many permutations, we see how privacy can be the wellspring of creativity—"I needed a quiet place for my work" (445)—but it is more often a space of terror: "she didn't like the darkness and fog and loneness" (396). Privacy can license murder and rape: "It would be lonely up here at night" (466). It can be a space of emotional trauma: "He had to get out, to be alone in his lonely place" (497). These different connotations tend to express the ways that private life can be: on the one hand, freeing for Dix as a man to perform license—Dix's bachelor life as a "lone wolf" (411), "the freedom" (395) he feels within the fog—but confining for others, especially women, as evidenced by Sylvia's terror at lonely places. As a maladjusted veteran, Dix's character also expresses one of the period's major concerns that soldiers returning home from war had been so irreparably damaged as to be incapable of fitting back into the private/public schema of liberalism.

Like many a detective novel, *In a Lonely Place* would initially seem to assuage anxieties about privacy's authorization of sexual license and deviance by bringing Dix to justice. The twist is that there are two female detective figures. They trap Dix, who takes advantage of privacy within public spaces for his murders, by confusing him about what is private and what is public.[51] Sylvia and Dix's lover Laurel lure Dix out of his private apartment and onto the semi-public space of the apartment's patio. With its blue-lit "artificial moonlight" (439) and its unused pool, it looks like "a stagy stage set" (439). Sylvia and Laurel use the apartment's patio, designed to confuse its experiencer as to whether he is in public or private, frontstage or backstage, before an audience or not. Dix thinks he is strangling Laurel in private, but it turns out that he's being watched by Brub and the police.

Dix might seem like the damaged or nefarious figure who haunts liberalism's private spaces, but he can also be read as the conservative man who is so threatened by women's autonomy and independent sexuality that he murders them. He strangles his first love Brucie during the war. She stays under an assumed name at a hotel and meets him for a tryst in a deserted rocky cove; he kills her, the narrative implies, because she still harbors an attachment to her husband. After Brucie, Dix murders the single women he picks up or encounters in public places—at bus stations and on the beach. Dix decides he wants to marry Laurel, but for Laurel it is the space of heterosexual security, not of untethered intimacy, that is terrifying. She is "trembling within the cup of his arms" (520) when he embraces her. Laurel has already realized how privacy can be damaging: she "took quite a beating" (511) in her first marriage. He decides to kill Laurel when he breaks into her apartment and uncovers a photograph of another man. Dix is so alarmed by a female sexuality that transcends the bonds of marriage, the traditional space of privacy, that he murders the women who embody it.

But it is precisely female sexuality, a transgression less spectacular than Dix's outrageous villainy, that is allowed to continue at the novel's end. Laurel can remain unmarried and continue her serial affairs. The replacement of male with female libido is in fact foretold in the book's epigraph: "It's in a lonesome place you do have to be talking with someone, and looking for someone, in the evening of the day." Though ostensibly indexing Dix's threat to nocturnal privacy, "talking" and "looking" for a woman to kill, the epigraph derives from J. M. Synge's play, *The Shadow of the Glen* (1903), where it is spoken by Nora, a young woman who has married an older farmer who has died (he is actually pretending to be dead). When a man comes to visit her, she admits to having an affair, and she refuses to marry again, wanting instead to stay on the lonely farm where men pass by frequently and where she will have sexual liaisons with them: "talking with someone" and "looking for someone" in her "lonesome place." At a moment of Irish nationalist sentiment, the play scandalized many for its bald depiction of female Irish libido.[52] What appears to be a reassertion of the proper order of public and private—as Dix's capture restores the dangerous "lonely places" to the more traditional private ones—is a covert assertion of female sexual desire.

In a Lonely Place imagines crime writing as uniquely able to conceal private immorality behind a respectable public persona. Dix is an author of the same genre in which he appears as a character: detective fiction. At one point Dix imagines his profession as an alibi to explain why his lights were on all night: he had pulled an all-nighter finishing his novel. The profession of the crime novelist is, Hughes suggested wryly, the public persona that licenses a private capacity to commit murder. In conversation with a suspicious Sylvia (who eventually captures him), Dix makes quasi-confessional comments—"I have a personal interest in the case" (433)—before explaining that he is, after all, a detective novelist. When Dix and Brub joke about writing crime fiction, they think about it not as individualized self-expression but rather as creative bricolage: "Who are you stealing from, Chandler or Hammett or Gardner?" (433). "Little of each," Dix agrees. "With a touch of Queen and Carr." The crime novel turns out to be the perfect place to hide transgressive desire beneath what was imagined to be entirely derivative fiction.

While Hughes used the overdetermination of the lonely place to show how privacy could be a space of terror and loneliness, Margaret Millar was interested in how privacy could be a place for the keeping of secrets. Whereas the period's literary critics believed that encountering the private lives of others could be the wellspring of empathy and a better liberalism, in *Beast in View*, Millar imagined privacy as more like the constraint of the closet, and she saw understanding others' interior lives as a way of humiliating and manipulating them—or, closer to the title, hunting them. Millar began writing crime fiction when she quite literally could not escape the privacy of the marital bedroom: she was bedridden not long after having an unplanned child with what was either a heart condition or a psychosomatic ailment. "Here I am—*stuck*," she imagined herself. Writing crime fiction was a means of self-actualization, of having a more public life. "I had to do something to get out of that bed," she said.⁵³ But she did not imagine the novel as a place for her to disclose her private self. Having grown up reading murder mysteries, Millar spoofed the ethos of an MFA program—the idea that literature should be a profound form of self-expression—in an interview: "They tell you always to write about what you know. What I knew was murder."⁵⁴ Instead of treating her fiction as representing the story of a private life that only she could tell, she believed that writing fiction would get her out of the domestic space and put her in a milieu in which she could imagine herself as a murderous figure invading the domestic interiors of others.

Her most famous work, *Beast in View*, follows Helen Clarvoe, a well-to-do woman who lives alone as a shut-in within a hotel room. Excessively jealous of her own privacy, she has thoughts like "skin on skin offended her" and "I must get back to my own room and lock the door against the ugliness."⁵⁵ Even the closets in her apartment are closeted: "All the doors in the hall were closed; it was impossible to tell what was behind any of them, a closet or a bedroom or a bathroom" (388). She is being stalked by Evelyn Merrick, a shameless exhibitionist, who threatens her over the telephone. As the novel continues, it is revealed that Helen Clarvoe suffers from a split personality: Helen is a repressed lesbian, while Evelyn, her uncloseted counterpart, is a shameless exhibitionist.

The telephone in particular becomes the trope in the novel that coordinates all of the ambiguities surrounding privacy. The phone gives Helen the cover—the private space—from which to project the queer persona of Evelyn, and to enter the private spaces of others, both literally (the phone rings in their apartment) and figuratively (she exposes their secrets). When Helen as Evelyn uses the public telephone, the man tells her that public does not actually mean for all to use indiscriminately: "a public phone, meaning it's for the public, for everybody. Someone like you ties it up and the rest don't get a chance" (443). Helen alleges that the operator is listening to her phone calls. Evelyn uses a telephone in a public place to reach into the private spaces of others and whisper their own terrible secrets back to them. Even the imaginary lost "shares of AT&T" that her mother hopes will be found "stuck in a drawer and forgotten" (427) remind us that the telephone that Evelyn loves to use represents a public utility that is privately owned. The shares lie, Helen thinks, in "a closetful of punctured dreams" (427), a phrase that also refers to her disappointment at her children's homosexuality.

What if, Millar wondered, privacy didn't refer to a space rooted in the home but was something people took with them wherever they went? When the Supreme Court eventually did constitutionally protect anywhere a person had "a reasonable expectation of privacy" over a decade later in *Katz v. United States* (1967), the Court, too, turned to the telephone booth—deciding federal agents could not bug a phone booth without a warrant.[56] If, as Millar realized and the Court eventually decided, a phone booth could be private—if privacy was something that could be distributed anywhere in society a person had a reasonable expectation of it—then privacy as a concept was something less like the home and more like the closet: it referred to secrets concealed in public view. As *Beast in View* progresses, we discover that the closet is also the governing psychic metaphor for nearly all the characters in the novel, most of whom Evelyn threatens to out. It turns out that there is a real Evelyn Merrick, who was briefly married to Helen's brother Douglas, but as a beard: Douglas is gay and is the self-described "wife" of Jack Terola (468), a pornographic photographer. Helen had a crush on the real Evelyn; the two were very close friends as children until Evelyn began dating boys while Helen failed to assimilate into heteronormative life. The real Evelyn currently stays with a married couple; the husband is often away, and Evelyn comes over to spend the night because Claire is "nervous about being alone" (496), faintly implying a romantic tryst.

The titular "beast" in view could refer not just to Helen/Evelyn but to any number of these secret-harboring characters. The term "beast" first appears when Helen's brother tells his mother that he is Jack Terola's "wife." She responds, "you filthy little beast" (468). But the more one looks, the more "beasts" become indistinguishable from hunters. The title derives from Muriel Rukeyser's 1944 poem, "Beast in View," in which Rukeyser writes: "I hunted and became the followed."[57] We begin with a sense of Helen being hunted by Evelyn, but it turns out that Helen really is Evelyn. Remembering her infatuation with the real Evelyn, Helen suggests as much in a brief recollection—"I would have followed her anywhere, like a sheep, the goat, the victim" (518). Having a beast in view is thus intimately connected to harboring a desire to be hunted by a dominant, sexual pursuer.

In the novel's closing lines, the beast/hunter metaphor shifts again: Blackshear, the financial advisor who assumes the role of the novel's detective figure, becomes the "hunter with a beast in view" (527). Blackshear seems to restore beast and hunted into its proper, heteronormative order, but Blackshear himself harbors an unsavory lasciviousness. In an earlier scene, Blackshear thinks to himself, shaking Helen's hand with a sweaty palm: "It gave him a kind of petty satisfaction to realize that he must have left some of his moisture on her" (397). When shaking her hand, Blackshear thinks, "The private I . . . always looking through a single keyhole" (397). He is the private eye (the detective, the voyeur) watching the private "I" (Helen). The play of "private I" with "private eye" invokes the act of reading, which has been analogized to voyeuristic keyhole-looking since the days of *Tristram Shandy*. Reading *Beast in View* testifies to a readers' desire to listen in on the phone calls and peer into the closets of others. If the imagined reader is the hunter with the beast in view, as suggested by the missing subject position in the title, then the reader is also drawn into the endlessly recursive logic of the novel wherein people who take pleasure at peering into private closets inevitably also harbor their own secrets.

At a moment when privacy seemed to be the overarching virtue of American society, Hughes and Millar were drawn to two of the scenes in the American landscape that exposed contradictions as to what counted as private—the lonely place and the telephone booth. They showed how those private or semi-private spaces could be sites of terror and domination. And, at a moment when literary critics celebrated fiction for providing an encounter with alterity in private that would lead to a transcendent vantage point on society, they did not imagine reading as an opportunity for moral self-betterment. They saw it as the immersion in the consciousness of stalkers and murderers who gloried in the destruction of privacy. While Hughes imagined the crime novel as a space to secrete taboo sexuality in public view, Millar saw it as speaking to the universality of the closet. In both instances, the pleasure a reader would take in watching a villain destroy privacy was licensed only by their murderous protagonist's eventual subdual. But to imagine the reader as taking delight in the destruction of heterosexual private space without even the ultimate expectation of the protagonist's punishment—this was the particular forte of Patricia Highsmith in the *Ripley* novels.

"One of the Most Innocent and Clean-Minded He Had Ever Known"

Hughes, Millar, and Highsmith all stood at the edge of mainstream literary fiction, but of the three of them, Patricia Highsmith especially longed to be seen as a member of it. After studying classic works of American literature at Barnard College in Manhattan, she applied to work at, and was rejected by, the *New Yorker*,

Vogue, Harper's Bazaar, and *Mademoiselle*—ultimately landing as an editorial assistant at the middlebrow publication *Jewish Morning Journal*.[58] After being laid off at the *Journal,* she stood outside a department store surveying customers about deodorant and liver pills while struggling to write fiction at night.[59] A few weeks later, she landed a job with Michel Publishers, a publisher of comics, and penned stories for pulpy comic books like *Jap Buster Johnson* for seven years.[60] Whether she liked it or not, she had an ideal vantage point from which to observe the development of mass culture—the commodified proliferation of advertising, popular comic books, pop music, pulp paperbacks, television, and movies that so many critics believed would obliterate the capacity for individual reflection in private.

As Highsmith became more established, her oeuvre was inevitably classed within that mass cultural milieu, even as she saw herself as a more elevated chronicler of the mysterious and the macabre. She continued to send the *New Yorker* her stories and cartoons but was published there only posthumously. "Remember," she wrote in her diaries, "you are in good company. Dostoyevsky, Wilkie Collins, Henry James, Edgar Allan Poe . . . there are hacks in every kind of literary field. . . . Aim at being a genius."[61] When Truman Capote recommended her to Yaddo, the selection panel felt that she was a talented writer but only when considered within the middlebrow. One judge wrote, "There is surely a very respectable place for such a writer . . . my own vote would be Yes—unless there is a great deal more pressure than there seems to be from really *very* extraordinary people."[62] In a letter to her friend Kate "Kingsley" Skattebol, she described Coward-McCann, the firm that published both *The Price of Salt* and *The Talented Mr. Ripley*, as "an inferior and not very honorable house"; after it was published, she called *The Price of Salt* "a stinking book."[63] Her other novels were published by Harper & Co., a reputable house, but as part of their new, pulpier Harper Novel of Suspense line. To establish her literary credentials, she familiarized herself with zeitgeists like quantum physics, special relativity, and existentialism and rubbed shoulders with the *Partisan Review* crowd at parties in New York. Highsmith even read some of Trilling's essays, "Art and Fortune" among them, and noted in her journal, "I follow ¾ of the way through his essays, and then have the feeling he is bashing his brains out at the end, still with the same sincerity and highmindedness, to sum it up concisely, which he can't."[64] She also pasted Faulkner's Nobel Prize speech into her diary, which follows the critical logic of the period; literature represents "the problems of the human heart in conflict with itself" and is one of the pillars that would help individual "man... endure and prevail."[65] Reading Trilling and Faulkner, she was directly exposed to the idea that reading fiction would help cultivate the private self-reflection so prized by postwar liberalism. But she also found herself classed as a writer of pulp.

Highsmith was doubly excluded from the normative ideals of privacy in midcentury society—not only because she was a pulp novelist, and therefore allegedly did not write about real people with real private lives, but also because she was gay and thus her expressions of love both depended on privacy and were not officially or legally protected by it. Private life, which postwar liberals theorized as the site of bountiful self-development, was for her stigmatized as immoral and unnatural. In 1948, the same year the Miller sexual psychopath act was passed, Highsmith underwent therapy that would help her enjoy sex with her boyfriend—which she called "a sensation of being raped in the wrong place." To pay for the therapy, she took a job at Bloomingdale's, inspiring the plotline that became *The Price of Salt*.[66]

The Price of Salt chronicles the ways her two queer protagonists seek, and often fail to find, private refuge in semi-public spaces. When Carol and Therese make love in a hotel room, the male private eye phallically penetrates their seclusion, listening in with a "spike" he drills in the wall.[67] As Tom Perrin points out, in a world in which the heroines are perpetually under potential surveillance, each seemingly innocuous public sign—town names like "Waterloo" or "Defiance"—threatens to become a symbol of their private tragedy, which will occur when their private moments are thrust into public recognition.[68] At the close of the novel, when Therese declines to live with Carol, the book suggests that their privacy will be won only through the repeated stagings of anonymous and public intimacies, as the two meet at a party:

> Oh, in a different way now, because she was a different person, and it was like meeting Carol all over again, but it was still Carol and no one else. It would be Carol, in a thousand cities, a thousand houses, in foreign lands where they would go together, in heaven and in hell.... [H]er hand waved a quick, eager greeting that Therese had never seen before.[69]

Leading up to this moment, Carol has agreed to stop seeing Therese to maintain the right to visit her child, and Therese wonders whether Carol's private life has changed along with her respectable-seeming public exterior. But at the novel's conclusion, she realizes that she and Carol will maintain their private identities ("it was still Carol") even as they will encounter each other with publicly different facades, as "different people" in different cities, performing new gestures and unfamiliar gestures in public—they will be the same people in private, while evading the moral judgment of "heaven" and "hell."

The Price of Salt is a realist fantasy story about a romance that never happened in real life: Highsmith became entranced with and later went to the house of a woman who shopped at Bloomingdale's. What does not emerge in the novel is that her impulses toward the mysterious woman were tinged with sexual and murderous desire. She wrote about her decision to wait outside the woman's home:

> Murder is a kind of making love, a kind of possessing. Is it not, too, a way of getting complete? And passionate attention, for a moment, from the subject of one's affections? To arrest her suddenly, my hands upon her throat (which I should really like to kiss) as if I took a photograph, to wake her in an instant cool and rigid as a statue.[70]

If queer sexual desire was bound up with murderous impulse, art was a sublimated record of that desire—a photograph, a statue, perhaps a story. One strategy was to try and tell this story in realistic terms—as she did in *The Price of Salt* or "First-Person Novel"—but her other strategy was to conceal it within genre fiction. The latter offered a way of publicly narrating that private desire; moreover, such a sideways telling came closer to the way she experienced sexual attraction—bound up with immorality, possession, even violence.

The animal story was one type of genre fiction that allowed Highsmith to obliquely represent images of queer intimacy. She was inspired to write "The Snail-Watcher," which her agent initially rejected as "too repellent to show editors," after watching *A Streetcar Named Desire*.[71] In "The Snail-Watcher," Peter Knoppert, a financial manager, is engulfed by the endlessly reproducing snails that he collects in his study. Highsmith's ending allows gender-defying reproduction to triumphantly destroy the private home, whereas at the end of *Streetcar*, middle-class heterosexual domesticity is unconvincingly reasserted in the figures of Stella and Stanley as Blanche (who represents transgressive desire) is carted off to a mental hospital. Knoppert watches the snails' queer (or, more accurately, hermaphroditic) reproduction, with "the ear-like excrescences . . . [pressed] precisely together rim to rim."⁷² The phrase echoes a love poem Highsmith wrote in her diary about Kathleen Senn, the mysterious woman who inspired *The Price of Salt*, in which she imagined their worlds as barely able to touch: "like the kissing rims of two circles."⁷³

While postwar culture was so often dedicated to the celebration of the liberal private individual over mass society, in stories like "the Snail-Watcher," the masses of animals triumph over the individual. In his posture of education and high culture, Knoppert assumes the liberal disinterestedness that critics like Trilling strove to cultivate, hiding his licentious interest in watching sex under the guise of aesthetic appreciation. "I never cared for nature before in my life," he tells friends at dinner parties, "but snails have opened my eyes to the beauty of the world."⁷⁴ He spends long hours watching the snails reproduce and lay eggs in his study, and he becomes excited when, while reading Darwin, he finds a description of snail sensuality in French: "The word *sensualité* made him tense like a bloodhound that has suddenly found the scent."⁷⁵ Though he is clearly interested ("tense" to say the least) in the erotic implications of snails having sex, he imagines himself, for being able to decode the French, as "one of the scholarly few now"—veiling a queer lust beneath the veneer of high culture.⁷⁶ Because watching the snails has brought him "relaxation," Knoppert is a better, more daring stock picker, and he sees himself, in good liberal individualistic style, as having as much agency over his stock picks as over his pets: "he saw his bank account multiplying as rapidly as his snails."⁷⁷ He finds, of course, that he lacks the control and disinterestedness that he once believed he had: the exponentially reproducing snails end up engulfing and killing him. The forces of biology, of the masses, of indiscriminate sexual desire, triumph over the lone individual with pretensions of acquiring "culture" in his private study.

For Highsmith, one strategy for making queer life public was to write under a pseudonym; another was to submerge queer desire in a story about animals; a third was to write crime fiction that rendered immoral and aesthetic impulses sympathetic. We have seen how privacy in the period was celebrated in two different senses—one referring to heterosexual values and the home, the other to literary interiority. Excluded from the heterosexual and the literary alike, Highsmith in *Ripley* tried to subtly cast doubt on both: covertly training readers to celebrate queer life while also dissolving the boundaries between literary fiction and mass culture.

At the beginning of the chapter, we saw how Ripley's irresistible attraction to artwork—which recurs throughout his pursuit, murder, and impersonation of Dickie—can be understood as a metaphor for uncontrollable queer desire. In interpreting artworks, he also practices a queer or camp reading practice, if we remember that for Susan Sontag the "whole point of camp is to dethrone the serious" or recall Michael Trask's assertion that camp "refuses to recognize any content as authentic."[78] When Tom goes to Palermo to visit the tomb of Santa Rosalia, a patron saint in times of plague, he giggles because he sees her as orgasming: "in a state of frozen ecstasy."[79] Near the beginning of the novel, Tom and his friend Cleo think of Tom's invitation to Europe as "just like out of Shakespeare or something," framing his pursuit of Dickie as a version of a gender-blurring identity plot like *Twelfth Night* (31). Ripley imagines himself as "crossing the wine-dark sea like Jason or Ulysses returning" (261) (an all-male voyage of monogamy-shirkers).

Highsmith encourages a mass cultural reader to adapt this very practice—to seek out all the ways in which "great art" can be recast or reread, with the aim being not the cultivation of heteronormative, moral private life but rather the pleasurable exploration of deviance. (Coward-McCann, which published the novel in hardcover, was a middlebrow publisher of assorted fiction, some poetry, Book-of-the-Month Club selections, and Thornton Wilder's *Our Town*.[80]) Thus, the plot of *The Talented Mr. Ripley* copies and takes to an extreme a novel by the quintessential art novelist and darling of critics like Trilling—Henry James. Tom Ripley, tasked like Lambert Strether of *The Ambassadors* with returning a wayward son to America, does not merely imitate his charge's infatuation with European culture; instead, he murders and impersonates the object of his mission, Dickie Greenleaf. The same point could be made about another classic of the American highbrow, *The Great Gatsby*, which explores similar themes of impersonation, emulation, and authenticity. The "heavy linen sport shirt with wooden buttons" (33) that Ripley eyes at Brooks Brothers evokes the finery of Gatsby's shirts; Tom's upper-class aspirations and homicidal urges are intensified versions of Gatsby's ill-gotten fortune and criminal past.[81]

The other way that Highsmith smuggled a queer reading practice into her mass cultural text was in her refusal of the moralistic ending. Having been deemed immoral by their society, queer readers, as David Halperin argues, tend to be suspicious of emotional power that leads to a "compulsory moralistic feeling."[82] Highsmith herself had been forced, in the words of Eve Kosofsky Sedgwick, to extract "sustenance from the objects of a culture ... whose avowed desire has often been not to sustain them [queer people]."[83] In her 1990 afterword to *The Price of Salt*, Highsmith observed that before her novel, lesbian pulps, which were most often penned as soft-core porn with heterosexual male audiences in mind, were forced to conclude with the protagonists "pay[ing] for their deviation by cutting their wrists, drowning themselves in a swimming pool, or by switching to heterosexuality (so it was stated), or by collapsing—alone and miserable and shunned—into a depression equal to hell."[84] And yet, since lesbian pulps were the only popular representations of lesbians available, queer women often overlooked the negative and unhappy characterizations of lesbians in an attempt at self-fashioning and self-understanding.[85]

Even among Highsmith's oeuvre, her refusal of the unhappy ending was unusual: it was only in *The Price of Salt* and *Ripley* (in contrast to works like *Strangers*, *The Blunderer*, *The Tremor of Forgery*, *The Cry of the Owl*) that she resisted the moralistic endings required by heteronormative culture. And her refusal of the moralistic ending was afforded to her only within the noir novel as opposed to the noir film; when *Strangers on a Train* was adapted into film, because of the Motion Picture Production Code, Guy is made even more heroic and moral: he refuses to murder Bruno's father—the crime for which he is caught by a detective at the novel's close. In *Ripley*, by contrast, Tom emerges unrepentant and unpunished. At the close of the novel, Tom, who has already murdered Dickie, inherits all his money. Relishing his ascent into a higher and more decadent European cultural strata, he cheerfully tells his Greek taxi driver, who mistakes him for a native Italian, "Il meglio albergo. Il meglio, il meglio!" ("The best hotel. The best, the best!") (274).

Highsmith's ending, like the rest of her novel, drew upon the legacy of modernism as well as queer culture. In works like *Ulysses*, obscenity—like Highsmith's representation of queer desire (Tom eyeing the "public urinals" or acrobats in G-strings)[86]—was too buried to be perceptible to most readers. It was also nominally excused by its pretensions to aesthetic value, the very same pretensions that Highsmith caricatures as laced with sexual intrigue.[87] Whereas modernism carried with it what Mark McGurl called "purported obscenity and seemingly unapologetic immorality," mass culture demanded endings that would "magically resolve" the tensions and difficulties that the novels produce, which led critics like Dwight Macdonald and Adorno to complain about their vacuity.[88] Dickie's murder, the most momentous event of the novel, occurs in the first third of the book, upsetting the typical middlebrow fictional plot embodied by Freytag's triangle. The rest of the novel is spent waiting for the police to arrest Tom, which they fail to do. Along the way, Highsmith pointedly riffs on another canonical text: Shakespeare's *Macbeth,* specifically the famous scene in which Macbeth expresses his guilt. For critics like Samuel Johnson, Macbeth's last soliloquy was crucial to understanding why we enjoy watching a murderer like Macbeth. Highsmith turns it into a scene of a murderer's triumph. "To think tomorrow and tomorrow and tomorrow of being Dickie Greenleaf," Tom says to himself (129). Audiences are interested in her art, Highsmith suggests, not so they can see evil punished (a magical resolution) but rather so they can witness "immoral" acts performed.

Because she reproduced modernist, queer techniques in books for mass cultural audiences, Highsmith came to think of forgery as the central metaphor for her artwork. In patterning her text off familiar literary narratives like *Gatsby* and *The Ambassadors,* she likens her crime novel to an illicit version, or forgery, of an art-novel. As *The Talented Mr. Ripley* opens, Ripley positions himself as superior to mere mass cultural artists. He defrauds bourgeois Brooklyn-based professional artists—journalists, musicians, photographers, illustrators, and comic book artists (an allusion to Highsmith's past career)—out of their taxes. He specifically chooses artists who make enough money to be "logically accused of having made a two- or three-hundred dollar error in their tax computations," but who will not have hired professional accountants to compute their taxes (19).

As Highsmith describes how Ripley takes special measures to imitate voices, forge signatures, and master the jargon of the IRS, she implies that his art, the art of forgery, is somehow more elevated than the arts of mass culture. Likewise, in the subsequent volume of the *Ripliad,* Ripley murders an art collector, Thomas Murchison, who, as a wealthy pipe manufacturer and a stickler for detail and authenticity, is a synecdoche for the crude middlebrow. What Ripley understands and Murchison misses is that the forgery can be just as great an artwork as the original. Whereas the artist does things naturally, without thinking, Tom prefers the forger, who "struggles, and if he succeeds, it is a genuine achievement."[89] Her elevation of forgery to the highest artwork contrasts with another contemporary text with more traditional literary credentials, William Gaddis's *The Recognitions* (1955), in which Wyatt Gwyon attempts forgeries of the Old Masters and then ultimately decides to expose them as inauthentic false pretenders. But Highsmith celebrated her fiction as a kind of forgery because it provided her with a form of concealed identity. As Joan Schenkar points out, Highsmith identified with Ripley, saying, for instance, "I often had the feeling Ripley was writing it and I was merely typing" and signing her name, "Pat H, alias Ripley."[90]

Highsmith imagined her work as a forgery not only because it encased modernist aesthetics and queer morality in a mass cultural package, but also because forgeries involve counterfeiting the private interiority of others. For Tom to sign his name as Dickie Greenleaf is for him to manifest through a public sign that his interior identity—his thoughts, feelings, emotions, consciousness—were those of Dickie Greenleaf. Murchison represents the opposing aesthetic tradition, the idea culled from Romanticism that art is the quintessential expression of individuality: "An artist's style is his truth, his honesty. Has another man the right to copy it, in the same way that a man copies another man's signature?"[91] By contrast, Ripley's art consists, not in individualist expression of private interiority, but in successfully masquerading as another. If, for a reader like Trilling, reading was supposed to cultivate "understanding and forgiveness," "human variety," and a "moral life," Ripley is the artist who gives the lie to that understanding: he shows how aesthetic appreciation can teach one to counterfeit the private life of someone else.[92]

In *Ripley*, Highsmith found herself able to channel sympathy for her villainous protagonist precisely because of her experiments with point of view. Ripley is largely sympathetic because Highsmith represents his private life as so earnest-seeming. When he spies the shirt at Brooks Brothers, Tom contemplates putting it on the Greenleaf tab, but he ultimately decides against it. He is determined to repay Mr. Greenleaf's kindness with kindness: "He wouldn't let Mr. Greenleaf down. He'd do his very best with Dickie" (17). Of course, a few paragraphs later, Ripley defrauds the Brooklyn and Bronx-based artists out of their tax money. Still, he never cashes their checks—he only exposes their carelessness and laziness. "It amounted," Ripley concludes to himself, "to no more than a practical joke, really. Good clean sport" (19).

For liberal critics in the period, privacy was synonymous with interior thought; exposure to the private life of another could produce empathy, which in turn helped create a better liberalism. But Highsmith was attuned to all the ways exposure to an interior life could create moral distortions. While Tom's interior reveals him to be fundamentally well intentioned, Dickie is repeatedly condescending and lacerating. When Tom suggests that the two ride into France illegally in some coffins, Dickie and Tom go to meet a bootlegger. Dickie is acutely conscious of "the man's dirty nails, dirty shirt collar, his ugly dark face that had been recently shaven though not recently washed" (86). After he finds Tom wearing his clothes, Dickie accuses him of being queer and then loses interest in Tom's friendship, disinviting Tom on a previously proposed trip to Cortina and choosing to go with Marge Sherwood instead. It is only after Tom offers Dickie "friendship, companionship, and respect, everything he had to offer," and Dickie replies with "ingratitude and hostility," that Tom dreams of murdering him (97). Readers are supposed to feel Tom's aggrievedness acutely precisely because they have spent so much time traipsing about in Tom's head.

A useful point of contrast to *Ripley* in terms of narrative style is Truman Capote's true-crime novel *In Cold Blood* (1965). In many ways, the two novels are diametrically opposed. *In Cold Blood* was critically acclaimed and published in the *New Yorker*, the magazine that rejected Highsmith throughout her career. Capote announced his sexuality in the epigraph—dedicating it to his partner Jack Dunphy—and actively promoted himself as a gay male writer while Highsmith shirked the limelight. And, in Capote's work, we are conscious always that the story is being told by a hyper-literate narrator capable of describing characters in language that would not occur to the characters themselves. Take, for instance, the following passage:

> Dick ordered another hamburger. During the past few days he'd known a hunger that nothing—three successive steaks, a dozen Hershey bars, a pound of gumdrops—seemed to interrupt. Perry, on the other hand, was without appetite; he subsisted on root beer, aspirin, and cigarettes. "No wonder you got leaps," Dick told him. "Aw, come on, baby. Get the bubbles out of your blood. We scored. It was perfect."
>
> "I'm surprised to hear that, all things considered," Perry said. The quietness of his tone italicized the malice of his reply. But Dick took it, even smiled—and his smile was a skillful proposition. Here, it said, wearing a kid grin, was a very personable character, clean-cut affable, a fellow any man might trust to shave him.[93]

The signs here that we are outside the characters' heads are numerous. There is the precise cataloguing of all the food Dick has eaten (three steaks, a dozen Hershey bars), bracketed by em dashes to generate a more complex sentence structure. The verb "subsisted," like the adjective "successive" before it, indicates a narrator who uses higher diction than the slang of the characters. Perry's tone "italicized the malice" (a phrase that makes us think of writing, not speech) and Dick's facial expression ("smile was a skillful proposition") become the subjects of the sentences, alienating the reader from the characters' actual thoughts. The effect of this hyperarticulate narrator is to create a distance between the reader and the character, who is inevitably viewed through Capote's lens. The reader is left to ponder the question, just as liberal critics and social theorists in the aftermath of the Second World War hoped: what kind of private life could have produced the unknowable, unspeakable horror? And, unlike Highsmith's *Ripley*, Capote ends *In Cold Blood* with the murderers punished and the sheriff imagining a scene of heterosexual futurity—Susan, "a pretty girl in a hurry, her smooth hair swinging, shining" who is dating boys but not married yet, leaving the gravesite behind.[94]

By contrast, Highsmith presents readers with a world in which there is no narrative distinction between public and private. We are hermetically sealed within Tom's head; even quotidian details are tinctured by his interpretation. While Tom and Dickie are together on the train and Tom thinks of murdering him, Highsmith presents a characteristically thorny paragraph for differentiating psychological judgment from objective narration:

> "Okay," Tom said, smiling a little. He saw Dickie sit back with an air of irritation, and Tom knew why: because Dickie had hated giving him even that much attention. Tom smiled to himself, amused at his own quick reflex in pretending to collapse, because that had been the only way to keep Dickie from seeing what had been a very strange expression on his face.
>
> San Remo. Flowers. A main drag along the beach again, shops and stores and French and English and Italian tourists. Another hotel, with flowers in the balconies. Where? (98)

There is not a single observation in these paragraphs that could be reliably ascribed to a perspective outside Tom's; the whole world is imbued with his consciousness. When Dickie is about to have a feeling ("irritation," "hate"), it is enclosed with a judgment from Tom: "He saw"; "Tom knew why." The other descriptions in the paragraph are subtly indicated as Tom's judgments, his smile bracketed by the past participle of "amused," to explain why he is amused.

As the passage continues and in subsequent paragraphs, the narrative dissolves even further into Tom's head as he imagines killing Dickie in narrative stream of consciousness. Unlike a first-person narrative that signals narrative bias and invites ironic judgment, Highsmith gives us interior judgment that is baked into the reality of the novel, where events are indistinguishable from their origin in Ripley's head. The novel is so saturated with free indirect style that readers are liable to substitute Ripley's private impressions for their own. In contrast to *Beast in View* in which the closet was a space of taboo secret-keeping, in *Ripley*, the closet is either everywhere or nowhere. There is arguably no hidden truth within the closet to confess—no latent meaning beneath the manifest sign; Tom maintains that he is, after all, "one of the most innocent and clean-minded [people] he [Tom] had ever known" (80). As Michael Trask observes, Highsmith imagines "a radically unencumbered fantasy of self-closeting."[95] Trask's observation is true, too, at the level of the sentence; the novel is not so much an imagination of queer identity bursting forth from the privative space of the closet but rather of enveloping a reader inside a closet from which there is no outside.

Highsmith's experiment with point of view undermined the stability of the boundaries between public and private; it was also, of course, a literary technique associated with modernism, particularly Henry James.[96] James's literary DNA is all over Highsmith's writing—as when she models *Ripley* off *The Ambassadors*, or in her "Notes from a Respectable Cockroach" where the insect protagonist has infested Washington Square (another imagination of her own aesthetic colonizing the highbrow).[97] Even the modernist logic that aesthetic value could excuse the representation of immorality—which Highsmith appropriates, gleefully showing how aesthetic value could rationalize obscenity—traces its origin back to James's essay "The Art of Fiction."[98] James was particularly beloved by critics like Trilling and Booth, but whereas they read his experiments in point of view as producing a sense of moral contingency and reflection, Highsmith read him as her bard of perversion, seeing his experiments with points of view and macabre stories (e.g., *Turn of the Screw*) as fodder for her own writing. (One could say the same thing about Ripley that Eve Kosofsky Sedgwick does about the James protagonist Marcher: "To the extent that Marcher's secret has *a* content, that content is homosexual," but queer sexuality is figured only as "a liminal presence."⁹⁹) Rather than imagine a narrative where dramatizing several opposing and unreliable points of view invites a reader to transcend any one, Highsmith saw her experiments in point of view as wholly immersing a reader within a world tinctured by someone else's consciousness.

Ripley epitomized the fears of critics of the day: that mass culture would immerse a reader unthinkingly in a work of art. But it was not the techniques they normally associated with mass culture—overplotted, stylized violence—that allowed Highsmith to provide that immersion. It was the free indirect style associated with James (or Faulkner or Joyce—not incidentally the last names of Guy Haines's lovers in *Strangers*). In refusing the public/private binary in her descriptions, Highsmith's narrative style ultimately paralleled her motive for writing genre fiction. She declined to participate in a confessional structure where the private naïvely become public and instead sought refuge in crime fiction, where the narrative details of her own life and sexuality were revealed only obliquely. She produced sympathy with immoral murderers instead of immoral sex acts, with uncontrollable aesthetic impulses instead of queer desire, with queer or camp reading practices divorced of their sexual context. And in her refusal to distinguish between public and private in her narrative voice, she showed how she could blur the line between modernist stream of consciousness and mass culture. Though she was ignored by liberal critics, she posed a challenge to their celebration of privacy as the foremost virtue of their literature and their heteronormative society, neither of which, as a genre writer and a queer woman, she was alleged to represent.

Altogether, Highsmith, like Hughes and Millar, used the villain-centered crime novel to challenge the reigning period's conceptions of privacy. As we have seen, privacy in the period was often conceived as an idyllic space centered around the heterosexual home—and the right to privacy would, over the course of the subsequent decade, become a more generalized right to self-definition. Literary critics believed that reading literature would enable readers to better understand the private lives of others and thereby create a better liberalism, a system in which individuals are imagined to collectively assent to a public form of self-government that ensures their private freedoms. By contrast, Hughes and Millar represented spaces of privacy as sites of terror and repression—more like lonely places among the cliffs or a telephone booth. Highsmith imagined the whole of her fictional world as imbued with pleasures of the closet: Ripley's unpunished, unrehabilitated private interiority was indistinguishable from the exterior setting and events of the novel. All three authors saw reading not necessarily as cultivating tolerance and understanding through the encounter with private interiority (as liberal critics claimed) but rather as a pleasurable form of immersion in another's private life that had something in common with stalking, manipulation, or identity theft. Their preferred mode of privacy was not a heterosexual "zone" or a "marital bedroom," but instead an encodedness hidden in public view. It was Highsmith in particular who stood at the nexus of postwar liberalism and heteronormativity. There, she imagined the genre novel as a form in which she could induce a reader to celebrate the destruction of the idols of midcentury private life, by transposing what was modernist best practice—the minute-by-minute representation of private thought as it collided with external reality—into mass cultural form.

2 Midcentury Black Cops

IN 1956, Chester Himes was down on his luck. The sales of his novel *The Lonely Crusade* had been disastrous. He went to talk to Marcel Duhamel of Gallimard about getting his novel about prison life—*Cast the First Stone* (1952)—translated into French. It had taken him a decade to publish it, even in bowdlerized form. The unexpurgated original, which included same-sex intimacy and prison brutality, would appear only many years later as *Yesterday Will Make You Cry* (1998). The publishers he shopped it with had called it "revolting," "morbid and moody," "too strong meat for public consumption," and "too vivid for the average reader's taste."[1]

Duhamel said he would think about getting *Cast the First Stone* translated, but that what he really needed was a crime novel with Black faces. Himes initially proposed a novel about a Black piano player falsely accused of raping and murdering a white woman, but Duhamel didn't like the piano player improvising on Chopin. He was too smart. Duhamel handed Himes a copy of a pulpy book called *Runaway Black* by a white writer with the pen name Richard Marsten. (Marsten, whose real name was Evan Hunter, would later write, as Ed McBain, some of the first police procedurals, the 87th Precinct series, concurrent with Himes's.) *Runaway Black* was more like what he wanted from Himes. "Put plenty [of] comedy in it, not too much white brutality," he said, "just an action-packed funny story about Harlem." Himes took *Runaway Black* home and read it. It was, he thought, "pretty shoddy stuff."[2] *Runaway Black* concerned Johnny Lane, a Black man on the run in Harlem for a crime he didn't commit, and it ends with Johnny facing off against a rodent in a sewer. Faced with the request to write a pulpy novel like *Runaway Black*, what was Himes supposed to do? The book seemed to imply that all there was to life in Harlem was poverty, degradation, and criminality. Himes reread Faulkner's *Sanctuary*, one of his favorite books, and thought back to an old pal.

Fifteen years earlier, in 1941, Himes had been invited, along with other promising young Black writers, to share a table with Langston Hughes at a Los Angeles dinner of the League of American Writers, an organization known for its left-leaning and Communist sympathies. One of those writers was Zora Neale Hurston, the anthropologist and novelist, who had just moved from Harlem out to the west coast; another was Jess Kimbrough, a burly man with a deep voice who had just retired from the Los Angeles Police Department and who was, like Himes, a writer of short stories.[3] Kimbrough and Himes, an ex-cop and an ex-con, became friends, met a number of times after the dinner, read each other's stories, and swapped tales of their exploits. Himes found that Kimbrough was a "much better writer than many of the writers whom [sic] got mention in" Sterling Brown's anthology "the *Negro Caravan*."[4] Himes alighted on Kimbrough and his partner Charles Broady—"pitiless bastards," he called them later[5]—and then dreamed into life the two characters for which he became most famous: Coffin Ed Johnson and Grave Digger Jones.[6]

Traditionally, detective novels had most often been written from the perspective of private investigators pursuing wrongdoers. In the previous chapter, we saw queer and female novelists like Hughes, Highsmith, and Millar narrate instead from the vantage point of villains because they wanted to inspect readers' desires to witness immoral behavior. They relished showing how the space of personal privacy, the putative font of white middle-class Cold War heterosexual morality, could be a place of fear and terror, and how readers could be led to enjoy watching the destruction of those private spaces. But in this chapter, we will see something quite different: in the Harlem Detective series, Chester Himes focused on neither criminals nor private investigators but on cops. He aligned his reader's perspective with two police officers who felt profoundly ambivalent about their complicity with state-sponsored racist surveillance.

While the legal right to privacy expanded in the 1960s and 1970s with cases like *Roe* and *Griswold*, the right to privacy, especially when understood as a right to self-definition, often seemed to be in abeyance or else diminishing to people of color.[7] The social programs of the War on Poverty brought the administrative state increasingly into the homes of low-income people of color; welfare, treatment, counseling, training, and rehabilitation all required intensive state oversight, even as those programs were supposed to guarantee personal autonomy.[8] While low-income women of color were granted rights to abortion under *Roe*, the Hyde Amendment of 1976 denied the financial means to procure them.[9] The year after the Court declared "a reasonable expectation of privacy" in *Katz v. United States* (1967), it found that "stop and frisk" was constitutional in *Terry v. Ohio* (1968), a decision that paved the way for the Court's allowance of the random police searches of people of color common during the War on Drugs.[10] The expanded scope of the surveillance state of the War on Poverty coexisted with the heightened police activity of the War on Crime.[11] As James Forman, Jr. argues, Black cops played a particularly important role in the expansion of the carceral state; in response to overly aggressive policing, many communities of color advocated for more African American officers on the force, but these middle-class officers turned out to be just as inclined to brutality toward working-class Blacks as their white counterparts.[12] At least a decade before most historians would mark the dramatic expansion of the carceral state, Himes was writing about two middle-class Black cops assigned with patrolling the working-class population of Harlem. In focusing on these violent African American cops, Himes might seem to have been remarkably clairvoyant. But as Kelly Lytle Hernandez has shown, mass incarceration began decades earlier in Los Angeles, long before the rest of the country. When Himes met Kimbrough in early 1940s LA, he was encountering one of the earliest avatars of the modern carceral state.[13]

Indeed, one of the great and perpetually unanswered questions posed by Himes's oeuvre has been why he chose to write detective novels about policemen. In 1954, the year Himes began writing the series, the police procedural was still in its infancy. Radio/TV shows like *Dragnet* (1949–1957, radio; 1951–1959, recurring, TV) had only just begun, and Ed McBain's 87th Precinct series wasn't yet released. There were only a few scattered popular representations of Black cops in African American literature—Rudolph Fisher's *The Conjure-Man Dies* (1934); Hughes Allison's "Corollary" (1948) and "Imposture" (1949). Even after the genre picked up more popularity, Black cops remained rare—the notable exception being Virgil Tibbs in *In the Heat of the Night* (1965) (written by the white author John Ball).

By contrast, in the aftermath of Watts, Black authors of crime fiction rarely imagined the police as potentially heroic protagonists. Sam Greenlee's *The Spook Who Sat by the Door* (1969; film 1973) follows fictional Dan Freeman, the first Black CIA officer, as he uses the skills he learned as a spook to organize Black teenage guerrilla forces to lead a violent rebellion in Chicago against white and

Black police officers. Writers like Iceberg Slim, Donald Goines, and Nathan Heard—and Blaxploitation films like *Sweet Sweetback's Baadasssss Song* (1971), *Superfly* (1972), and the LA Rebellion film *Bush Mama* (1975; released 1979)—all follow Black criminals (or accused criminals) contending with ruthless, corrupt cops who were mostly white. When Black cops do appear in these works, they often turn out to be worse than the white ones.[14] Coffin Ed and Grave Digger, who evolved between 1957 and 1969, occupy an intermediary position between the few good Black cops of the 50s who tried to protect their neighborhoods from crime and the bad cops of the 60s and 70s who destroyed them with viciousness and corruption. The duo are heroic but also heartless and trigger-happy.

If one question was why these particularly conflicted cops, another was: why did his two fictional cops seem to lack any meaningful private life—perhaps even less than their notoriously laconic forebears like Sam Spade and Philip Marlowe. As Sean McCann observes, Grave Digger and Coffin Ed "seem throughout Himes's series to have no 'interior life' whatsoever."[15] For Hilton Als, too, they lack "the unsettling complexity of Himes's autobiographical heroes."[16] While we do find out a bit more about their family lives (they live on Long Island, for instance) as the series progresses, their thoughts are rarely narrated. Critics have responded to Coffin Ed and Grave Digger's flatness by reading them as allegorizing an intellectual position, whether Himes's waning faith in New Deal liberalism, his engagement with the selective statism of the civil rights movement, or his interest in French surrealism.[17]

In this chapter, however, I will argue that we should read Coffin Ed and Grave Digger as responding to a literary marketplace that demanded stories that would conjoin race and criminality, a marketplace that, as we have begun to see, would not bear his more realistic depictions of Black life. In what follows, I will argue that we can better understand why Himes chose to write about cops by reflecting on the three main influences—*Runaway Black*, Faulkner's *Sanctuary*, and the life of Jess Kimbrough—that he contemplated as he created them. Himes saw a doubling between the middle-class figures of the Black cop and the Black crime writer: both were tasked with surveilling working-class African American life for a white establishment. With publishers and readers unwilling to treat his characters as real people with authentic private lives, Himes instead used his flat characters to reflect on the constraints of the literary marketplace that had produced them. In uncovering

Jess Kimbrough's lost life and literary output, we begin to see what Coffin Ed and Grave Digger's flatness was designed to conceal—and what a rounder picture might have looked like.

Man on the Run

To understand the genesis of Himes's characters, we need to first understand the cultural field in which he wrote. It was a field that often participated in a certain kind of racial surveillance: the alignment of skin color with criminality. This cultural logic aligned an exterior feature (skin pigmentation) with a private, interior sensibility (the propensity to commit crime). Khalil Gibran Muhammad has chronicled the emergence of the cultural link between race and criminality between 1890 and 1940 as progressive reformers and social scientists produced new statistical data that framed Black people as criminals.[18] By midcentury, as Theodore Martin writes, crime novelists, too "could not avoid the uncomfortable yet implacable fact that being black in the US was often synonymous with being seen as a criminal."[19] The cultural logic that linked race with criminality had a profound effect on the way African American authors writing about crime or urban settings encountered the literary field at the time: their work was often misinterpreted as revealing their capacity for criminal behavior.

Richard Wright, for instance, found that *Native Son* was misread as furthering the conjunction between race and crime. In 1944 the sociologist Gunnar Myrdal wrote that in the "Negro slums of American cities," there was a "growing generation" of "individuals like Bigger Thomas." While *Native Son* was meant to show how Bigger's lack of educational and economic mobility turned him into a criminal, Myrdal instead focused on his capacity for anger and violence.[20] "It is," Myrdal wrote, "not so much discrimination which distorts the Negro's criminal record, as it is certain characteristics of the Negro population."[21] Midcentury sociologists like Myrdal enlisted Wright's novel on behalf of what Daryl Michael Scott calls "the damage thesis": the idea that Black people and communities had been psychologically damaged by their exposure to poverty.[22] While "the damage thesis" was meant to encourage social reform, it often ended up reinforcing the stereotype that people of color were culturally or psychologically inclined to crime. Even those writers like Ralph Ellison who critiqued Bigger for being essentially too flat, who strove to create characters who were more "human," still struggled more generally with the racialized demands of the literary field.

If novels "depict too much of reality they frighten us by giving us a picture of society so far from our optimistic ideal," Ellison wrote, but "if they leave out too much we cannot take them seriously for very long."[23]

Writers of crime fiction, too, had to contend with a white audience that did not readily accept stories of Black heroism. In Hughes Allison's two short stories, "Corollary" (1948) and "Imposture" (1949), a Black cop named Joe Hill's unique knowledge of the Black population enables him to solve crimes that the white cops could not. In 1948, Allison struggled with a white audience—he found that white readers were incredulous of Hill, who not only possessed a keen intellectual discernment but who was also "six feet one inch in height, with two hundred pounds of solid muscle appropriately strung along an excellently developed frame."[24] Allison said in an interview that it was

> a battle to get a story about a Negro detective published in a national magazine, you know. I send the publisher a page-by-page explanation of what I'm doing in the story, and how I know what I'm talking about. He has to be ready in case some letters of protest arrive from Mississippi or Georgia.[25]

Writing naturalist fiction about the social forces that produced Black criminality turned out to essentialize that criminality; writing crime stories about heroic Black cops was supposedly unrealistic.

Himes experienced the market's desire for stories conjoining race and crime throughout his career, first as a literary writer and then as a writer of crime stories. His first novel, *If He Hollers Let Him Go* (1945), was already attuned to the idea that naturalist novels like *Native Son* would be either occluded from view or else misread as conjoining race and criminality. A white character, Polly, reflects the white readers who don't want to read about crime in a conversation about Richard Wright's *Native Son*. "All Wright did was write a vicious crime story," she says. A Black female character, Arline, responds that the book "just proved what the white Southerner has always said about us; that our men are rapists and murderers." Echoing Himes's viewpoint, Bob Jones, the protagonist, disagrees; he sees the book as an indictment of the social circumstances that produced Bigger: "you couldn't pick a better person to prove the point [of Negro oppression]."[26] In its form, *If He Hollers Let Him Go* ultimately disputes the association of race and crime: it is a novel about how easy it is for a Black man to be accused of a crime he didn't commit—the rape of a white woman. Like *Native Son*, Himes's next novel, *The Lonely Crusade*, was also received as linking race and criminality. It concerned the travails of Lee Gordon, an African American working as a union organizer at an aircraft plant in wartime Los Angeles. Conjoining Wright with Myrdal with an improbable hyphen, Lloyd L. Brown, the African American reviewer for the *New Masses*, saw it as belonging to the "Myrdal-Wright school" insofar as Lee Gordon and Bigger Thomas both represent "the basic character of the Negro people in America."[27] (Himes believed the novel was, in fact, designed to emphasize Gordon's decision to turn from selfishness to self-sacrifice in a labor riot at the end of the novel.)

In his speech "The Dilemma of the Negro Novelist in the U.S." (1948), Himes, reflecting on some of these critiques, claimed that audiences simply did not want to hear honest stories of Black life. For the writer, "delineat[ing] the degrading effects of oppression will be like inflicting a wound on himself." Publishers, he said, consider honest novels by Black authors "bad ventures" in general. Liberal white publishers, familiar only with middle-class Black people, concluded that the "honest negro" writer must be "psychotic."[28] In his next novel *The End of a Primitive* (1956), Himes satirized the market in which he wrote. His editor asked the protagonist, "Why don't you try writing about people, just *people*?" to which he replied: "White people, you mean?"[29] There was no room in the literary marketplace for Himes's stories about working- and middle-class Black life.

When Duhamel asked Himes to write a novel like *Runaway Black*, it was the culmination of Himes's decade-long struggle with a literary marketplace that refused his stories or else misinterpreted his fiction as essentializing Black criminality.[30] *Runaway Black* follows Johnny Lane who is wrongly accused of murder. Halfway through the novel, the cops beat a confession out of the real perpetrator, but they don't tell Johnny, who keeps running. Black women appear in various stages of undress as exotic dancers and prostitutes. Johnny is stabbed in the arm by a junkie in an alley whose syringe he accidentally breaks. The novel ends with Johnny in a dumpster heap facing off against a rat. *Runaway Black* is manifestly designed to appeal to a voyeuristic white audience who expected to see exaggerated scenes of sex, criminals, and drugs. Duhamel wanted Himes to be a native informant for this same milieu.

Runaway Black imagines itself as sympathetic to the plight of Black life in the city. "When cops are involved," Johnny thinks to himself, "it's better to run first and think about it afterward." The Black characters frequently bemoan their own stereotyping. "And they call *us* the happy people," thinks Johnny, looking at wealthy white people in evening clothes.[31] When a cop tells a Black man, "Every Nigra carries a razor," he responds, "You've got a pretty stereotyped picture of the Negro, I'd say."[32] The trouble is that, in articulating a social problem, the novel implies that all there is to Black life is criminality. The characters are stereotypes: an accused criminal on the run, a hopped-up junkie, an ignorant but well-intentioned adult dancer, a corrupt gangster, and so on. A review by Gertrude Martin, in the *Chicago Defender*, said that "there is a sense of hopelessness from the very beginning which gives the book its tragic tone."[33] Another review called it "a novel of fear and terror and at all times harrowing."[34] Mostly, reviewers came away feeling that Harlem was a place of fear and terror; it was a place that suffered both from too much surveillance (Johnny is on the run because he is Black) and also too little (the cops do not bother to tell Johnny that the charges have been dropped).

In some respects, Himes's first novel in the Harlem Detective series, *For Love of Imabelle* (later republished as *A Rage in Harlem*), resembles *Runaway Black*; both follow hapless innocent protagonists on the run. Only over time did Coffin Ed and Grave Digger's viewpoints expand so that they occupied more than a few chapters in each novel. Both novels allude to the African American folk song "Run, Nigger, Run"—a vestige of a world in which Black people trying to escape slavery were criminals eluding the "patter-roller." Certain sentences could plausibly belong to either novel. "You did a lot of running in Harlem," Marsten writes;[35] Himes's version is "Somebody was always running in Harlem." Himes's Jackson thinks, "He had forgotten why he was running. Just running." Marsten's Johnny thinks, "He'd run and he was still running. . . . For Johnny Lane had just realized with a sudden clarity that he'd been running all his life."[36] There were, of course, many key differences between the novels—perhaps most notably Marsten's salacious and sorrowful tone contrasted with Himes's absurdly comic one. But a crucial one was that, in a small portion of Himes's novel, there were two Black cops, two characters who rebutted the presumption that Black people were simple or criminally inclined. These cops' viewpoints eventually enlarged to become the lens through which the rest of the series is viewed.

Himes's most overt response to *Runaway Black* came a few years later in his career when he returned to the basic story in *Run Man Run* (1959). It was inspired by Himes's last experience while living in America: in December 1955, on the eve of his departure to France, a drunken white policeman stumbled into the Horn & Hardart automat cafeteria, where Himes had worked as a janitor and was saying his last goodbyes. The cop falsely accused Himes and the other staff of stealing his car.[37] Having seen firsthand how his skin color could mark him as a criminal in front of a white police officer, Himes reflected on the experience in *Run Man Run*. Like Marsten's book, *Run Man Run* follows a falsely accused Black man on the run, but Himes made the cop in question not merely negligent but sociopathic. Walker, the white cop, pursues the Black protagonist Jimmy, the last witness to Walker's drunken murders of Black bystanders. Walker uses his authority as a cop and his brother-in-law's status as police chief to pursue and try to murder Jimmy. *Runaway Black* had pointed to lackadaisical law enforcement as producing Johnny Lane's plight—the cops forget to notify him he's been exonerated. *Run Man Run* points to the way the police state enables a cop to hunt down and try to kill an innocent man.

But to audiences the genre and the cover mattered more than the actual details of the story. When William Targ, his editor, asked him to explain the origin of the detective's racism, Himes demurred, claiming that he was not trying to write a work of "literature," as American readers had not appreciated his attempts to do so. American readers knew more about white detectives than he did, he claimed, and "the majority of readers would be more interested, for one reason or another, to read of 'a scared nigger.' I may be wrong, but I believe that would be my most successful story in the U.S."[38] The original US cover of *Run Man Run* featured a Black woman in a striped shirt, apparently naked from the waist down, with the caption "Lush sex and stark violence, colored Black and served up raw by a great Negro writer." Responding to the American paperback, Himes wrote to Dell, his publisher, in protest: "if it is necessary to put this type of cover with this descriptive copy on the book in order to sell it to the American people, the American people are really truly sick." Himes could write to his publisher, but he couldn't shake the problem that dogged him throughout his career: how do you write novels about Black life for an audience that only wanted to see "lush sex and stark violence"?

To understand how Himes imagined characterization within the Harlem Detective series, it is worth looking at the book he reread before creating it: Faulkner's *Sanctuary*. From *Sanctuary*, Himes learned how to embed social critique in mass cultural forms. *Sanctuary* conjoins modernist techniques with mass appeal; Faulkner called it "a cheap idea . . . deliberately conceived to make money."[39] Himes didn't see it that way. "His portrayal of Black people is so masterful," Himes thought fondly.[40] The influence of *Sanctuary* and its characterization appears frequently at the level of the sentence in Himes. In *Sanctuary*, Faulkner often anatomizes his characters into inanimate objects: "Popeye's eyes looked like rubber knobs, like they'd give to the touch and then recover with the whorled smudge of the thumb on them."[41] Himes uses a similar technique: "Reverend Short's nearsighted eyes began bulging like bananas being squeezed from their skins, and all they could see was the livid scar on Johnny's blood-purple forehead, puffing and wriggling like a maddened octopus."[42] These metaphors naturalize violence by making it comic; they make the characters seem less than human, more like caricatures, dissecting them and transforming them into hyperbolic objects and animals: knobs, bananas, and octopuses.

One of the most resonant images in *Sanctuary* is that of an unnamed Black man in the prison who is supposed to be hanged—perhaps the figure Himes was recollecting. The man "slashed" his wife "in the throat with a razor so that, her whole head tossing further and further backward from the bloody regurgitation of her bubbling throat, she ran out the cabin door and for six or seven steps up the quiet moonlit lane."[43] It is an image so gruesome that, as with much of the violence in Himes's novels, one is inclined to raise an eyebrow. In Faulkner as in Himes, violence is absurd, grotesque, excessive—a barbed comment on the mass cultural reader's desire to witness it.

In *Sanctuary*, the murderer himself turns out to be an incisive commentator on the racial politics of the novel. The Black laborers come together in the darkness after work to sing spirituals underneath the window, and the white folks stop to "listen to those who were sure to die and him who was already dead singing about heaven and being tired."[44] The murderer, like the other Black laborers, is "sure to die." He is a double, too, for Lee Goodwin, who is wrongly accused of raping the novel's southern heroine with a corn cob and murdering the man trying to protect her. He is eventually lynched.

Even though Goodwin is innocent, he dies, too. Guilty of the most heinous crime or not guilty at all, it makes no difference in the South if your skin is not the right color. And lest the reader rest too easy in an eloquently described moment of pathos ("a rich, sourceless voice coming out of the high darkness"), the murderer bursts out in dialect that he shouldn't be killed because he's the best baritone singer in north Mississippi ("Fo days mo! Den dey ghy stroy de bes ba'ytone singer in nawth Mississippi!").[45] In response, Goodwin thinks, "Damn that fellow. . . . I ain't in any position to wish any man that sort of luck, but I'll be damned . . ."[46] The convict's call is a reminder that their two fates are unfairly intertwined. It is the moment when structural racism intrudes on liberal proceduralism, when the shadow of the system that treats people as flat caricatures or stereotypes intrudes on the system that claims to treat them as fully autonomous private individuals with differentiated private lives. *Sanctuary* may be darker, more cynical, more disgusted in tone, and even more misogynistic than anything Himes produced, but it also gave him the idea that he didn't have to passively accept the flatness that was forced upon him by the literary field. He could embrace it as a stylistic choice. Flat characters placed an emphasis not on individuals' choices and private emotions but on the literary form (the cheap violent potboiler) and the political system (the structural racism) that produced their flatness.

The Forgotten Career of Jess Kimbrough

While he was trying to figure out how to write a crime story for Duhamel and rereading *Sanctuary*, Himes also thought back to a real-life person he knew—Jess Kimbrough. From the very beginning of his career, Himes had imagined Black cops as figures whose personal, private allegiances conflicted with their professional ones. In "He Knew" (1933), Himes represents two Black cops, John Jones and Henry Walls, who are tasked with investigating two murders in the Black district of Harlem. When they arrive on the scene, they follow some gunshots, end up in a standoff, and return fire, only to find they have killed Jones's sons. Himes saw writing a story about cops as the perfect way to dramatize a conflict between professional duty—to police Harlem—and private allegiances—to race, to family. He would return to this same plotline in *The Real Cool Killers*, in which Coffin Ed's daughter turns out to be involved with a criminal gang of Muslims. The captain asks Jones and Walls to police the "Negro neighborhood" because they are fellow "plodders." They imagine initially that the crime is unrelated to them. They think they can separate the performance of their public duties to police from their private lives. "God, the pity of this new crop of youths turning to crime," Jones remarks, only to find that the youths he encounters are his sons, whose lives he has ended.[47] Himes's acquaintance with Kimbrough brought him a living example of what he had imagined back in 1933: a Black police officer who was conflicted about surveilling his own neighborhood on behalf of a white establishment. When he was contemplating participating in a different kind of surveillance—representing Black life for an audience looking to associate race and criminality—Himes imagined a homology between the Black cop and the Black writer. Recovering Kimbrough's life and art gives some additional texture to the characters of Coffin Ed and Grave Digger; it can help us see what the flat characters were designed to shield from view.

While Grave Digger and Coffin Ed often give expression to a sense of conflictedness, particularly as the series progresses, their conflicted mindset was matched if not surpassed by their real-life counterpart.[48] Jess Kimbrough was secretly a socialist while he was on the force. Born in 1892 in Texas, Kimbrough moved with his family to California when he was four. He dropped out of school in the eighth grade to provide for them but continued to read as many books as he could by night. He spent the next decade or so shoveling sand in a riverbed. At the age of twenty-four he took the entrance exam to become a police officer and passed because of his reading ability. He stood to earn twenty dollars a week as a cop, in contrast to the two dollars weekly he made shoveling sand—assuming the weather held out.[49] Kimbrough was a fellow traveler of the Communists the LAPD assaulted and belonged to the very unions the cops busted. As a police officer, he was circumspect about revealing this fact. But at least in a biography he supplied to *International Literature*, a Moscow-based English-language magazine (and in which he makes no mention of his career on the force), Kimbrough claims to have become a Socialist after hearing Eugene V. Debs speak on his presidential tour in 1910. He embraced the Marxist tenet that "the working class and the ruling class had nothing in common and that the war between them must go on until the workers came to power."[50] After joining the IWW (Industrial Workers of the World), he wrote that he met Bill Haywood and Ben Fletcher and participated in the Fall River textile strike in Massachusetts. His fellow IWW members inspired him to be a writer, because they taught him to imagine "a better way of life."[51]

Kimbrough was an active participant in organizing activities. He was close friends with Hugh Gordon, one of the Black organizers of the strike on Llewellyn Iron Works in 1916, and one of his stories imagines a Black veteran trying to commit violence against the white, American Legion–affiliated strikebreakers of the Imperial Valley lettuce strike of 1930.[52] The anti-labor white faction of the

American Legion, which he decries in that story, was the LAPD's close ally.[53] A drum major, he helped found a Black musicians' union, the American Federation of Musicians, Local 767, in the 1920s—which, having merged with its white counterpart Local 47 in the 1950s, still endures today.[54] Kimbrough was also a member of the Executive Committee of the California chapter of the progressive League of American Writers and an editor of the affiliated west coast magazine *The Clipper*.[55] When he joined the LAPD in 1915, Kimbrough would likely have witnessed other officers doing things that would have seemed anathema to him: strike-breaking, rounding up leftist radicals and vagrants, and even persecuting the IWW.

Kimbrough's time on the force should be understood in view of the white urban segregation that began in LA in the late 1910s when Kimbrough joined the LAPD. With a new influx of Black settlers, racial segregation in Los Angeles increased; Blacks were confined to the Central Avenue district, Watts, and a few other areas. Many homes outside of the Central district had restrictive covenants placed on their deeds so that no people of color could own them, and the Ku Klux Klan played an active role in harassing Black homeowners living outside the district. Police often took kickbacks from organized crime that operated prostitution, gambling, and racketeering within Black districts. The middle-class Black citizens living in these districts agitated for better policing, less corruption, and for more Black police officers, but what they got instead was often police brutality.[56] Kimbrough was thus tasked with enforcing and policing a segregated Black community, charged by a white establishment with rooting out crime while also looking the other way at organized crime.[57] (In their first appearance, Coffin Ed and Grave Digger take "their tribute, like all real cops, from the established underworld.")[58] He became a plainclothes detective investigating homicides after his service in World War I and was promoted to lieutenant in 1925.[59]

Many of the crimes that Kimbrough solved on the force were chronicled in the *California Eagle*, LA's leading Black newspaper.[60] They sometimes seem as full of pathos or absurdity as the crimes that Himes wrote about in his novels. For instance, on February 26, 1926, Kimbrough arrested a man named Matthew Gibbs, who had wanted to open a grocery but didn't have the money. Gibbs robbed a bank, but he panicked and left before he could collect the money because the teller was too slow.[61] On another occasion, in a plot with notes of Himesian absurdity, an innocent embalmer named Melvin Griffin was standing on a street corner when a man offered to buy him a drink. At the bar, the man pulled a gun on Griffin and insisted that he assist in a bank robbery. Once the man's partner arrived, the partner bewailed that his "girl" had taken all of his money; he mistakenly identified Griffin as having "procured" her for him. Together, the three went around LA in search of the girl until Kimbrough apprehended them while they were peering into some bushes in search of "the elusive 'femme.'"[62] Other cases were more tragic: on May 23, 1930, Kimbrough apprehended a man who emerged from Delphinia Jackson's closet and stabbed her with a knife; it was thought that she had refused his sexual advances.[63]

These stories give us a sense of the real-life material that Himes may have heard from Kimbrough, and we can think about his novels as struggling with the problem of how to represent them for a white audience. The edgy mix of violence and humor that he developed after reading Faulkner was designed to prevent the reader from attaining a stable emotional repose, whether in a sense of pity or laughter. The reader was stymied from accessing too much of the private lives of the characters. If these characters were realistically depicted, they might be seen as reinforcing racist stereotypes about Black simplicity or sexuality or depravity; instead, they are described or even blazoned through Faulknerian comic similes and metaphors. Imabelle, the femme fatale of *A Rage in Harlem*, appears as "a cushioned-lipped, hot-bodied, banana-skin chick with the speckled-brown eyes of a teaser and the high-arched, ball-bearing hips of a natural-born *amante*."[64] When the reverend in *The Crazy Kill* is brought into the police room, "His eyes protruded behind his gold-rimmed spectacles like a bug's under a microscope, and his Adam's apple bobbed like a float on a fishing line."[65] Rendering them flat and comic could sometimes make them seem like caricatures, ones that reflected more on the motives of the reader who wanted to be entertained by watching Black crime. This is not to say that Himes's stories were written exclusively for white audiences. In interviews, he imagined a white audience looking for scenes of Black criminality, sexuality, or just general absurdity: "the majority of white readers are just looking for the exotic episodes. They're looking for things that will amuse or titillate them. The rest of it they skip over and pay no attention to."[66] But he also hoped that Black readers would see the realism beneath what might seem like absurd characterization: "the people of Harlem can recognize each spot in their city, and see themselves mirrored in one character or another in my books."[67]

While uncovering the details of some of the crimes Kimbrough thwarted might give us better insight into Himes's other characters, was Kimbrough as brutal as Coffin Ed and Grave Digger? Would his pistol kill a rock and then bury it? While his political sympathies ran contrary to his duties, there are other signs that he could be an aggressive cop. In a history of the Black cops on the LAPD, Kimbrough was listed by fellow officer Homer Broome as one of the Black officers who "proved a menace to the shiftless," along with his partner of nine years, Charles Broady.[68] Broady was accused of excessive brutality on more than one occasion. In an incident in 1916, he shoved a woman's head against a fence so hard that she was in the hospital for over seven weeks. Witnesses saw her lying bleeding on the ground and claimed that Broady initially would not let them assist her. Broady was acquitted of charges because the woman was still in the hospital and thus unable to testify at his hearing.[69] But even though he was on the LAPD during what historian Gerald Woods called one of "the lowest depths in its dreary history," Kimbrough also remembered later in life that "police brutality was not an issue in those days," because "everybody was more or less afraid."[70]

In Kimbrough's writing, he struggled to balance his leftist allegiances and the racist ideas of the police force on which he served. In 1925, Kimbrough published a series of essays entitled "The Psychology of the Negro Criminal" in a California government publication called the *Municipal Employee*; as a Black officer patrolling a Black district, he was imagined to have special insight into that psychology. The essays are elliptically worded and sometimes give voice to racist stereotypes and preconceptions. The articles explore possible explanations for African American crime—citing botanists, geneticists, British explorers, and psychologists—as he considers genetic, social, and psychological motivations for crime. Kimbrough suggests that heredity plays a part in transmitting mental diseases and even goes as far as to approve of the idea that African American passivity as a trait has been hereditarily passed down. "The ancestral strain of the Negro in the United States," he initially speculates, "is very essential as a basic cause of criminal tendencies." But then he tacks away from the idea that Black people are inherently violent or criminal. As the essay progresses, Kimbrough writes wryly, "psychologists have come to our rescue and have conclusively proven this to be without foundation, and the criminal of this nature is in reality suffering from some form of mental disorder." He concludes that certain inherited traits, when combined with poverty, lead to "Negro crime" and not that African Americans are genetically disposed toward criminality.[71]

For a white audience, Kimbrough tried to suggest that Black criminality was caused by a combination of poverty, mental disease, and ignorance. But, while writing poetry for a Black audience during roughly the same period, he showed that urban segregation is the cause of crime. In "The Lure of the Black Belt," a 1930 poem he published in *Flash* (a short-lived magazine for Black intellectuals identifying with the New Negro movement), he imagines the inefficacy of the urban segregation he was tasked with enforcing.

> They set it aside in the city, like a cancerous thing accurst,
> Hemming it in with a yawning wall, the last of its kind and the first.
> They blocked it 'round with factories grim, with the busy clash and din,
> But they forgot that cloudless roof of blue that lets the sunshine in.[72]

Even if white America has isolated and forgotten "The Black Belt," Kimbrough believes in a natural order, sunshine, that is more just. The implications of this poem are that Black life might seem to be ignored and benighted, but, in fact, is blossoming in ways to which the white population is completely oblivious: "They did not know that flowers that grow, in the gardens rich and fair, / Would blossom bright, in the same sunlight, as they blossom over there." Contrasting the two pieces of writing suggests that as a cop Kimbrough urged gradual reform, but when writing for a Black audience, his more politically subversive opinions came through.

Kimbrough would continue to display his rebellious face for a left-leaning audience in the next decades. In 1937 and 1938, he sent two book manuscripts to *International Literature* (*IL*). One, "Brown Doughboy," about a Black World War I veteran, he hoped would show "the Negro's reaction to a war that meant nothing to him" and imagine the birth of "a new idealogy [sic] of world socialism."[73] The other, "A Path Upward," was intended to describe "the early awakening of class consciousness in the Negro masses," "how a capitalist society, with its many contridictions [sic], has demoralized Negroes."[74] Writing to *IL* in 1938, the year of his retirement, he enumerates his various occupations as an itinerant manual laborer: stable boy, bricklayer, blacksmith's assistant, and cement layer, but he does not ever mention his years on the force in his two-page biography.

Kimbrough wrote only one story that was explicitly about policing, "Humpy" (1939), which was published in the League of American Writers' *Clipper* next to an essay by Dalton Trumbo. A white man comes into the police station, and, to the Black detective, accuses a "brown" woman with an "enormous hump" of pulling a knife on him and stealing twenty dollars. But when the white station chief asks him to testify, he refuses and admits that his story was "cock-and-bull." The Black cop brings the woman into the station, and she claims that the man is her john and that she was paid only a dollar. At the end of the story, once the john leaves, she pulls out a ten and offers it to the station chief, because she is in the habit of giving cops kickbacks. "I don't hold out on the law, and I don't play smart. You get half of all the money I make," she says. In response, the cop is "helplessly dependent, like some animal caught in a snare."[75] As in certain of Himes's later Harlem Detective novels like *The Heat's On* or *Blind Man with a Pistol*, the police officer is nominally the one with the power, responsible for enforcing the law. But in "Humpy," he finds that he is powerless to do so—and is faced only with a chain of illegal deeds he cannot address: a white john who refuses to testify in court, a Black prostitute who falsely denies stealing from him, and a police force that is in the habit of taking bribes.

Kimbrough was a World War I veteran, and in a story and a play, he told of a veteran returning home and being forced by southern racists at gunpoint to remove his uniform. "Brown Doughboy," the excerpt from the novel he sent *International Literature*, chronicles a young serviceman, Jed, journeying to Alabama to give a fallen soldier's mother news of his death; on his way he is intercepted by "the shambling champions of white supremacy" and forced to return home with his uniform tucked away. For a Soviet audience, Kimbrough represents how Black people in America were instrumentalized, used to commit state-sponsored violence, and then abandoned by the state. His one-act play *Georgia Sundown* (1940) (published alongside another by Julius Pinchev) told a similar story. Jed Daniels, a Black soldier and war hero, returns home to his family in Georgia. "What do they care about us?" his wife opines, "Other than to use us." The family, it turns out, has ancestors who have fought in the Civil War, in Cuba, and in the Philippines.[76] But in this version, the character has grown more militant: instead of giving up his uniform, Jed takes out the racists with his hand grenade in a suicide bombing. After living a double life for many years on the force, Kimbrough took off his own uniform and reflected on his role as an agent of state violence. He retired from putting people of color in jail and instead fantasized about a character who blew up white racists.

In his second career as a writer, Kimbrough struggled with the same problems as Himes: his fiction was also expected to shore up the link between race and criminality. After he retired from the force, Kimbrough worked as a carpenter at a VA hospital, but he continued to be a prolific writer—authoring a collection of World War I poems, a western, a recollection of his grandmother's life in Texas, and more. His unpublished book of poetry provided a record of his experiences as a Black officer in World War I. *Enoch Dawson*, a western, is a kind of novel of ideas set on the range, as a Black man freed from a white wagon train learns about liberation, freedom, and racial history from his mentor, the titular Enoch Dawson. Dawson gives his protégé the name Anthony Copeland after one of the members of John Brown's group at Harpers Ferry. *A Kitchen in Sandton* describes Kimbrough's childhood and a story of his grandmother's romance with a white man.[77] In spite of his attempts, publishers would not accept any of these works.

In fact, they turned out to want only one thing: realistic stories of Kimbrough's life as a cop. In the 1960s, Kimbrough got in touch with a publisher at Macmillan named Alan Rinzler, who agreed to publish a novel based on Kimbrough's time on the force—*Defender of the Angels* (1969). Around the time Kimbrough contacted him, Rinzler was in the midst of publishing one of the most famous works about a Black private investigator—*Shaft* (1970). He had noticed that many Blacks saw Virgil Tibbs, of *In the Heat of the Night*, as, essentially, "an Oreo." "What about a black policeman who is not a sweetheart?" Rinzler wondered.[78] So Rinzler contacted Ronald Hobbs, the only prominent Black literary agent working in New York at the time, and Hobbs introduced Rinzler to a white man, Ernest Tidyman. Tidyman had read William Styron's *The Confessions of Nat Turner*, which he viewed as melodramatic and unrealistic, and wanted to write about "a black hero who thinks of himself as a human being, but who uses his black rage as one of his resources, along with intelligence and courage."[79] But while Tidyman thought he was depicting realistic intelligence and courage, the character he created, John Shaft, was regarded by many readers and some film viewers as an oversexualized and thuggish figure who glorified violence.[80]

This is not to say that Rinzler hawked stereotypes of Black people—the year after *Defender of the Angels* he also published *The Bluest Eye* and had released Claude Brown's *Manchild in the Promised Land* (1965). Rinzler, a self-described "red diaper baby," had participated in the civil rights movement, helping the Student Nonviolent Coordinating Committee (SNCC) register Black voters. Rather, if *Shaft* is any indication, Rinzler as a publisher may have thought of himself as dispelling stereotypes or revealing new perspectives, but the books he released—*Shaft* and also *Defender*—nonetheless appealed to a certain audience that had an appetite for depictions of Black sex and crime. Even though Kimbrough enjoyed a pleasant relationship with Rinzler (in Rinzler's recollection), in his personal letters Kimbrough questioned the way that he was being pigeonholed. The letter he sent to his friend Adina Williamson while waiting for publication is lost, but she wrote back to him: "As you so ably put it you are Mr. Rinzler's Black Boy! He is your Mister Charlie, the one that through his great white goodness allows you to reap a part of the action."[81] He felt like he was being tokenized.

Because Himes and Kimbrough had lost touch, Kimbrough never knew that he had inspired Himes's detective series, but he realized that they both struggled with similar obstacles in the literary marketplace. At the end of his life, Kimbrough owned a copy of the *Lonely Crusade*, and he spoke admiringly of Himes as "the best Negro writer in America alive," but nonetheless "confined to a certain feeling and a certain limit." He remembered lamenting with Himes, "We could only really write about Negro life as it dovetailed or as it strove to become a part of American life."[82] In 1969, he published an account of his time on the force as *Defender of the Angels*. Kimbrough, too, felt that he was received in terms of shoring up the link between race and criminality, that he was "accused of degrading my race by writing about hustlers and pimps."[83]

The protagonist of Kimbrough's narrative, Strite Hinton, may seem to take on a "genocidal" cast, as Kelly Lytle Hernandez, one of the only scholars to write about the novel, argues. Hernandez indicts Kimbrough's memoir as a reflection of the vicious mentality of the police officers in Los Angeles in the first half of the twentieth century. But Kimbrough consistently uses a darkly ironic tone, subtly mocking the idea that Black people are naturally more prone to crime. Here is the passage from *Defender of the Angels* that Hernandez critiques as "genocidal":

> Negroes in the mass are lawless and irresponsible. One writer has summed up the situation quite aptly: "The American Negro is man-made rather than God-made." Since this is historically true, then the descendants of the slave masters have unloaded a monstrosity of their own making on the whole nation. The grave question that confronts white America at this late day is whether to take

on the almost impossible task of remaking Negroes, or the easier method of eliminating them completely.[84]

The passage begins by embracing the widely held stereotype among the LAPD of his day that "Negroes" are lawless. But in contrast to the officers he served with, Kimbrough imagines race as a "man-made" social construction.[85] It is, in fact, a white construction that begins with slavery. The passage then descends into the mockingly self-serious and stentorian: "grave question" on a "late day." He describes "white America" paternalistically as the sole arbiter of social change, and finally he urges genocide by rhetorically supposing a false choice: remaking (which must be "almost impossible") or "eliminating."

This passage is an example of the complex, darkly ironic tone Kimbrough adopts in the early pages of the novel. By the end of the book, readers will have seen so many examples of racism, of pointless crimes, and of Black/white misunderstanding, that it would be difficult to maintain that the novel is espousing the genocidal views that already seem sarcastically adumbrated at the beginning. This tone is also potentially a way of solving a representational problem: illustrating the complex subjectivity of the Black police officer. Kimbrough refuses to ask for sympathy (look what violence they made me do to survive) nor does he practice confessional self-repudiation (look what a monster I was then). His bitter irony allows him to show the racist imaginary he took on as an agent of the state as well as what very limited resistance he was able to exert by overdramatizing and mocking that position. Kimbrough's ominous tone has a similar effect as Himes's flat caricatures: both thwart a reader's attempt to view interiority and instead reflect their own desires to witness it.

As another instance of Kimbrough's tone, we might turn to an earlier passage in the preface to the novel. Kimbrough plays on "Los Angeles" in his title, *Defender of the Angels*; Hinton claims he was tasked with defending the white population of LA, the "angels" from the "imps":

> ... below heaven's height lie the grottoes of hell, all anguish and confusion, sooty, fork-tailed imps, frantically beating their membranous wings, trying to escape the pit of fire and brimstone. And since pictures that illustrate the words of Holy Writ have had far more influence on human behavior than the written word itself, it appears that the eternities are definitely marked on the basis of color. All the redeemed of heart in heaven are white, and all the damned in

hell are black. And with a background so firmly rooted in antiquity, it is not at all surprising that the same demarcation of color is a fact of life in the City of Angels.[86]

The language of imps and angels may seem to mark Hinton as having internalized and naturalized racism. But the tone here is more clearly hyperbolic, even sarcastic. There is overwriting in the "grottoes of hell," "sooty, fork-tailed imps," and "membranous wings." We see also a bitingly sarcastic idea that pictures must be more significant than the word of God—and then an equally sarcastic "so firmly rooted in antiquity." Kimbrough mocks the essentialized vision of race created by white Americans that he is tasked with upholding and defending.

Throughout his novel, Kimbrough expresses a good deal of ambivalence about his role as a cop. At its conclusion, reflecting on the 1965 Watts riots—which he sees as the natural consequence of the aggressive policing and ghettoization of the Black community in the 20s and 30s—Hinton narrates: "Jail is the only American institution where we are admitted in considerable number without a loud cry about getting out of our place."[87] When Hinton is still getting used to wearing his badge, he says ruefully: "I was sworn to uphold the laws that denied me so many rights."[88] Nearly every crime in the novel that Kimbrough mentions turns out to be less a struggle between good and evil and more a result of accident, tragedy, or police corruption. Hinton watches the extradition and life-sentencing of a Mexican criminal who shot a cop, not knowing in the darkness whom he was shooting. He hauls to jail a man who euthanizes his wife because she has cancer. He helps a friend hide money from crooked cops who are demanding tribute. Other police try to extort him on more than one occasion, deliberately shoot at him while on the job, and reveal their membership in the Ku Klux Klan. One gets the sense that, like Coffin Ed and Grave Digger, Kimbrough was faced with crimes where the genesis extends far beyond right and wrong. They were freak accidents or else moments of pathos produced by larger social structures.

At the conclusion of the novel, Kimbrough reveals how Hinton has, in effect, been shoring up the link between race and criminality as a police officer—confining the Black population to the Central Avenue district, thereby making them more vulnerable to state surveillance and incarceration. By the novel's end, when retired and roaming the streets during the Watts riots, he encounters some police officers who stop and frisk him and wonder why he would spend time in the district. He responds: "My people are down here. Where else would

I go?"[89] As in his earlier stories, once he takes off his uniform, he is subject to the same state surveillance and urban segregation as any other Black man. Having protected the "angels," he has once again become "an imp." Once the uniform is gone, he is as subject to the link between race and criminality as any other Black man encountering the police in the wrong part of town.

Coffin Ed's Scar

If we return from Kimbrough's narrative in 1969 to the moment of Himes creating Coffin Ed and Grave Digger some fourteen years earlier, we see that Himes settled on his two flat cops after contemplating several influences. Marsten showed him what he did *not* want to do: conjure pity for inner-city life. Reading Faulkner gave him a better alternative: the flat characters of mass-market fiction could reflect the social structures that engendered them. Kimbrough further refined his thinking, revealing to him a parallel between the Black cop and the Black writer, both tasked with representing their race for a white establishment. And, if *Defender* is any indication, Kimbrough saw flatness and a bitingly sardonic tone as a way of surviving the impossible position of being tasked with incarcerating Black people in order to make money.

Coffin Ed and Grave Digger's flatness reflects two larger systems in particular: a police force that stationed Black cops in Black neighborhoods and a literary marketplace that demanded stories of race and crime. Their defining characteristic, and indeed practically the only thing that distinguishes the two of them, is Coffin Ed's scar, which he receives in the first novel, *A Rage in Harlem*. Hank, a counterfeiter, throws a beaker of acid used to test the purity of gold into Coffin Ed's eyes after Grave Digger fires his gun wildly. The scene is a rewrite of "He Knew." Two cops approach a hideout and discharge their weapons too quickly. But while "He Knew" ended tragically in a moment of recognition, with Jones killing his sons, Coffin Ed's scarring underscores the futility of policing. In a windowless shack next to an abandoned church called "Peace Heaven," Coffin Ed is blinded by acid and ends up knocking his partner unconscious while some of the real villains escape. "Are you hurt, Digger? . . . Where are you Digger?" the blinded Coffin Ed asks as he stumbles over Grave Digger, whom he has accidentally pistol-whipped unconscious. Himes's two detectives' primal scene is a reminder of the vaudevillian slapstick, futility, and violence that characterize their situation as cops. Jonathan Eburne rightly calls Coffin Ed's scarring moment "antioedipal": it is a moment of blindness but without any kind of larger recognition.[90]

The scar, a reminder of that anti-oedipal moment, lingers throughout the series and underscores Coffin Ed's murderous sensibility. After receiving the scar, Coffin Ed becomes trigger-happy, and he expresses his rage through the scar's twitching. In *The Real Cool Killers*, a Muslim youth sprays him with perfume, and he shoots the young man because he thinks he's being attacked again with acid. His anger is narrated: "Quick scalding rage turned his acid-burnt face into a hideous mask."[91] When he interrogates suspects, his face looks "like a Mardi Gras masque to scare little children." In another scene, "[h]is acid-burned face was jumping as though cooking in the heat and his eyes looked insane."[92] "His acid-scarred face" looks "sinister" when he says that he prefers a long revolver, because white cops don't realize "how hard these Harlem Negroes' heads are."[93] Out of his woundedness emerges his aggressive masculinity and brutality.

Coffin Ed's scar is also the sole outlet through which the character can express his private life. His scar spasms when he experiences stress—and when he approaches the site where he was scalded previously. When he finds out his daughter is locked in a shack with a shotgun-toting gangster, his burned face becomes "hideous with fear."[94] When he thinks that Grave Digger has been shot, the emotion seems again as if it is coming through his scarred face, so much so that his tears seem to emanate from the wound: "Tears were seeping from his eyes and catching in the fine scar ridges between the patches of grafted skin on his face as though his very skin was crying."[95] While the scars are what make Coffin Ed unique, they also make him ordinary. Standing in a crowd with their uniforms off, Coffin Ed and Grave Digger's "faces b[ear] marks and scars similar to any colored street fighter."[96] His scars bind him to and distance him from the other Black people in Harlem; they represent his position as a middle-class Black cop standing amid the Black working class—distinct and yet alike.

Coffin Ed's scar can also be read as an expression of Himes's emotions about an event in his own life. At the age of thirteen, he and his brother Joe created a homemade "torpedo" for a chemistry presentation, which went horribly wrong and exploded in his brother's face. The large white hospital nearby refused to treat Joe, who was permanently blinded. In his autobiography *The Quality of Hurt*, Himes suggested that this was key to the "hurt" of the title: "That one moment in my life hurt me as much as all the others put together. It still does, a half century later."⁹⁷ The incident gave Himes a sense that even though he grew up in a middle-class family, his skin color inevitably bound him together with working-class Black people. It was one of his first awarenesses of the situation that the whole series explores—the porous boundaries and uneasy relationship between middle-class Black professionals (cops and authors) and the Black working class. In the Harlem Detective series, he found a way to write about that private tragedy, but he made it unrecognizable, transmuting it into the semi-comic, violent form of the crime novel.

In "The Dilemma of the Negro Novelist in the U.S.," Himes expands upon the metaphor of hurt—a wound or a scar—to describe the challenges a Black writer faces in telling an honest story of Black life. For the writer, "delineat[ing] the degrading effects of oppression will be like inflicting a wound on himself." Middle-class Blacks, too, he writes, will seek to hide their "scars of oppression" and condemn the Black writer. To the white population, he argues that "the scars of those assaulted persons are not only reminders, but affronts."⁹⁸ To Himes, the scars that no one wants to look at represent why it is difficult for the Black author to find a place within the literary field. But the scars also refer to the liminality of the middle-class Black author with respect to his own race. He is willing to expose the scars that no one else will show.

Not unlike Coffin Ed's scars, Himes's imagination of the Black writer's scars connects him to the rest of the Black population in a shared condition of oppression, even as they also distance him from it. Himes imagines the honest, middle-class "negro writer" as chronicling the lives of working-class Blacks—a story no one wants to hear and that seems "psychopathic." Similarly, Coffin Ed is the middle-class professional who is responsible for completing a task no one else, Black or white, wants to do—overseeing the working-class Black population of Harlem. The key difference is that whereas Himes describes a victimized writer who tries to bare his scars, Coffin Ed turns his scars, his damage, into ruthlessness. Whereas Himes tries to chronicle the woes of the Black population, Coffin Ed tries to police them. And yet, we also might think about the solution Himes finds to "the dilemma of the negro novelist"—writing crime fiction—as itself masking woundedness or "hurt" by turning it into violence. In moving from prisoners to cops, he shifts from the victimization no one wanted to read about to the violence everyone wanted to behold. "Start with action. . . . We don't give a damn who's thinking what. Only what they're doing," Himes remembered

Duhamel telling him.[99] The fact that Coffin Ed expresses his emotions through his wound is a result of Himes's perception of a literary marketplace in which he can express his character's emotions only through a flat caricature, a leitmotif like a scar. Himes saw a homology between the liminal positions of the cop and the middle-class Black writer: both were parts of and distanced from the working-class population they were said to represent.

Later in life, Himes claimed to have been quite content writing detective stories. "I was very happy writing these detective stories, especially the first one, when I began it," he said. By 1973, he claimed that his detective fiction constituted "the best of my writing and the best of my thinking." But records from the period indicate he did not always feel that way. He originally contracted to write the Harlem Detective series at a period of one novel every two months—eight novels over less than a year and half. "The idea has soured," he wrote to Carl Van Vechten in the midst of the series, "and the fun of writing them has gone and now it is hard-hard work, and I don't want to do them anymore. But I must until something better comes along." "At first," he claimed, "they were an amusement (besides being a source of vital income) and I enjoyed creating the grisly fantasy. But then they became—I don't know how to describe it—a bone of contention."[100]

His books sold poorly in the United States and were published as cheap paperbacks with Avon; they were more popular in France, but Le Serie Noire undersold them to keep them from outselling the series. His first book, *La Reine de Pommes* (published also as *For Love of Imabelle* and *A Rage in Harlem*), did win Le Grand Prix de la Littérature Policière, an award for the best detective fiction in French, and it received high acclaim from renowned French writers like Jean Cocteau and Jean Giono. At the same time, he was stung by the reactions of American critics who saw his French approbation as a kind of tokenism—as accentuating America's race problem for a French audience. The critic for the *New York Times* who specialized in crime fiction, Anthony Boucher, imagined him as describing an "America that a European likes to believe in . . . a lurid world of squalor and oppression and hatred and meaningless violence."[101] Even as late as 1961—three books into the series—he was referring to *The Primitive* and *Pinktoes* as better than his Harlem Detective series.[102] "In the U.S." he wrote before beginning his last published novel, *Blind Man with a Pistol*, "they are essentially 'Negro books' and appeal only to the audience interested in 'Negro books.'"[103]

Toward the end of his life, he received some of the wider critical acclaim he longed for. The tragicomic violence of the novels seemed to grow only more pertinent in the 1960s with Watts, the civil rights movement, and Black Power. But even in 1964, he still longed to write "a good book"—a realist representation of his own experiences as opposed to the detective stories he had called "cheap."[104] For a writer contemporary with Richard Wright and Ralph Ellison, his decision to write crime fiction must have come at great cost. To write the novels that would pay his bills, he had to give up on his aspirations to represent Black life in the more venerated naturalist or realist tradition and instead write novels that he feared would be misinterpreted as salacious depictions of Black life. The record of that choice is publicly inscribed only in the scar on his character's faces.

At the same time, the narrative focus on two flat and brutal cops, on ruthless violence, on vaudeville-esque comedic action could also bring out, in the background, the motives and feelings of the ordinary Harlemites to which city officials, like Himes's readers and editors, remained callously indifferent. In *Cotton Comes to Harlem*, for instance, we see at the beginning the hopes and dreams of people being swindled by the Reverend Deke O'Malley, who has begun a fraudulent Back-to-Africa movement:

> Bottles of wine, beer and whisky were passed about. Here and there a soul-brother cut a dance step. White teeth flashed in black, laughing faces. . . . Sad-eyed Puerto Ricans from nearby Spanish Harlem and the lost and hungry black people from black Harlem who didn't have the thousand dollars to return to their native land congregated outside the high wire fence, smelling the tantalizing barbecue, dreaming of the day when they could also go back home in triumph and contentment.[105]

Himes writes here not of individuals, but of groups animated by fundamental emotions and states of being: camaraderie, hope, desire, hunger, dissatisfaction, striving. A little later in the passage, in an extended reflection, we learn their motives for leaving: "They had not found a home in America. . . . Everyone has to believe in something; and the white people of America had left them nothing to believe in."[106] On adjacent pages, we see tough cops bemoaning going "soft on crime," hyper-calisthenic violence, women in varying states of undress and arousal, an action-packed heist, but when imagined as a collective, the individuals in Harlem in Himes's novels have powerful, meaningful desires, emotions, and goals, even if they are invisible to the white establishment and to the readers looking for sex and violence.

If one of the central questions of this book is "How did authors navigate genres where they did not or could not write about people with realistic private lives?" the central answer is they reimagined the functions of those genres by drawing on contemporary issues that raised questions of what it meant to be in private or who had privacy. In this chapter, we have seen how Himes navigated a literary marketplace in which white readers would interpret stories about Black crime as revealing Black people's capacity for criminality. Himes tried to manage his predicament by writing instead about flattened cops—two officers engaged in public duty and who had little private interiority to speak of. Remembering his old friend Jess Kimbrough, Himes imagined the middle-class Black police officer as like the middle-class Black writer—conflicted, ambivalent, complicit, unable to represent his true sentiments. His profession made him both a representative of his race and temporarily removed from it. Himes's characters' lack of earnest private lives reflected the larger systems of surveillance that created them: a police force tasked with watching for Black crime and a literary establishment that wanted to witness stories of Black depravity. While the right to privacy nominally expanded in the years during and after which Himes wrote to guarantee a right to define or express oneself, Black people could find themselves unable to do so when subject to the gaze of the surveillance state, their race imagined as an indelible sign of their criminality. Himes's novels, like Kimbrough's, grappled with how to escape that gaze and the fear that he would inevitably be complicit in perpetuating it.

The Science Fiction of *Roe v. Wade*

PRO-LIFE ADVOCATES OFTEN INSIST that the unborn fetus resembles nothing so much as a slave. To President Ronald Reagan, that resemblance was abundantly clear. In his 1983 essay "Abortion and the Conscience of the Nation," Reagan wrote that "we cannot survive as a free nation when some men decide that others are not fit to live and should be abandoned to abortion or infanticide."[1] He explained that he was channeling Abraham Lincoln, who had said that the nation could not endure "half slave and half free."[2] As recently as 2015, the Republican presidential candidate and neurosurgeon Ben Carson compared women who have abortions to "slave owners," and as early as 1971, the authors of the pro-life publication *Abortion and Social Justice* compared the situation of the fetus, deprived of its rights, to "Negro slavery of the nineteenth century."[3] In a seemingly disparate context, in *Do Androids Dream of Electric Sheep?* (1968), Philip K. Dick reanimates slavery over a hundred years after its official end. The novel tells the story of androids who are designed, according to their advertisements, to evoke "the halcyon days of the pre-Civil War Southern states."[4] A group of androids tires of performing forced labor on Mars, and so they escape to Earth and attempt to live human lives while eluding capture. One by one, they are terminated by the novel's protagonist, Rick Deckard, who is unsettled by the thought that he might be killing beings who are "*genuinely alive*" (125, emphasis in the original).

The connection between *Androids* and the discourse of fetal slavery might seem incidental, except that Dick was adamantly pro-life. He became particularly disheartened when, in 1960, his wife Anne had an abortion against his wishes, and in 1978, he donated money to the Crusade for Life, a pro-life charity.[5] In *Roe v. Wade* (1973), the Supreme Court expanded "the right to personal privacy," which I have been tracing through previous chapters, to encompass a woman's right to an early-term abortion. In the previous chapters, we saw how crime novelists developed creative ways to imagine subjects excluded from that expanding right—queer people and people of color—in part because they were thought to be writing about people who weren't fully realized, without private interiorities. As the right to privacy expanded further in *Roe* and became understood as a right to define oneself as a person, it drifted into the realm of a question that had long been posed by science fiction's aliens, androids, and extraterrestrial squids: who or what counts as a person? Dick took up this question the year after *Roe* when he published a dystopian story entitled "The Pre-Persons" (1974), about a world in which Congress passes a law where children under twelve and incapable of doing "higher math like algebra" can be taken away in "an abortion truck" and "put to sleep." The protagonist of "The Pre-Persons" insists that the Supreme Court's ruling that "an embryo is not entitled to American Constitutional rights" is entirely "arbitrary."[6] Dick believed that if the Court was going to claim that an embryo's rights suddenly began at three months of gestation, it might as well declare that a child acquired rights only once he turned twelve. The context of abortion, which would become highly explicit in "The Pre-Persons," is implicit in *Androids*, its predecessor. Like the society of "The Pre-Persons," which turns to algebra as an arbitrary standard of personhood, the world of *Androids* uses the Voigt-Kampff empathy test as a capricious and invalid measure to determine who counts as a person.[7] Pro-life advocates would imagine the fetus as a human slave denied of its rights to life and thus unable to develop its potential; so too does Dick imagine the android.

For Dick, there was a special homology between science fiction and abortion, revealed as two of his passions converged into one. The android represents a being to whom society does not accord full rights (the fetus, the slave, the disabled person), as well as science fiction (SF), the type of writing that is not supposed to deal with actual humans. Art-novelists, literary critics, and creative writing programs from midcentury onward criticized SF precisely for being unable to provide the nuanced, layered characterizations that populate more self-consciously literary fiction. As we saw in the introduction to this book, Mark McGurl describes the university creative writing program as defining itself against what was characterized as "the machine-made quality of formulaic genre fiction."[8] Midcentury critic Dwight Macdonald complained, "I never read science fiction. It bores me and it's not about people."[9] Preferring to call her own work "speculative fiction," Margaret Atwood echoed his sentiments in 2009 when she criticized science fiction for being about "rockets, chemicals, and talking squids in outer space."[10] Just as the realm of the human, of deep emotional interiority, is denied to the supposedly mechanistic automata in *Androids*, so too has that realm been historically denied to genre fiction, which was itself often seen as android-like, as an interminably reproducible commodity of the mass market.

Science fiction has been concerned with both pregnancy and "the rights of man" from its very inception: as Ellen Moers argues, Mary Shelley's *Frankenstein*, the story of an artificially created, unacknowledged monster, reflects the guilt she experienced when thinking about her stillborn daughter.[11] In linking SF's foundational pregnancy story with abortion in the 1960s, Dick was remarkably prescient. In the years after *Roe v. Wade*, Dick would become one of a whole array of SF authors who wrote stories and expressed vociferous opinions about abortion: Octavia Butler, Ursula K. Le Guin, Harlan Ellison, Kurt Vonnegut, James Tiptree, Jr. (Alice Sheldon), and (despite her resistance to the genre) Margaret Atwood.[12] What has often seemed like SF's abstract, metaphysical exploration of what it means to be a human or posthuman was frequently anchored in the real, historical context of the abortion debate.[13] Fictional aliens, androids, and animals all served as tools for these authors to reflect on the notion of the person—and by extension, the fetus. This chapter charts science fiction's engagement with abortion, beginning in the early 1960s when the question of fetal personhood started to become a national issue.

Though it rarely discusses genre fiction as such, previous literary criticism about abortion has revealed how language, gender, historical discourse, and technology all mediate our understanding of abortion. In her landmark essay, "Apostrophe, Animation, and Abortion," Barbara Johnson argues that fetal personhood may be inextricable from linguistic expression, residing in "the ineradicable tendency of language to animate whatever it addresses."[14] Feminist scholars working at the intersections of cultural and media studies, history, and literature—such as Rosalind Pollack Petchesky, Barbara Duden, Lauren Berlant, Valerie Hartouni, Christina Hauck, Karen Weingarten, and Heather Latimer—have since shown that fetal personhood is neither a moral absolute nor a rhetorical inevitability, but rather a historical construct, brought about by changes in technology and medicine and inflected through pronatalist and paternalist cultures.[15] Analyzing the science fictional texts of this study will contribute to this feminist project of historicizing fetal personhood and its surrounding concepts:

as early as the 1960s, American SF writers contested definitions of the fetus that were becoming part of law and popular culture alike.

Yet, in their focus on speculative analogy, SF texts often engage legal reasoning more closely than other cultural representations do. Legal reasoning characteristically yokes together two cases to generalize them into a legal principle, and in the years before and after *Roe v. Wade*, legal reasoning about abortion often relied on producing an analogy (e.g. to slavery) to characterize the sui generis relationship between a woman and her fetus, to suggest that a fetus is or is not a rights-bearing person. Because speculative analogies are their stock in trade, SF authors have been able to directly grapple with the legal and cultural analogies that establish personhood, more so than their counterparts in lyric poetry, visual culture, and literary fiction.[16]

In their explorations of the language establishing personhood and privacy, both SF and lyric poetry differ from the fetal images displayed in the anti-abortion film *The Silent Scream* (1984) or in the 1965 *Life* magazine photos, which, as Rosalind Petchesky notes, naturalize the humanness of the fetus as they omit the pregnant woman.[17] For Barbara Johnson, lyric's apostrophes reveal how those fetal images rely on hidden structures of rhetorical address, which animate and anthropomorphize their object.[18] For Deborah Nelson, confessional lyric reveals how legal privacy at midcentury was achieved through language, through disclosure and withholding, in the conversation that takes place in the intimate space between a woman and her doctor.[19] But whereas Nelson and Johnson argue that poetry's apostrophes illustrate that privacy and personhood depend on an address to a doctor or to a fetus, SF serves as a kind of laboratory in which the proliferating cultural and legal analogies establishing personhood can be tested, affirmed or discarded. SF argues for or against the validity of specific analogies between the fetus and the person by making those analogies the premise of extended speculative narratives. Following Dick, who took the analogy between slaves and fetuses and wove it into his fiction, his contemporaries also spun fictional worlds out of the myriad analogies characterizing fetal personhood in law and popular culture—comparisons of the fetus to a piece of meat or of the woman's body to a baby-making machine.

The greater and more immediate contrast is between SF and its counterparts in literary fiction. John Barth's *The End of the Road* (1958, revised 1967), John Updike's *Rabbit Run* (1960), Joan Didion's *Play It as It Lays* (1970), and Richard

Yates's *Revolutionary Road* (1961) all depicted the inner psychology and social circumstances of women who considered or had abortions, as well as the role that men played in their lives. These novels incited the reader to sympathize with the plight of a real-seeming character. Judith Wilt subtitles an excellent study of some of these novels "the Armageddon of the Maternal Instinct," because these works narrate a woman's "punishment" and "self-punishment" as she departs from maternity "towards infanticide and abortion."[20] But whereas these literary novels depicted the fine-grained emotions of human characters grappling with abortion, SF authors wondered whether and how the very category of the person should matter in the context of the abortion debate. Excluded from the art-novel's domain of humanizing truth and beauty, pro-life and pro-choice science fiction writers alike used their writing to speculatively extend and examine the cultural and legal analogies that established personhood in the years surrounding *Roe v. Wade* (1973).

Not only did SF writers temper their genre to reflect on the analogies of the abortion debate, but authors of SF also imagined the historical and cultural forces shaping the literary field as continuous with the ones shaping the debate about abortion.[21] The law tied personhood to the capacity for self-definition, and SF authors, because of their marginalized positions in the literary field, were especially conscious of the ways self-definition and self-expression could be misrecognized and constrained by law and social norms. One of the earliest postwar SF writers to approach abortion, Dick felt it natural that the unfairly maligned genre of SF would speak up for the forgotten fetus. By contrast, a later SF writer, Octavia Butler, imagined the marketplace for her fiction as permeated by the social power structures that controlled female reproduction. But both articulated their views about legal personhood in science fiction.

Abortion and Science Fiction: An Origin Story

When does the link between science fiction and abortion begin? Shelley's *Frankenstein* (1818) has been read as an allegory of pregnancy and childbirth since Moers's famous essay "Female Gothic" (1974). Moers sees the novel as rooted in Shelley's postpartum depression and in the self-reproach she experienced when thinking about her stillborn child. Frankenstein's monster is, after all, a child abandoned by his creator.[22] Although *Frankenstein* is often read in terms of pregnancy, early nineteenth-century obstetrics, and spontaneous abortion, many critics have overlooked that it was also written in the wake of Lord Ellenborough's Act of 1803, which made abortion at any stage of pregnancy a felony for both medical practitioners and pregnant women.[23] The act, which tried to clarify vague and ineffective law outlawing abortions in Britain, was also likely influenced by contemporary medical practitioners who asserted that life begins at conception and not at the fetus's "quickening."[24] Frankenstein's monster calls himself an "abortion" (a term, added to the manuscript by Percy Shelley, that had a freer usage in the nineteenth century), and at one point in the novel, Victor Frankenstein is coerced by his monster into creating a female counterpart. He ultimately refuses and destroys his "half-finished creature" in secret, feeling "as if I had mangled the living flesh of a human being," a moment that suggests the experience of many women who took abortifacients or committed infanticide of unwanted children.[25]

Still, the public controversy surrounding abortion did not assume its polarizing modern form until the latter half of the twentieth century. Though not absent elsewhere, this polarization has been particularly virulent in the United States. American physicians led the effort to pass "right to life" laws, which made abortion illegal after conception, in every state between 1860 and 1880, and these laws went unchallenged until the 1960s. Right-to-life laws carried one important exception: they allowed doctors to perform abortions to save the life of the mother. Because childbirth was inherently dangerous, many doctors used their discretion to perform abortions more frequently than official laws and moral strictures may have seemed to condone.[26] In the 1930s and 1940s, childbearing itself became safer, thus eliminating the argument that women's lives were potentially being saved by performing abortions. With the mother's life less often at stake, the philosophical question of fetal personhood became salient. Legal medical abortions moved out of homes and into hospitals in order to prevent infection, making it more difficult for doctors to practice abortion without the awareness of their colleagues.

In the 1960s and 1970s, abortion was taken out of the discretionary hands of physicians and returned to the public spotlight. In the early part of the 1960s, many news outlets covered cases of women unable to abort babies who would be born without fully formed limbs because their mothers took thalidomide. The media also followed mothers who contracted German measles during their pregnancy, and would give birth to blind, deaf, and cognitively disabled babies.

As I've noted, innovations in ultrasound and other imaging technology made pictures of uncannily human-looking fetuses available to a large public in the 1965 edition of *Life* magazine. Feminist organizing throughout the 1960s also helped to raise national consciousness about abortion and to generate ballot initiatives.[27]

Alongside advances in science, the inadequacy of existing legal frameworks to address pregnancy also stoked the controversy surrounding abortion. In adjudicating *Roe v. Wade* (1973), the Court argued that a woman's right to privacy ensured her the right to an early abortion. They compared *Roe* to the other cases establishing a right to privacy, which dealt with contraception, interracial marriage, home invasion, compulsory sterilization, and the education of one's children.[28] But the justices also qualified their comparisons by alleging that the fetus was enough of a person, that abortion was sufficiently unlike these other cases (or in its words, "inherently different"), that a woman could not be afforded a blanket right to choose abortion at any stage in her pregnancy.[29] In other words, in the Court's eyes, a pregnant woman choosing an abortion was similar to a woman choosing to purchase contraception—but only until the pregnant woman's second trimester, when the fetus began to seem more like a rights-bearing person.

While the Court compared choosing abortion to choosing contraception or educating one's children, legal scholars, philosophers, and ordinary citizens concocted their own analogies and generated hypotheticals to make claims about abortion and fetal personhood. Perhaps the most well-known hypothetical regarding abortion is that provided by the philosopher Judith Jarvis Thomson. Imagine that one day, you awake to find that your circulatory system has been attached to a famous concert violinist who is ill—and you will be forced to sustain him for nine months. This would, Thomson argues, be an unjust imposition on a person's life; ergo, a mother should have the right to terminate her pregnancy. Thomson thus claims that even if the fetus were fully a person, its rights would still not trump the rights of the mother to control her own body.[30] Other legal scholars and philosophers have compared the fetus to a body part, a parasite, an ailing individual that a Good Samaritan encounters, an acorn that will one day be an oak tree, and a draft card—and the mother has been likened to, among other things, the subject under a totalitarian state.[31]

A broader public also participated in the legal competition to use analogies to characterize the fetus, albeit in a form that was often more rhetorically impassioned. Pro-life advocates called the fetus a slave, while pro-choice advocates claimed that the pregnant woman was the real slave.[32] Pro-lifers characterized abortionists as treating the fetus as if it were "a mass of cells" or a "piece of meat."[33] While SF gave pro-lifers a dystopian language to contend that people were being needlessly murdered, it also helped women express the helplessness they felt during pregnancy and abortion. The poet Adrienne Rich drew on SF when she compared the unwanted fetus to an "alien" invading a woman's body in *Of Woman Born* (1976).[34] In a pro-choice amicus brief for *Thornburgh v. American College of Obstetricians and Gynecologists* (1986), one woman said that she felt like a "baby machine—an incubator without feelings," trying to represent how she felt coerced into bearing a child.[35] Likewise, in an anonymous 1976 article in the *New York Times* describing an abortion (an uncommonly early testimonial), the author wrote that "my body felt mine again instead of the eggshell it becomes when it's protecting someone else." She almost seemed to compare abortion to alien abduction, as she described how small black spots in the ceiling seemed to swell into "the shape of saucers" that "quiver[ed] in the air." The abortion itself, she claimed, felt like "the vacuuming of my uterus."[36] The tropes of SF have provided women with a language to represent the experience of losing personal autonomy: being probed, being controlled or dominated, and forced to produce children.

As the proliferation of analogies intensified, legal scholars tried to formulate a more precise definition of personhood. "The right to personal privacy" established in *Roe* seemed inadequate or opaque, and so these scholars began speaking of a generalized "right to personhood."[37] In his treatise on constitutional law, Laurence Tribe defines this right to personhood as a right "to be master of the identity one creates in the world."[38] Theorists like Tribe supposed the decisions to use contraception or to have an abortion were so intimately connected to who we are as people that the state could not interfere with them. But legal scholar Jed Rubenfeld has noted that the defense of abortion through a right to personhood—through a woman's right to self-definition—also smuggled in a conservative logic: it suggested that bearing children was intimately, inextricably connected to female identity.[39] Personhood was often spoken of in terms of a person's right to "self-definition," and SF writers of the same period were acutely interested in the ways that allegedly free self-definition could be circumscribed either by the law or else by the cultural field, both of which shared exclusionary norms about who and what counted as a person.[40]

Philip K. Dick's Pro-Life Imaginary

The great irony of Philip K. Dick's reception is that while critics on the Left like Fredric Jameson champion him for his progressive politics, he is also beloved by the evangelical Right for his pro-life stance.[41] In N. Katherine Hayles's influential reading, Dick is on the side of posthumanism, a philosophy that rejects the autonomy of the liberal person in favor of an understanding of "human life [a]s embedded in a material world of great complexity, one on which we depend for our continued survival."[42] But while Hayles never considers Dick's pro-life stance, much of Dick's oeuvre can be read as an extended meditation on abortion and the rights of the fetus. Dick's version of posthumanism entails expanding the category of the person to include two beings without their own fully human bodies: the android and its counterpart, the fetus.

Dick articulates his pro-life views most strenuously in the "The Pre-Persons" (1974). Nearly all of Dick's male characters criticize abortion during the story, but Walter, a child who has just turned twelve, is particularly incensed. Contemplating a passing abortion truck, he rails against abortion:

> Why is it, he wondered, that the more helpless a creature, the easier it was for some people to snuff it? Like a baby in the womb; the original abortions, "pre-partums," or "pre-persons" they were called now. How could they defend themselves? Who would speak for them? All those lives, a hundred by each doctor a day . . . and all helpless and silent and then just dead. The fuckers, he thought. That's why they do it; they know they can do it; they get off on their macho power. And so a little thing that wanted to see the light of day is vacuumed out in less than two minutes. And the doctor goes on to the next chick.[43]

Many of the signature themes of Dick's oeuvre appear in Walter's monologue; we see the redemptive power of love and concern for the downtrodden, as well as suspicion of the establishment. Not only does the story apply those themes to defend the fetus, but "The Pre-Persons" also paints women as having abandoned their natural maternal duties. In another moment in the story, Walter's father asserts: "It's a certain kind of woman advocating this all. They used to call them 'castrating females.'" Walter even tells his mother that he'd like to commit acts of terrorism on an abortion clinic: "I'd wait until there were no kids in there, only county employees, and I'd firebomb it." As fanatical as Walter and his father may seem, the narrative's other perspectives ultimately vindicate a pro-life position. Cynthia, the wife and mother in the family, says to her husband: "Let's have an abortion! Wouldn't that be neat? Doesn't that turn you on?" Ed Gantro, another father, is only slightly more detached than Walter; he complains that "the organism that is killed had no chance, no ability, to protect itself."[44] Dick wrote an afterward to the story in 1978, in which he insisted on his "love for the children" and position against "abortion on demand." He quoted from Martin Luther: "Hier steh' Ich; Ich kann nicht anders" ("Here I stand; I have no other choice").[45]

The full-blown outrage at *Roe v. Wade* that appears in "The Pre-Persons" gradually developed over the course of Dick's career. Dick's very first novel that concerned abortion, *The Man Whose Teeth Were All Exactly Alike* (written in 1960; published in 1984) was a realist one. The novel is sometimes compared to Richard Yates's *Revolutionary Road* (1961) in its narration of the claustrophobia of suburban life. Through a series of chance events, Walter Dombrosio (perhaps the predecessor to the Walter of "The Pre-Persons") loses his job and is replaced by his wife Sherry. When Sherry misbalances their checking account, Walter rapes her twice, denies her requests for an abortion, and hits her, ultimately forcing her to bear his child and lose her job. In one dialogue, Walter threatens violence when Sherry thinks about getting an abortion:

> "You can't keep me from getting my abortion. Dolly got an abortion a year ago when she was pregnant."
>
> He said, "I'll keep you from getting it. You don't think I can? I'll drive you over to Sheriff Christen and have him arrest you for trying to commit a felony. For trying to murder my child."
>
> "You liar," she said.
>
> "I'll kill you," he said. "I'll beat the living hell out of you. And everybody'll be on my side because it's natural. Natural for a father to feel like that. With a wife like you, wanting to do a hideous unnatural act like that."
>
> "It's just your word," she said. "I'll deny it. You know what I'll say? I'll say you got mad when you heard I was pregnant; you beat me up so I'd have a miscarriage."[46]

In light of Walter's violent temper and Sherry's sympathetic desire for an abortion, Dick may seem to be pro-choice in this early novel. But the novel also undercuts its apparent pro-choice sentiments by demonstrating Sherry's willingness to lie about the circumstances of her abortion. She later concedes, apologizing for herself: "If I was any real mother I wouldn't even consider getting an abortion."[47] This paternalistic view was Dick's own in 1973, and it was likely his view in 1960 (when he wrote the novel) as well. Throughout the novel, several characters express the opinion that a woman's place is in the home, and at least one commentator has felt that the novel sides with Walter over Sherry.[48] Others have felt that the quarrels between Walter and Sherry were based on Dick's own relationship with his wife Anne.[49]

A few months after Dick finished the novel, his wife Anne became pregnant unexpectedly. The two already had four children, and on the $2,000 Dick made cranking out two paperbacks a year, they could not see their way to raising a fifth child. They argued about whether she should get an abortion before he finally capitulated. Anne explained to Dick's biographer Lawrence Sutin, "He finally did think it was for the best—he said, 'I agree'—and then we went up to Seattle, went to this nice restaurant." Not long after, Dick wrote *We Can Build You* (1962), a novel set in Seattle when, at a nice restaurant, a cold, uncaring femme fatale named Pris Straton kills a half-finished John Wilkes Booth android—one that she had created. "It's all in *We Can Build You*," said Anne about her abortion, "in the novel Pris kills a little robot with her high heel."[50] This is the passage to which she was referring:

> The shoe smashed down on the head of the Booth simulacrum. Its heel burst into the thing's head, right behind the ear. "There," Pris said to Barrows, her eyes shining and wet, her mouth a thin contorted frantic line.
>
> "Glap," the Booth simulacrum said. Its hands beat jerkily in the air; its feet drummed on the floor. Then it ceased moving. An inner wind convulsed it; its limbs floundered and twitched. It became inert.[51]

Dick had been attuned to the theme of prenatal vulnerability for his whole career—he had had a stillborn twin sister, and for his whole life he was haunted by guilt that he had somehow killed her in the womb. But in the lines from *We Can Build You*, Dick expressed a particular rage about his wife's abortion, which he channeled into science fiction; he imagined a vindictive, beautiful woman in Seattle stepping on a half-formed being that she had created, which "floundered and twitched" before becoming "inert."

In light of Anne Dick's comments, what seems at first glance to be a murder can actually be read as an abortion: a half-formed being is cruelly beaten to death by a "mother" of androids.⁵² Both figures in the scene—the Booth simulacrum and Pris—are designed to ask us to question our definition of personhood. The poorly constructed Booth simulacrum might be human; it seems to exhibit a kind of pain as it drums and jerks, but elsewhere in the novel, it is capable only of grinning emptily. By imagining the android as John Wilkes Booth, Dick gestures at the question of whether it is fair to kill a humanoid being who has not fully developed cognitive capacities and who will also likely turn out to be evil. Pris herself, though a flesh-and-blood human, seems cold and impersonal when she aborts the android Booth. Her shoe becomes the subject of the sentence, and while the android seems to display something resembling response to pain, Pris's mouth is "a thin contorted frantic line." After the scene, we are told, she "sipped her drink expressionlessly."⁵³ Louis, the first-person narrator and protagonist of the story, may be a double for Dick: he is unsure how to feel about the act, oscillating between queasiness—"I did not feel able to stand any more"—and indifference: "I wondered if I cared whether it could be repaired or not."⁵⁴ But Dick's cruel representation of Pris suggests Dick's ultimate lack of sympathy for a woman who, like his own wife, chooses an abortion and foreshadows his later misogynistic entrenchment in the pro-life camp.

This earlier novel anticipated many of the aspects of *Do Androids Dream of Electric Sheep?*: sentient automata, a Rosen corporation, and a femme fatale named Pris. Louis explains that in this world, H-bomb testing has caused many congenital disorders. He describes one that particularly "depresses" him: "the embryo disintegrates in the womb and is born in pieces, a jaw, an arm, handful of teeth, separate fingers."⁵⁵ This Rosen Corporation creates androids in a barren, radioactive world of human sterility, just as a different Rosen Corporation will in *Androids*. For Dick, machine life arises in worlds characterized by the failed reproduction of human life. As Dick abandoned realist fiction and began writing exclusively SF, he moved away from representing the specific situation of a woman who wanted an abortion and turned instead toward more abstract and existential questions. Thinking about abortion in the absence of its realist particulars enabled him to substitute the drama of undesired maternity for the metaphysics of fetal personhood.

In a subsequent book, *Dr. Bloodmoney, Or How We Got Along After the Bomb* (1965), Dick attempts to change the narrative around a powerful pro-choice image—the thalidomide baby. *Dr. Bloodmoney* features a little girl who lives with a conjoined twin inside her—another birth disorder caused by radioactive fallout. This fetal-like being ("a homunculus") is eventually able to exit her body and save the world by inhabiting the body of an evil man, Hoppy Harrington, who, armless and legless, appears to have been modeled after a thalidomide baby ("a phocomelus").[56] The events of the novel can be understood as referring to an incident in 1962, when the story of Sherri Finkbine helped make abortion a countrywide issue. Finkbine was a minor celebrity from a children's television show who had taken thalidomide before understanding its effects. She was denied an abortion by her hospital in Arizona and had to travel to Sweden for her procedure; her story was covered on national news.[57] In Dick's novel, Hoppy, the phocomelus, represents the image that would drive women to want access to abortion—the thalidomide baby. Growing up ignored and neglected, Hoppy takes his revenge on society by establishing complete control over the media via satellite. His counterpart is Bill, the heroic fetal homunculus, who is able to stop Hoppy by taking possession of his body. The novel thus displaces one widespread pro-choice cultural image—the thalidomide baby, who threatens to dominate the media (and who is unfairly spurned)—with a pro-life one—the good-hearted and talented fetal being who is able to make the best of a limited body once he inhabits it.

In *The Crack in Space* (1966), Dick takes on fears about overpopulation that helped to lend further cultural support to the pro-choice cause. Stanford professor Paul Ehrlich's bestselling *The Population Bomb* (1968) was one prominent narrative suggesting the right to an abortion as a potential remedy to an impending Malthusian population crisis.[58] In Dick's futuristic novel, the world is massively overpopulated, many people of color have decided to put themselves into cryogenic suspension to wait for a better era, and "abort-consults" are widely and readily available in the phone book. Poor people are taken off government aid unless they have abortions; the novel opens with a couple of color who want to freeze themselves because of a pregnancy. Myra Sands, the novel's abortionist, is troublingly blithe when the couple reluctantly approaches her in her office: "It's routine. We can arrange for it by noon today and have it done by six tonight. At any one of several free government abort clinics here in the area."[59] She then takes a phone call. Dick's novel imagines abortion as a deeply flawed solution to the overpopulation problem, because concerns about overpopulation might disproportionately drive poor people and people of color to abort.

Looser, more implicit references to abortion characterize Dick's oeuvre, in which the theme of conjoined persons frequently recurs, reflecting both his guilt about his twin sister and his distress about Anne's abortion.[60] In *Ubik* (1969), for instance, many of the characters are suspended in half-life, stored in cryogenic tanks while on the verge of death. The teenage Jory gains energy by eating the other people in suspension. At the denouement of *Ubik*, the heroic Ella Runciter is going to escape Jory and half-life when she is "reborn into another womb," as if she and the other people in half-life were frozen embryos struggling to survive.[61] For Dick, when the experience of conjoinment involves an attempt to dominate the weaker conjoined person, it is terrifying and awful. When characters resist being terminated, conjoinment becomes a blessing, since it inevitably results in hope, love, and interdependence. Hayles is not wrong to note that Dick, ambivalent about liberal personhood, asks for "tolerance and affection for the creatures, biological and mechanical, with whom [his characters] they share the planet."[62] But Hayles fails to note that the fetus is emphatically included as one of those creatures—and that urging care and affection for the fetus can unfairly stigmatize those women who choose abortions. His posthumanism was also pro-life.

In other works, Dick seems more of a gender essentialist than Hayles and others acknowledge. In a 1972 speech entitled "The Android and the Human," he imagines a world in which there is an increasingly troubling blend of android and human—"artificial constructs masquerading as humans." He takes a thought experiment from Stanislaw Lem about a man trying to rape a sewing machine and imagines a dystopia where there are "abortions for sewing machines which have become pregnant against their will" in addition to "birth control pills" and "Planned Parenthoods" for those sewing machines.[63] Against the ominous, sterile, aborting sewing machine, another figuration of the android, Dick recounts his experience of caring for an eighteen-year-old girl who had an abortion at five and a half months. Rather than reproach her, he remembers being solicitous for her well-being. Her breasts bear milk, because her body is unaware that her fetus had been aborted. Dick uses this milk as a symbol of the resilient life force flowing through her, which Dick hopes human beings will carry into the future:

> But—I think, I believe—the force that is her, so to speak the swelling into maturity of her breasts, the looking forward into the future of her physical body, even at the moment that mentally and spiritually she was virtually destroyed—I

hope, anyhow, that that force will prevail. If it does not, then there is nothing left, as far as I am concerned. The future as I conceive it will not exist.[64]

Dick asserts a paternal affection that uncomfortably verges on voyeurism; he tries to show that the girl's abortion is a tragic decision that reveals her humanity. The legal defenses of a right to personhood that are released over the next few years similarly suggest that a woman's identity is defined by her capacity to reproduce.[65] But Dick takes the essentialist reasoning of those opinions to a logical extreme. If a woman is defined by the mandates of her physical body, then she must be mother to the future of humanity whether she wants to be or not. For Dick, a woman's reproductive organs represent not just her own identity, but the character and future of the human race.

In *Do Androids Dream of Electric Sheep?* (1968), the androids evoke the figure of the enslaved African, a trope that, as I have argued, was often rhetorically leveraged by pro-life advocates to argue for fetal personhood. The Voigt-Kampff test, which is used to detect and exclude androids, suggests race and slavery, since it measures the androids' blushing reaction. Eighteenth-century philosophies of sympathy contrasted the transparent, blushing white face to the inhuman, opaque Black one.[66] As Michael Bérubé points out, the Voigt-Kampff test also suggests eugenics of mentally disabled people, since it was developed to identify and sterilize "specials," people neurologically damaged by radiation.[67] The persecution and extermination of the androids in the novel thus loosely correspond to a pro-life position, which indicts abortion both for treating humans like slaves and for its potential eugenics of disabled people.[68]

The androids further bring to mind the enslaved African insofar as the novel foregrounds their capacity to respond to aesthetic stimuli. Simon Gikandi has argued that eighteenth-century enslaved Africans attempted to stake claims to personhood and the public sphere by showcasing their aesthetic sensibilities. White thinkers like Thomas Jefferson claimed that enslaved Africans could not be rights-bearing people because they had no capacity for the aesthetic. But the aesthetic also became a route through which Africans and others excluded from personhood could demonstrate their own deservingness to be included in the category of the person. Gikandi argues that, for instance, "when slaves in the Dombi plantation in Suriname or the South Carolina rice country rehearsed elaborate Kongo dances or danced the Juba, they were staking a moral claim to the public sphere."[69] A similar logic—by which the androids demonstrate their own unique personhood by relating to a series of artworks—takes place in *Androids*.

In particular, two of the androids, Luba Luft and Phil Resch, demonstrate that they deserve to be included in the social polity by defining their android identities in relationship to artworks. At the same time, they imply the literary legitimacy of science fiction. Luba Luft stakes her claim to personhood when she becomes an opera singer on Earth. Her participation in *The Magic Flute* represents her own desire for freedom from her chattel status as an android, since the opera itself is about a woman who is rescued from imprisonment by a magic flute. Mozart's highbrow opera *Magic Flute* is also notable among operas for its broad appeal, a detail that suggests Dick's own attempt to combine his literary ambitions and the mass form of the SF novel. Not long before Deckard retires her, Luba asks him to buy her a reproduction of Edvard Munch's *Puberty*, a painting that represents a young girl's isolation and discomfort with her own naked, pubescent body. Insofar as the print is a mechanical reproduction, it becomes an expression of Luft's own feelings about her existence as a female android, removed from naturalized heterosexual reproduction. Phil Resch, the android hunter who doesn't realize that he himself is an android, also betrays his own identity in his relationship to Munch. Resch prefers modernist artists who represent fragmented individuals like Picasso, claiming that "realism in art doesn't interest me." When he sees Munch's *Scream*, he thinks "this is how an andy [android] must feel," and he claims that the portrait isn't "representational."[70] Resch marks out a lineage of artworks that, like the SF novel, upset the realist representation of characters as humans with coherent identities and rich interiority, in favor of fragmentation and distortion. While he establishes the SF android within a lineage of fragmented, anti-realist characters that include Picasso and Munch, he also stakes a claim to social personhood by showcasing his aesthetic sense.

Dick imagines personhood and self-definition as intimately connected to human fertility, as when the android Rachael Rosen gives the following speech:

> "How does it feel to have a child? How does it feel to be born, for that matter? We're not born; we don't grow up; instead of dying from illness or old age, we wear out like ants. Ants again; that's what we are. Not you; I mean me. Chitinous reflex-machines who aren't really alive." She twisted her head to one side, said loudly, "I'm not alive! You're not going to bed with a woman. Don't be disappointed; okay? Have you ever made love to an android before?" (193–194)

Rachael cycles through various terms to indicate her lack of personhood—"ant," "chitinous reflex-machines," "not alive"—because she is outside the ostensibly holistic process of childbirth, neither able to be born nor to give birth. Rachael's questions transition between those of the infertile or aborting mother ("How does it feel to have a child?") and the unborn fetus ("How does it feel to be born?") precisely because, for Dick, both figures are elements of a cold, dystopian world characterized by infertility, surveillance, and impersonality. Rachael is thus a figure for a fetus who is never born and for a mother who is unable to give birth.

For Dick, both the aborted fetus and the infertile mother are subversions of their natural, human functions. If, when Deckard administers the Voigt-Kampff test, Rachael seems as if she speaks "from personal experience" about getting an abortion, the reason is that as an android, she has been permanently sterilized (50). Rachael has, in other words, had her personhood taken away from her—understood here as a right to define herself by having a child. Rachael's oppression, she suggests, is her exclusion from the cycle of birth, life, and death—but implicit in such a suggestion is Dick's familiar idea that a natural woman is a childbearing woman. This deprivation is further highlighted by the fact that Rachael's name is probably a biblical allusion to Rachel, the wife of Isaac, who is seen as the childbearing mother of the Jewish people. Rachel was infertile until God allowed her to become pregnant; the biblical story emphasizes pregnancy as a divine gift. Rachel also literally means "ewe,"[71] a subtle reference to the electric sheep of the title; Deckard owns an electric "black-faced Suffolk ewe" (43). Rachael should be the mother to a nation, she should be a childbearing ewe, but as a woman cut off from her biology, she is closer to the mechanical sheep, unable to truly be alive.

While Dick may have seen a natural woman as childbearing, Deckard, like Louis in *We Can Build You*, must struggle with a seemingly inhuman, murderous woman to whom he is nonetheless sexually attracted—an imagination that, as we have seen, was catalyzed by Anne's abortion. *Androids* opens with Deckard and his wife Iran (who is also without child) using the "mood organs" that are designed to calm them down to instead trigger reproach and depression as they fight with each other. After the quarrel with his wife Iran, Deckard becomes sexually attracted to the android Rachael Rosen, and he begins to wonder whether the quasi-humanoid beings he's terminating are, in fact, people. His consideration of personhood is bound together with his desire for a woman who is cold and sterile. After sleeping with her, he finds, to his distress, that Rachael cannot be bent to his will; Rachael struggles with him over the radio (just as Iran had previously struggled with him over the television), and ultimately attains her "victory over him" (202). The scene is a harbinger to her killing his most prized possession—his goat, which she throws off the roof in her final appearance in the novel. As a result, Deckard reconciles with his wife, who has become more dutiful and reinforces his masculinity. She purchases some flies and a fake puddle for Deckard's toad, because "my husband is devoted to it" (243). Ironically, the conflict that may have been most important to Dick—between Deckard and the cold, unfeeling android-woman—was erased from *Blade Runner,* in which he has no wife, and the film instead concludes with a moment of moral clarity: Deckard and Rachael running away in love, having overcome doubts about her lack of humanity.

Dick thought that his science fiction could teach readers to recognize that life and female pregnancy are divine gifts. The fact that SF's detractors habitually critiqued the genre as mechanistic or android-like meant, for Dick, that SF authors were uniquely capable of appreciating beings like the fetus, whose personhood went unacknowledged and unfulfilled. In fact, later in life, Dick would devote much of his writing to trying to understand the events he called "2-3-74," a series of mystical, theophanic visions he experienced over the months of February and March of 1974. He had many explanations and descriptions of these visions, among them: contact from God, from a cosmic source known as VALIS (Vast Active Living Intelligence System), or from the late Bishop James Pike.[72] But he also thought of the visions as tantamount to God's endowment of the fetus with a soul, explaining the experience in an unpublished segment of his "Exegesis": "a Soul can enter a full grown body as well as that of the fetus."[73] At certain moments in his career, Dick cast doubt on the category of the autonomous liberal person in favor of a pro-life posthumanism that would require people to care for beings like the fetus who might not fully qualify as persons. But particularly in texts like *Androids* and "The Pre-Persons," Dick seems less to want to abandon the category of the person altogether than to suggest that it rightly encompasses beings without their own fully human bodies—a description that applies to both the android and the fetus. As he advocates for fetal personhood, he also defines a woman's personhood according to her capacity to bear children.

Abortion Science Fiction After *Roe v. Wade*

In the years that followed, many SF writers would follow Dick in extending cultural analogies that justified or denied fetal personhood into their fiction. One group of SF authors magnified the popular fear that fetuses are full persons, frivolously being killed. In Harlan Ellison's "Croatoan" (1975), a woman demands that the protagonist, Gabe, go into the sewers and find an aborted fetus who has been flushed down the toilet. Gabe eventually becomes the father figure to a population of fetuses and alligators living in the sewers beneath the city in a colony they call Croatoan, after the lost settlers of Roanoke. Likewise, in Kurt Vonnegut's "The Big Space Fuck," published in Ellison's second landmark anthology of New Wave science fiction, *Again, Dangerous Visions* (1972), any woman who volunteers for a free abortion receives her choice of "a bathroom scale or a table lamp"—because of overpopulation.[74] Later in life, Vonnegut would make statements in support of a woman's right to choose, and Ellison claimed in his introduction to "Croatoan" that he was not "anti-abortion" but that he was "anti-waste, anti-pain, anti-self-brutalization."[75] But both men still used science fiction to depict imagined scenes of deviant maternity and callow disregard for human life.

In her fiction, Alice Sheldon (who published most of her SF as James Tiptree, Jr.) contested the pro-life accusation that abortions treated human fetuses as if they were pieces of meat. In 1973, the year of *Roe v. Wade*, she wrote to her congressman to tell him about her abortion, insisting that her "embryo . . . was a rudimentary blob of flesh no bigger than a lima bean."[76] "Morality Meat" (1985), a story that she published under the pseudonym Raccoona Sheldon, criticizes the Right for its focus on fetuses and relative apathy for the fate of infants. Sheldon describes a world in which cattle and poultry are mostly extinct, and the law has rendered abortion illegal. As a result, a cabal of men has been secretly eating unwanted babies. Much of the story focuses on an adoption center as it is toured by victorious pro-life advocates, who do not realize what will happen to the babies who are not adopted. One of the visitors has delivered televised congressional testimony, holding up fetuses preserved in bottles, asking "who in the audience could 'deliberately tear apart this beautiful little person?'" But this same man, when finding that one of his bottles broke in his pocket, also said, off camera, "Get this *thing* off me!"[77] By a concealed and abstract analogy, fetuses can be made to seem like people, but in material reality, Sheldon believes that the fetus is closer to a gross thing ("a lima bean"); and the adoption center is exactly what pro-life advocates call abortion centers: a butcher shop or meat market. "Morality Meat" is thus a cautionary tale against those, like the visitors, who would forget the materiality of the fetus's body, as well as the body of the adopted infant, in favor of an abstract discourse of personhood.

Octavia Butler's "Bloodchild" (1984) can be read as the fictional incarnation of and precursor to Catharine MacKinnon's claim that "on the biological level, the fetus is more like a parasite than a body part."[78] The story concerns an isolated colony of human beings who are driven off their home planet and find themselves placed in a preserve on a planet of giant insect-like aliens, the T'lic. "Bloodchild" is, as Butler puts it, a "pregnant man story."[79] On this preserve, male humans are inseminated as hosts for parasitic alien babies or "grubs," while female humans continue the human race. If the male host is not cut open in time, these grubs will devour the man hosting them. The story follows a young male human, Gan, as he comes to terms with his obligation to carry parasitic alien babies. As with Shelley and Dick, part of Butler's interest in tragic and complex pregnancy stems from her biography: Butler was born only after her mother had given birth to four stillborn children.[80]

Throughout her work, Butler returns to the scenario of alien impregnation; the *Xenogenesis* trilogy (1987–1989) tells the story of Lilith, a female protagonist who is unwittingly inseminated with a human-alien hybrid. At various moments in the *Patternist* series (1976–1984), too, Butler's characters find themselves involuntarily impregnated with four-legged alien hybrids and explicitly consider abortion.[81] But they decide nonetheless to keep their babies. In "Bloodchild," by inflicting pregnancy on a male character, Butler forces the traditionally male SF readership to imagine the situation of a pregnant woman who appears to give consent and to love her partner but who is also coerced into bearing children.[82] The aliens seem like menacing, insect-like creatures who implant eggs in humans while coercing consent, but Gan also realizes that he has deep feelings for T'Gatoi. When T'Gatoi contemplates giving her eggs to his sister instead, he protests—partially because he doesn't want his sister to bear the parasites, but also because, as he tells her, he wants "to keep you for myself" (28). Butler notes in an interview that "men tend to see [the story as] a horrible case of slavery, and women tend to see that, oh well, they had caesarians, big deal."[83] What seems like a case of domination and oppression to men seems, to women, like an experience of love and pregnancy.[84]

Thinking about the experience of pregnancy as bearing a parasite under conditions of slavery allows Butler to approach the radical feminist critique of the liberal rhetoric of choice and personhood. T'Gatoi tells Gan in "Bloodchild": "You were the one making the choices tonight" (28)—when his choices involved being impregnated with an alien baby, delegating the pregnancy to his sister, or suicide. T'Gatoi further implies that the real choice was already made when she selected Gan at birth: "I chose you. I believed you had grown to choose me" (28). In the afterword to "Bloodchild," Butler describes the story as that of "a man becoming pregnant as an act of love—choosing pregnancy in spite of as well as because of surrounding difficulties" (30). But it can never be entirely clear whether Gan has chosen to conceive out of love for T'Gatoi or out of something like an adaptive preference—because loving T'Gatoi best enables him to survive. The conditions of alien matriarchy belie the putative freedom of Gan's choice. And yet, the interpretive question the story provokes is: does Gan truly love T'Gatoi? If MacKinnon, in calling the fetus a parasite, does not seem to imagine much love between mother and her unborn child or between a mother and father, Butler's task, in fictionalizing a parasitic fetus over an extended narrative, is to represent how love can both sustain gendered power imbalances and maybe even exist despite them.

As she reveals the limitations of "choice," so too does Butler ironize the word "person." The giant insect-like aliens, the T'lic, seem to have the fullest understanding of the word; they claim that they saw the humans "as people and gave them the Preserve when they still tried to kill us as worms" (25). "Do you care?" demands Gan of T'Gatoi, "Do you care that it's me?" Gan suggests that what seems like a valuation of specificity and uniqueness in the T'lic's preservation of human personhood may simply be a way of ensuring quality, compliant breeding stock, who are ultimately interchangeable (28). Though Butler has insisted that the story is not about slavery, she does include the detail that Gan's ancestors were "fleeing from their own kind, who would have killed or enslaved them" (24). Her ironizing of terms like "choice" and "person" was rooted not only in an intellectual position approaching radical feminism but in the particular experience of African American women. Post-*Roe*, African American women have had the legal right to choose abortion, but their choices have been even more socially controlled than those of other women, whether through racially targeted birth control and eugenics or through Supreme Court decisions like *Maher v. Roe* (1977) and *Harris v. McRae* (1980). These decisions denied poor—and disproportionately Black—women economic access to abortion.[85] Butler followed the plight of these women, saving clippings in her archive about abortion, including several about regulators excluding abortion from Medicaid.

Just as *Frankenstein* can be read as an allegory of both childbirth and female authorship, "Bloodchild" might also be said to represent childbirth in terms of the literary marketplace that constrained Butler's ambitions as an SF author.[86] As Gerry Canavan observes, Butler's repeated scenes of women slowly and reluctantly coming to terms with their duty to bear alien hybrids often look much bleaker in draft form. Butler felt torn between the desire to write what she called a "NO-BOOK," which would realize her ambition to represent reproductive failure, and a "YES-BOOK," a bestseller that would appeal to a marketplace that demanded narratives of successful reproduction. In the original draft of *Xenogenesis*, written just after "Bloodchild," the alien-human hybrids echo thalidomide babies—they are "armless, legless horror[s]" who are often stillborn—but Butler revises this narrative to be, like "Bloodchild," a story about reconciling oneself to an involuntary pregnancy.[87] In her afterword to "Bloodchild," Butler would call it a story about "paying the rent," about what humans stranded on a foreign planet could trade with their alien overlords (31). In light of the years that Butler spent working blue-collar jobs and her own struggles to make a living as an SF writer, to pay her own rent, it does not seem unreasonable to read "Bloodchild" as an allegory of artistic production. Like Butler, who feels coerced by the marketplace into crafting narratives of reproductive futurity and not of abortion or failed childbirth, Gan is similarly forced into the painful production of creatures that are not his own, and that will satisfy the demands of others, in order to survive. This allegory contrasts with the post-*Frankenstein* SF narratives like *Androids* that neglect both the physical demands of parturition and the material conditions of imagination.

Butler's story "The Evening, the Morning, and the Night" (1987) continues to explore the idea that to achieve personal autonomy, people need economic support, but she turns away from pregnant women and writes about children who would have been aborted, coming closer to the terrain of Dick or disability studies.[88] The characters of her story have the fictional Duryea-Gode Disease (DGD); at some point in their adulthood, they will begin to feel compelled to hurt themselves, to tear open their skin, because they feel that "they are trapped, imprisoned within their own flesh." DGD, she claims, was inspired by several genetic diseases (Huntington's, phenylketonuria, and Lesch-Nyhan), but it is actually an acquired disease that more closely resembles the effects of thalidomide on fetuses. It stems from a parent taking the prescription drug Hedeonco, a perceived "magic bullet" for cancer and other diseases. One character says about his parents: "If they had any sense, they would have had me aborted the minute my mother realized she was pregnant."[89] The only way that DGD characters can prevent mutilation turns out to be to produce artwork. But their compulsion (which resembles Butler's personal graphomania) makes them produce artworks and inventions above and beyond what the market will bear. In contrast to the government-funded facilities where patients languish and commit suicide, the privately funded and donated mansion-turned-"retreat" enables DGD artists to survive and flourish.[90] Only when they are given generous financial support are her characters able to produce artwork that is not to pay the rent but is rather a form of self-expression that helps them combat their desire to self-destroy. For Butler, autonomy was achievable only with the financial and material aid to promote flourishing. This was true equally for pregnant mothers ("Bloodchild") as it was for unwanted, abandoned, or disabled children ("The Evening, the Morning, and the Night").

Butler, then, like Dick, commented on the abortion debate in her imagination of the literary field. Dick imagined that both the fetus and the SF novel suffered from a lack of social recognition; Butler, by contrast, viewed her SF as constrained by the market's need for pro-natal stories. Whereas Dick's androids seem only to need to be recognized as human in order to become people, Butler's characters need, more than the negative rights that come with legal recognition, financial independence to be truly free. This was, for Butler, not merely an issue of theory; it was an urgent complaint about a world that imagined privacy as the freedom to choose without imagining the institutions of social welfare and equality that make genuine choice possible.

SF and *Planned Parenthood v. Casey*

During a crucial period in the development of the modern genre of science fiction, its preexisting speculative character co-evolved alongside abortion law, which traded routinely in speculative analogy. In the 1960s, Philip K. Dick would often seem to uncannily anticipate some of the rhetorical moves in much of the next decade's legal discourse about abortion. But close observation of historical timing reveals that Dick's lifelong residence in California, one of the first states to loosen restrictions on abortion, had him thinking about the problem ahead of much of the rest of the nation.[91] His imagination had been schooled early by personal experience and state politics.

That imagination still lingers with us today. As the debate about abortion continues, contemporary science fiction authors in a variety of different media have been no less active in fictionalizing the discourse surrounding abortion. Following Dick, a number of SF writers imagine abortion along pro-life lines, excising the woman's body and comparing the fetus to a persecuted, independent being. For instance, a variation of "The Pre-Persons," Neal Shusterman's young adult novel *Unwind*, concerns a society where parents cannot have abortions, but they can choose to "unwind" children between the ages of thirteen and eighteen. Shusterman asks his young adult audience to identify with fetuses by imagining abortion as if it were happening to someone their own age.[92]

Other writers follow Octavia Butler in using SF to represent the experience of pregnancy as invasion or infestation. Like Butler, the films *Alien 3* (1997) and *Prometheus* (2012), as well as an episode of *Star Trek: Enterprise* entitled "Unexpected," conceive of the fetus as a parasitic alien, but these pregnancies all result from cases of rape or involuntary insemination; they do not dramatize the underlying power structures that routinely marginalize women through the rhetoric of choice and personhood.[93] Margaret Atwood's *MaddAddam* (2013) features a character, Amanda, who is accidentally inseminated by bioengineered humanoid "Crakers." As in Butler's fiction, in the post-apocalyptic world of the text, abortion is not an option for Amanda. But instead of channeling the terror of conceiving an alien baby, Atwood has Amanda and her friends prefer that the baby be a child of the Crakers. They shun the other possibility, that the child is the spawn of the psychopathic humans who have raped Amanda repeatedly. The novel becomes an affirmation of posthumanist interdependence and comingling among species—even bioengineered ones. If in *The Handmaid's Tale* Atwood's dystopian imagination was fueled by evangelical threats to a woman's right to choose, *MaddAddam* has her more concerned about a future when the human race has to come to terms with bioengineered humanoid hybrids.[94] Unlike their predecessors, many of the more recent mass cultural imaginations of abortion in SF exist alongside questions of bioethics begotten by new technologies like stem cell research, cloning, and surrogacy.

With *Planned Parenthood v. Casey* (1992), the law's imagination of abortion became more firmly tethered to science. *Casey* affirmed a woman's right to an early-term abortion but observed that viability—and thus the permissibility of an abortion—was shifting earlier to twenty-four weeks. Justice O'Connor noted that viability may become "even slightly earlier if fetal respiratory capacity can somehow be enhanced in the future."[95] The decision invited the public to imagine speculative futures as advances in science render fetal viability a possibility earlier and earlier in pregnancy.[96] In a famous and peculiar formulation in *Casey*, the Supreme Court described the liberty to choose an abortion as entailing "one's concept of existence, of the universe, and of the mystery of human life."[97] In the Court's eyes, abortion was not just a woman's choice, but rather a demonstration of one's beliefs about humanity's place in the universe. For the Court as for many Americans, abortion had become an issue of liberty imagined on a cosmic scale. As the genre that also conceives of human life on a cosmic scale, science fiction has both reflected and abetted this cultural evolution.

One might see this evolution as predicted by the end of Stanley Kubrick's *2001: A Space Odyssey* (1968), when a giant fetus, the Star Child, approaches Earth. Diegetically, the Star Child represents the rebirth of the human species, but the moment also shows the capacity of the SF film to represent the cosmos and the evolution of human life on a grand scale.[98] And yet in celebrating science fiction, Kubrick channels the 1965 fetal photos of *Life* magazine, which helped to spark the abortion debate and also omitted the woman's body parts. This celebration of the SF genre is thus linked to an implicitly pro-life imagination of birth that does not include women.[99] But looked at in retrospect, the Star Child also seems to allegorize the way that science fiction has helped to make fetal personhood a metaphysical, cosmic issue.

The fact that science fiction has helped to make abortion a question of the meaning of humanity and the universe may explain certain feminist SF writers' ambivalence about the genre. In 1992, the same year as *Casey*, Ursula K. Le Guin traded SF for realism in "Standing Ground." "Standing Ground" is the story of a teenage girl, Delaware, who takes her pregnant, mentally disabled mother Sharee to an abortion clinic. The story features a familiar competition of analogies to characterize the fetus and the abortion. Pro-life evangelists dub the clinic "a

Butcher shop," whereas the doctor compares "aspiration" to "a haircut." The callousness of these metaphors suggests that each fetus is different and that only the mother can characterize her relationship to it. Whereas her last fetus was like a part of her, Sharee expresses that this fetus is "like a hangnail," "a wart," or "a scab" that's preventing her from being "whole."[100] The speculative analogies that science fiction relies on help Sharee characterize her own pregnancy, but they seem invalid when others apply them to her body. In the same year that the Supreme Court would imagine abortion as a mystery of the cosmos, Le Guin seemed to believe that it was no longer conscionable for her to do so.

Though science fiction seems partially responsible for making the abortion debate metaphysical, science fiction about abortion may still have lessons of value. Even though analogies continue to characterize the rhetoric around abortion, perhaps the sole point of agreement between the two sides is that the abortion debate should not be based in any kind of analogy. For pro-lifers, fetuses are not *like* humans; they *are* humans. "These people kill babies," the writer Patricia Lockwood remembers her pro-life mother telling her as a child in the early 1990s.[101] For pro-choicers, fetuses are not people. The feminist legal theorist Drucilla Cornell claims that any analogy between the fetus and the person reduces the woman to "a mere environment for the fetus." For Cornell, even late-stage abortions should be legal in order to preserve a woman's "most basic sense of self."[102]

Both viewpoints diverge from Barbara Johnson's claim that "arguments for and against abortion are structured through and through by the rhetorical limits and possibilities of something akin to apostrophe."[103] In approaching abortion through aliens, cyborgs, and talking squids, SF retains a consciousness that we need a language to talk about beings who both do and do not resemble humans. To Johnson's emphasis on apostrophe, the genre of science fiction adds the awareness that the rhetoric of the abortion debate has historically been rooted in analogy.

 # Exorcising Child Abuse in the 1970s

THE POSTERS FROM THE most notorious horror films of the 1970s suggest that a great number of them summoned fears about child abuse and domestic violence. The poster for *Rosemary's Baby* (1968) positions a baby stroller abandoned on a craggy landscape, with a drugged-out-looking Mia Farrow in the background. "Holland—where is the baby?" asks the poster for *The Other* (1972), forebodingly dramatizing the harm visited on a child. These posters also summon sympathy for parents tempted to abuse their children. "There's only one thing wrong with the Davis baby . . . It's Alive!" reads the tagline for the Larry Cohen film *It's Alive* (1974).

In *The Exorcist*, a few scenes imply that demonic possession is a metaphor for domestic abuse. In one scene, Chris MacNeil, the mother of the girl who is possessed, appears with a black eye, barely shielded by her sunglasses. Approaching the priest Father Karras, she seems as if she's about to tell him a secret. "What if," she asks, "a person, let's say, was a criminal, like maybe a murderer or something, you know? If he came to you for help, would you have to turn him in?" Perhaps, Karras might reasonably be thinking, she is going to tell him about the event that engendered her black eye. But instead of revealing a secret of domestic violence, she asks "How do you go about getting an exorcism?" and the story is deflected into literal demonology.[1] At the end of the film, the possibility of abuse surfaces once again; Regan and Chris move away from their home, both with the faded marks of physical violence on their faces, as if leaving behind an abusive man. In all these instances, helpless women and children are being harmed, parents have become violent, horror has invaded the space of the private home.

The genre's turn, or more accurately, return to privacy was a recent one. Horror had taken up dangers in private homes since the genre's inception in Gothic novels like *The Mysteries of Udolpho* (1794), which involve a woman being trapped in a castle or house by an ominous man. Charles Brockden Brown's

FIGURE 4.1 Movie poster from *The Other* (1972).
Source: The Everett Collection. Reprinted with permission.

Wieland (1798) imagined violence against women and children, and sensation novels like Wilkie Collins's *The Woman in White* (1860) had narrated domestic violence against women. But in the years immediately preceding the works of this chapter—the 1930s, 40s, and 50s—the most high-profile horror novels and films specialized in public spectacle: gruesome, external monsters like Frankenstein, Dracula, and their associated brides. There were precursors to the more restrained domestic horror I discuss here, including *The Curse of the Cat People* (1944), *The Bad Seed* (1956), *Psycho* (1960), and *Marnie* (1964), representing turmoil and even violence within the family. Still, with the notable exception of Alfred Hitchcock, horror was largely a niche genre, more appreciated by devoted aficionados than the general public, with H. P. Lovecraft, Ambrose Bierce, and William Castle being some of the most noted practitioners of tentacled or fanged gruesomeness. Beginning in the late 1960s, a new wave of mass cultural horror—epitomized by books like *Rosemary's Baby*, *The Exorcist*, *Carrie*, and *The Shining*—achieved greater sales than ever before by turning to the space of the private home. These books seemed almost designed to be adapted into film, which, as a medium, was especially effective at dramatizing anxieties about the privacy of the home. They took domestic scenes and brought them into what was quite literally a public space—the theater—and the films were accompanied by advertising campaigns that further saturated public spaces with fear.

As we saw in the last chapter, when privacy was imagined as a right to personal self-definition or autonomy, science fiction's flat characters, mixed with speculative thought experiments about who or what counted as a person, turned out to be particularly generative. But as the right to privacy expanded and conservative family values resurged, horror imagined the backlash against privacy—how private spaces could become haunted.[2] How much autonomy was too much autonomy? What happened when privacy wasn't anchored in the values of the traditional middle-class nuclear family? Horror authors examined how certain flattened character tropes could acquire a peculiar admixture of fear and delight. What was it about these unreal figures—a little girl walking backwards up the stairs or a family of blood-drinking Satanists—that seemed particularly gripping in the 1970s?

Previous commentators have noted that 1970s horror novels and films express male concerns about female sexuality and feminism—the same values of autonomy that *Roe* was designed to protect.[3] The priests in *The Exorcist* strap

Regan MacNeil down after she masturbates with a crucifix. Stephen King's Carrie discovers her telekinetic powers when she gets her first period. But these films also tapped into a simultaneous cultural anxiety—an ongoing national panic about child abuse and domestic violence. *The Exorcist* (1973) was released a little more than a month before Congress passed the national Child Abuse Prevention and Treatment Act, appropriated $60 million to create the National Center on Child Abuse and Neglect, and funded programs to identify abuse in all fifty states.[4] As I will show in the chapter, the key assumption behind this panic was that child abuse was equally present everywhere, but because middle- and upper-class families enjoyed more privacy, abuse in their homes had been shielded from view. The horror of the period spoke to the fears underlying this assumption: the works imagined (and sometimes challenged) the untold terrors that had been concealed by middle- and upper-class privacy.

The Invention of Child Abuse

The phenomenon of child abuse is surely very old, but the term itself did not become widespread until the 1960s.[5] Victorians conceived of child abuse as associated with poverty (as in works like *Oliver Twist*), but it did not conjure up the same horror that it does today. As Ian Hacking writes, "Cruelty to children was bad. But it was not an ultimate evil, inducing thoughts of horror and disgust."[6] While social reformers agitated for children's welfare in the nineteenth century, cruelty to children was rarely discussed in the first half of the twentieth. Freudian psychology discredited many who claimed to be abused, saying that they were producing unreal fantasies. Child abuse also fell out of the public eye as it was taken over by the profession of social work and as movements to strengthen the nuclear family dominated the nation, extinguishing nineteenth-century feminism.[7]

In 1962, the physician C. Henry Kempe claimed to discover child abuse, publishing an article with collaborators entitled "The Battered-Child Syndrome" in the *Journal of the American Medical Association*. Kempe and his co-authors described how, by using X-rays, they had been able to uncover the repeated abuse of children. "To the informed physician," they wrote, "the bones tell a story that the child is too young or frightened to tell." For Kempe and his collaborators, child abuse was not a socioeconomic problem; it could occur to anyone, anywhere, and at any time. Its factors were psychological, rooted in childhood.

Individuals who abused children tended to have been abused themselves—or else suffered from feelings of neglect or contempt.[8] After Kempe's article, national media coverage of child abuse began in force; child abuse seemed to be epidemic.[9] While all fifty states passed child abuse reporting laws by 1967, many of these laws did not provide any extra funding for the overwhelmed welfare agencies receiving those reports; they required only constant vigilance against the specter of child abuse.[10] As child abuse reporting improved and the definition of child abuse was expanded to include neglect and sexual abuse, incidences of child abuse would seem only to go up.

Child abuse became an issue of congressional concern, when, in 1972, Walter Mondale attempted to pass the Comprehensive Child Development Act, which would have ensured universal access to preschool regardless of income through multibillion-dollar funding. But even though it passed in both the House and the Senate, it was vetoed by Richard Nixon, who raised the familiar objection of the privacy of the family, worrying about the "family-weakening implications" of a "communal approach to child-rearing."[11] What Mondale did next illustrates the way that the period's understanding of privacy had shifted since the 1960s. He could no longer appeal to the values of personal dignity and autonomy that had anchored Great Society social programs; instead, he had to turn to more conservative fears about the privacy of the home—the dissolution of traditional family values.

Mondale engineered a new bill in 1974, the Child Abuse Prevention and Treatment Act (CAPTA). It was designed to be a bill that Nixon could not veto, because it was directed not at helping the poor but against the virulent and abhorrent evil that affected all classes equally—child abuse. "Not even Richard Nixon is in favor of child abuse!" he averred.[12] Testifying before Congress, David Gil, a professor of social policy at Brandeis, agreed with Mondale that child abuse could be found among all classes and races. But Gil had also published statistics indicating that non-white children were more than three times as likely as white children to be abused and that families making less than $5,000 a year underwent almost half of all abuse.[13] As he attempted to explain that "the poor have many more factors" that could lead them to child abuse, Mondale insisted, "This is not a poverty problem; it is a national problem."[14]

To frame the bill as partly addressing a socioeconomic concern would have smacked of social welfare legislation; instead, child abuse became a demon that could be found anywhere and everywhere, one that needed to be exorcised from society through constant vigilance.¹⁵ Mondale's argument was that because the police and social welfare organizations were already more involved in the lives of the poor, reporting of child abuse among poor families tended to be higher.¹⁶ Middle- and upper-class privacy shielded the epidemic of child abuse, which affected all classes equally. Consciousness of domestic violence followed a similar trajectory, with the term "battered woman" emerging as a variation of "battered child." Mary Jane Cronin, who worked in the federal government to coordinate legislative efforts, commented, "If domestic violence affected only poor women, it would have been dismissed."[17] Predictably, domestic violence legislation, too, met with New Right opposition about the breakup of the family; Senator Gordon Humphrey decried those working in battered women's shelters as "missionaries who would war on the traditional family or local values."[18] Buffeted by concerns about the vanishing nuclear family, liberals turned from imagining privacy as a liberating form of autonomy to a dangerous space that could shield the horrific specter of violence.

The media took up a version of the same narrative, telling an alarmist story of how the traditional space of middle- or upper-class privacy concealed scenes of bizarre, even satanic violence or decadence and drug abuse. "How could this happen here," Geraldo Rivera asked in his special two-hour report on satanic ritual abuse, "to a nice boy from a good Catholic school and a fine middle-class family?"[19] In 1987, the trial of Joel Steinberg for killing six-year-old Lisa Steinberg was one of the first to be entirely televised, receiving coverage on all three major networks in New York—ABC, NBC, and CBS.[20] His wife, Hedda Nussbaum, was an editor and author of children's books, and Steinberg was a defense attorney.[21] Similarly, interest in the longstanding case of the murdered six-year-old beauty pageant queen JonBenét Ramsey in the 1990s was so fervent in part because of the family's wealth.[22]

Audiences marveled at how seemingly placid exteriors could conceal horrific abuse (and perhaps experienced a tinge of schadenfreude too, at seeing the privacy of the upper classes exposed, their domestic lives immersed in turmoil). Anxieties about child abuse spoke, in particular, to a postwar middle-class parenting culture that was constructed around the idea of "permissiveness."[23] This culture taught that parents were not supposed to spank or command their children; they were instead supposed to let them grow and develop as autonomous beings. This new middle-class culture contrasted with an older style of parenting, once shared by both the working and middle class, in which children were left alone and taught to respect hierarchy and authority.[24] The child abuse scandals provoked shock and terror because they revolved around those in the middle and upper classes who had deviated so far from the permissive parenting culture—their horrific abuses hitherto shielded from view by their privacy.

Aristocratic Child Abuse: *Rosemary's Baby* and *The Exorcist*

The horror of the period took up the imagination that middle- and upper-class privacy concealed domestic turmoil. Previous criticism has emphasized that horror since the eighteenth century has dramatized the fears of liberal middle-class viewers and readers about the classes adjacent to them. Horror descended from Dracula channeled middle-class fears about decadent aristocrats who flouted staid bourgeois mores, while horror descended from Frankenstein represented anxieties about primal working-class culture overwhelming middle-class domesticity.[25] While liberalism in the eighteenth century had been oriented around the idea of middle-class people using their reason in private and coming together to form a public system of government to protect private life, the emotions of terror, disgust, and even pleasure conjured in horror threatened to unseat liberalism's emphasis on humans as rational creatures cultivating reason in private. In some respects, the works I discuss here update those older theories, representing those who flout the "permissive" values for an audience of middle-class viewers and readers. Horror like *The Exorcist* and *Rosemary's Baby* imagine how the private homes of celebrities or aristocrats could conceal scenes of abuse produced by decadent or immoral lifestyles. By contrast, stories like *The Shining* and *Carrie* shift the focus away from the hitherto unseen child abuse in spaces of abundance; instead, they dramatize brutal violence in the private spaces of the struggling working class.

We can read these works as speaking to the cathected emotions around privacy not just in their content but also in their form. Their representations of privacy invasion were accompanied by public advertising campaigns and displayed in the public environment of the theater. These works created middle-class publics who felt terror and delight at watching the horrific scenes of private life revealed. At the same time, we should not understand these works solely as opportunistically exploiting middle-class fears about the destruction of family values. Annie McClanahan has argued that horror's capacity to produce both terror and pleasure suggests its polyvalence: horror expresses unresolvable social contradictions, lending itself to multiple possible conflicting interpretations by different groups.[26] Close attention to the authors and works will reveal, in fact, that the works engaged with the logic of privacy in the period in complex ways, with *Rosemary's Baby* borrowing critiques of privacy from feminism and *The Exorcist* exhibiting the influence of Blatty's Arab background and working-class upbringing.

Rosemary's Baby has often been "read" as a film about child abuse. Not only does the one-shot stage anxieties about what might be happening to children, but real-life people have interpreted the film as encoding abuse. In 1980, Michelle Smith published, with her therapist Lawrence Pazder, *Michelle Remembers*, a bestseller about how she had recovered memories of being abused in a *Rosemary*-like satanic cult as a child. In the 1990s, a series of day care centers across the country were falsely accused of participating in a cult of satanic ritual abuse that seemed to take its script from *Rosemary*.[27] But the film itself imagines the abuse of children as one of several possible failures of privacy. Of all horror of the period, *Rosemary's Baby*, more a product of the radical 60s than the conservative 70s, may have approached most closely the feminist idea that the newfound freedoms of privacy in the postwar era were ciphers for older forms of patriarchal authority.[28] Like Octavia Butler in the previous chapter, Ira Levin was initially inspired to write the novel because he wanted to represent how giving birth to an unwanted or alien fetus could be terrifying to a woman: "Nine whole months of anticipation, with the horror *inside* the heroine!" he commented.[29] He wanted to explore what it felt like not to have one's own body protected as a "zone of privacy." Levin continued to imagine the staid middle-class community oppressing would-be feminists in his subsequent novel *The Stepford Wives* (1972).

As a novel and film, *Rosemary's Baby* raises anxieties associated with many of the most prominent areas of privacy concern in the postwar era—pregnancy, marital relationships, architecture, and telephone conversations—and shows how they fail to protect women. The personal relationships that the Supreme Court had protected as private in *Griswold*—"the sacred precinct of the marital bedroom" and would protect in *Roe*, that of "a woman and her responsible physician"—are precisely the relationships that prove most constraining to Rosemary.[30] Colluding with the Castevets, her husband Guy drugs and rapes her to impregnate her, and she wakes up with scratches on her. Rosemary feels intuitively as if something wrong has been done to her, but she cannot articulate what it is. (The novel predated the first conviction for spousal rape by more than a decade.)[31] Guy, who "married her to have an audience, not a mate,"[32] sells their baby to the Castevets in exchange for fame or wealth, showing how a husband can leverage his private life to further his public one. Six years after the novel, *Roe* would protect the privacy of abortion as a decision made between a woman and her doctor. But doctors are of little help to women here: Rosemary's doctor straps her into her bed to force her to bear a baby.

The apartment building where the Woodhouses and Castevets live also suggests the illusion of newfound postwar privacy in middle-class urban residences.[33] The Bramford has more "charm and individuality" than the "nameless white cellblock" that they had originally planned on renting. The Bramford was built for wealthy aristocrats (of whom the Castevets are relics), but then partitioned into middle-class apartments, which are supposed to have more privacy and distinctiveness than the rows of adjacent rooms they would have found in the "cellblock." As it turns out, Rosemary can hear through the walls, and the Castevets can burst in and out of the Woodhouses' most intimate private lives through their closet (suggesting a queer sexuality intruding on heteronormative, middle-class space). The phone booth also proves to be an area of illusory privacy. As we saw in earlier chapters, in *Katz v. United States* (1967), the Supreme Court considered a phone booth that FBI agents had bugged without a warrant and declared that privacy protections extended outside of the home—to anywhere that people had a "reasonable expectation of it."[34] In a famous four-minute long-take in the film, the camera is suspended in the phone booth with Rosemary as she calls a new doctor. Not only does it turn out that a man (a cameo by horror producer William Castle—and a missed signal of what genre she is in) is listening in to her conversation, but her new doctor is in cahoots with her husband and her other doctor.

At the root of all these invasions of her privacy are the Castevets, the decadent Dracula-descendants who shun middle-class values in favor of a longstanding satanic cultish religion. The young, chic Woodhouses represent the values of a late-1960s, middle-class, youthful viewing public—fashionable clothing, a Chemex coffeemaker, and a haircut by Vidal Sassoon—who celebrated the expansion of privacy into newfound areas like a woman's right to choose. By contrast, the

Castevets represent an older, aristocratic idea of privacy, in which the home licenses patriarchal authority. Roman is a well-to-do elderly businessman from the previous century (born in 1886) whose father was involved in theater and, it turns out, nineteenth-century European Satan worship (in Stockholm and Paris). As holdouts from the Bramford's more patrician days, their preferences initially seem garish and anachronistic—running toward overcooked steak, saccharine Boston cream pie, and lime-green toreador pants. It turns out that the previous generation does not merely suffer from bad taste; they find middle-class permissive and heteronormative values anathema. They indulge in orgies and harm children in the privacy of their apartment. Rosemary tells Guy, "They use blood in their rituals, because blood has power, and the blood that has the most power is a baby's blood, a baby that hasn't been baptized; and they use more than the blood, they use the flesh too!"[35] Several years before they move in, "a dead baby wrapped in newspaper" was found by their apartment building.[36] They provide one imagined explanation of how child abuse could emerge in private, middle-class spaces, which were infected with a culture of upper-class decadence and debauchery that was especially destructive to women.

The advertising campaign for *Rosemary's Baby* was effective at raising potential viewers' hackles that their privacy was illusory. The film was marketed to speak to concerns about subliminal advertising, which had first been stoked nearly a decade earlier by Vance Packard in *The Hidden Persuaders* (1957) before he took on the death of privacy in *The Naked Society* (1964). Previous advertising campaigns for horror films had emphasized the hideous monsters on view; they were often structured around three imperative sentences, each beginning "See the . . . !" The revolutionary advertising campaign for *Rosemary's Baby*, engineered by Steve Frankfurt of the firm Young & Rubicam, was far more subtle.[37] It focused on what viewers could not see, what they could only imagine. Advertisements for the film were integrated seamlessly into everyday media. Casual readers of newspapers would see, scattered amidst birth announcements or the classified ads for babysitters and piano teachers, the ominous "Pray for Rosemary's Baby."[38] Scrawled in the bottom corner of the *New York Times* in tiny print were just four semi-cryptic words: "Pray for Rosemary's baby."[39] In the one-shot, the Gothic-looking stroller combined with the prone, catatonic Mia Farrow suggested that a woman had been drugged, a baby abandoned or harmed: female autonomy and progressive middle-class childrearing somehow

FIGURE 4.2 Movie poster from *Rosemary's Baby* (1968).
Source: The Everett Collection. Reprinted with permission.

overcome by older, traditional values represented by the stroller. The whole campaign emphasized its capacity to overwhelm reason, to implant irrational fear in the viewers' psyches: somewhere, somehow the privacy of the middle-class home was being violated, a child was being harmed.

In abjuring special effects and depending instead on the viewer's psyche to represent the threat of child abuse, *Rosemary's Baby* also helped inaugurate a new genre of "serious horror," one that depended for its aesthetic not on public monsters but on private horrors. *Rosemary's Baby* is often regarded as the moment when the B-grade horror movie of producer William Castle met Roman Polanski's art-film.[40] The film's deliberately "realistic" setting, one that made sure to interpolate actual events—the pope's visit to America in 1965, the transit strike, and an actual issue of *Time* magazine—made it seem as if the horrors could actually enter the private lives of those young middle-class viewers who identified with the up-and-coming Woodhouses. Most notably, and in contrast to the novel, the film never showed the satanic baby but asked the viewer to imagine it instead. Contrast the understated, "psychological" horror of *Rosemary's Baby* with the grotesque, oversized, fanged baby of Larry Cohen's B-horror movies, *It's Alive* (1974) and *It Lives Again* (1978). Placing the demon in the audience's heads underscored horror's threat to privacy. It could invade the privacy of the imagination and cultivate there the unreasoning emotions of terror and pleasure.

Released a few years later, *The Exorcist* similarly imagined itself as exposing how unseen horrors could take place in wealthy families. It seemed to take advantage of the same kind of hysteria surrounding a saga like JonBenét Ramsey's: fear and perhaps vicarious enjoyment at watching an upper-class family overtaken by abuse. But when read against William Peter Blatty's background, the story can also seem tongue in cheek: an over-the-top, even satirical indictment of the hysteria surrounding abuse shielded by privacy in affluent communities.

Blatty had a unique career that positioned him to understand, and view with a skeptic's eye, the hold that images of heterosexual private family life had on the national imagination. He was himself no stranger to single parenting: Blatty's father abandoned him when he was seven.[41] As a Lebanese American writer for the United States Information Agency (USIA) and an editor and writer for the Lebanese propaganda magazine *News Review*, Blatty saw the cultural imagination of the American nuclear family as the bedrock of society.[42] While the particular issues of *News Review* that he edited are mostly lost, images of the family were

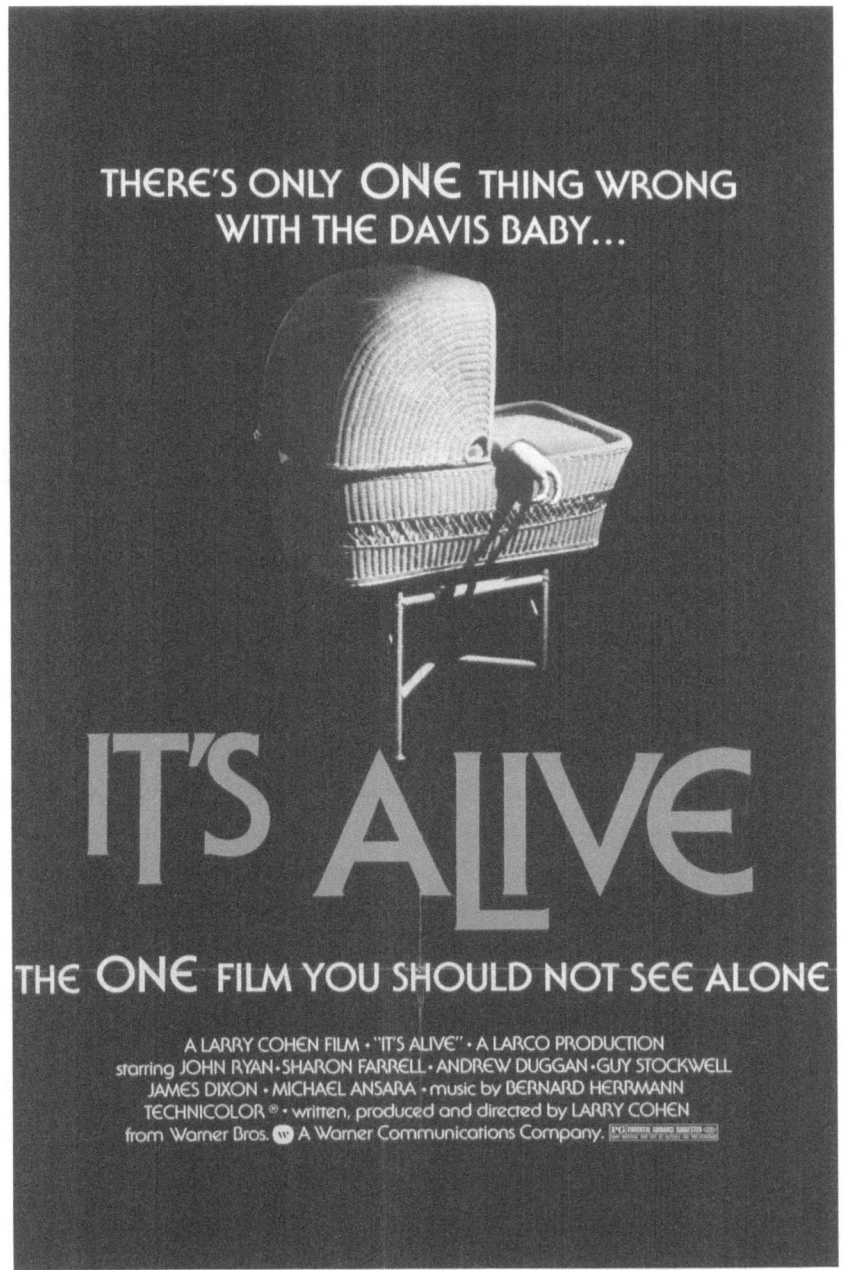

FIGURE 4.3 Movie poster from *It's Alive* (1974).
Source: The Everett Collection. Reprinted with permission.

common in the propaganda of the time. For instance, in 1958, two years after Blatty left, the USIA sponsored a tour in Lebanon of Edward Steichen's *The Family of Man* exhibit, designed to emphasize the family rather than class as the constitutive unit of society.[43] The fact that the demon Pazuzu comes from northern Iraq is a knowing nod to Blatty's understanding of how Americans imagined their homegrown family values as under threat from foreign cultures. It is both a political and personal allegory. Politically, Pazuzu reflects the American fear of the Arab Other; personally, Pazuzu reflects Blatty's father—whom he remembers his mother calling a "DEVIL" right before he left the family.[44]

Blatty also gained familiarity with the unique anxieties surrounding middle-class parenting culture by ghostwriting a book for Abigail Van Buren of Dear Abby fame, entitled *Dear Teen-Ager* (1959). Sections like "My Parents Are Nosy" and "My Parents Don't Trust Me" reveal that Blatty had his eye on the experience of middle-class teenagers seeking personal autonomy. In the afterword for *Dear Teen-Ager*, a section entitled "P.S. For Parents Only," he lists, among the ten things parents should understand teenagers want: "Trust" and "Understanding" as well as "PRIVACY. 'We need a room of our own to retreat to, a place to store our junk and pursue our hobbies. And we don't want any of this nonsense of reading our letters and listening in on our telephone conversations.'"[45] There was, however, a limit to Blatty's celebration of teenage privacy and autonomy. In another section, entitled "I Think I'm in Trouble," "Abby" advises a potentially pregnant girl to go to her mother once she knows she's pregnant, or "as a second choice confide in your clergyman." He continues about abortion: "There's a law against it, and the reason for the law is that quack doctors, pills and abortions kill people—people like *you!*"[46] Blatty understood the central premise of permissive middle-class parenting culture—that children's individual personalities should be given privacy to grow—and the anxiety surrounding that culture—what children might get up to in private.

Blatty likely viewed anxieties about single parenting, the problems of celebrity life, and foreign Arab invaders with a certain amount of skepticism, and we should read *The Exorcist* as dramatizing exaggerated versions of those anxieties. He took his understanding of the deep-seated emotions surrounding familial privacy and conjured up fear in *The Exorcist* by placing suggestions of abuse in the context of single parenthood and celebrity culture. As celebrities, Chris MacNeil and her daughter Regan live inescapably public lives. The two are featured together on the cover of Hollywood magazines. Chris is recognizable everywhere on the street. She is unmarried, a single mother with two servants. The demon appears for the first time when Chris is hosting a boisterous cocktail party for her celebrity friends; while Regan is supposed to be asleep, she comes downstairs and urinates on the carpet. The demon can be read as a dark underside to Hollywood celebrity; he is an actor who performs the different roles of Satan: Burke Dennings (Chris's director and potential paramour) and Mary Karras (Father Karras's mother), among others. Father Merrill speaks of the demon as audience-directed; he describes the demon's target as "not the possessed; it is us . . . the observers . . . every person in this house."[47]

While *The Exorcist* is often read as describing paternalistic alarm at a young girl's sexual maturation, one can also understand the demon as produced not by privacy but by too much publicity. Regan's bedroom suffers from a profound loss of privacy; the characters who go traipsing through it include her mother, her mother's two servants, her mother's friend (and possible lover), a doctor or two, and two different priests, not to mention the demon himself, who is repeatedly characterized as containing multiple people. The conundrum that Blatty grappled with in *Dear Teen-Ager*—how to give middle-class teenage girls enough privacy but without giving them too much—found a new and different expression as the film turned her bedroom into a space of publicity available in the theater.

Evoking fears about single parenting, the demon also has much in common with Regan's absent father. As Ann Douglas points out, he enters her life as an imaginary friend, "Captain Howdy," a name derived from her absent father Howard.[48] When the priest, Damien Karras, asks Chris to send for Regan's father, Chris responds by comparing the father to the demon possessing her: "I asked you to drive a demon *out*, not to drive another one *in!*" (277). Chris's comment invites us to imagine Regan's symptoms of demonic possession as representing her abuse at the hands of her father. She wails out to her mother, "Please make him stop hurting me! Okay, Mom? Please?" (128). In other places, Blatty writes, "'Oh, Mother, make him stop!' Regan was screeching. 'Stop him! He's trying to kill me! Stop him! Stoooppppp hiiiiiimmmmmmmm, Motherrrrrrrrrrrr!'" (113) or "Oh, he's burning me . . . burning me!" (114). Scratch marks appear on her face and cuts on her lips.[49] In the possession, Blatty imagines the spectacular hysteria surrounding parental abandonment or abuse when placed in a celebrity milieu, and he shows how throwing open that bedroom to a public audience could produce terror but also delight.

While *The Exorcist*'s domestic turmoil is primarily imagined as a product of decadent celebrity and absent or negligent parents, there is also a suggestion that it may resemble struggles in the life of the working class. Though omitted from the film for time constraints, the novel also imagines a poorer girl—Elvira, the daughter of Karl, one of Chris's servants—as a double for Regan. Elvira is addicted to heroin, and the detective investigating the murder convinces her to check into a rehab clinic.[50] Elvira's addiction has much in common with Regan's possession; she has "hollow eyes," "puncture scabs on her arm," and echoes Regan's deep voice, coughing "rackingly" (270). By juxtaposing Regan with Elvira, Blatty shows that the demonic possession of the story represents how social problems acquire spectacular hysteria when placed amid upper-class life. In the logic of the novel, the problems of the working class can be solved through state involvement—the detective persuades Elvira to check into a rehab clinic—but the state proves ineffectual when it comes to the upper class because of their privacy. The one person who is not allowed to see Regan is the detective. He begs entry to Regan's bedroom, but he is told that she is too sick to see him. Imagining child abuse as a form of demonic possession taking place in private means that the state is helpless to do anything about it; instead, it becomes a matter of family and religion.

While Blatty may have been at least partially satirizing anxieties about celebrity child abuse and single parenting (he was otherwise a comedy writer), in its advertising and presentation, *The Exorcist*, like *Rosemary's Baby*, showed how easy (and gratifying) it was to overwhelm the individual's capacity for reason, to take the space of the private psyche and turn it into one of irrational emotion. There was perhaps no more visceral, clear-cut example than the many reports of viewers who involuntarily vomited upon seeing the film. (There were also reports of fainting, nausea, heart attack, and a miscarriage.)[51] *Psycho* (1960) had made the film an event with a concrete and shared beginning and end (with Hitchcock refusing to let anyone enter the theater). *The Exorcist* built on this legacy, marketing itself as a mass cultural spectacle that would consolidate a viewing public around especially horrific images of private life.[52] The trailer refused to show the horror. It presented a series of reaction shots: the mother holding a torch; looking at her daughter's bed; doctors gathered around her bedroom; priest and mother discussing the girl's situation. It invited the viewer to participate in a public event and witness what lay behind respectable-seeming closed doors. Newspaper reports emphasized the sensation and spectacle of going to see the movie. In New York, people stood outside in the rain, sleet, and December cold for up to four hours.[53] In Los Angeles, director William Friedkin hired a coffee cart to cater to the immense queue.[54] In its story, *The Exorcist* dramatized a little girl's bedroom thrown open to a large public—priests, boyfriends, doctors. In its production, it put images of her middle-class privacy on display in the public space of the theater. It lured people in with the promise to gratify their urges to see privacy made public spectacle.

Also like *Rosemary*, *The Exorcist* made its horror more effective by combining the more spectacular elements with realistic-seeming restraint. The most notorious images associated with the film are the scenes of spectacle: a little girl vomiting and walking up the stairs backwards. But the film's grotesque elements were surrounded by pretensions to aesthetic seriousness and moderation. It was the oscillations of real-seeming referents and aesthetic elevation with carnivalesque thrills that made these works particularly engaging. *The Exorcist* had just enough apparent aesthetic seriousness to offset its gross spectacle, to prevent it from being rated X or treated as trash—though many critics did take a hatchet to it for purported crudeness.[55] It was made by William Friedkin, the New Hollywood auteur behind *The French Connection*; the score was a modern classical one, the introduction was filmed on location in Iraq, and, unthinkable for a horror movie, it won an Academy Award for Best Adapted Screenplay.[56] This quasi-aesthetic seriousness, this mix of bourgeois restraint with horrific spectacle, made its discovery of the horror within private life seem more real and thus more engrossing to a middle-class audience.

In fact, the terror and superstition that the films conjured were so effective that everyday people have imagined the Satanism depicted in works like *Rosemary's Baby*, *The Exorcist*, and *The Omen* as somehow true. In addition to spawning *Michelle Remembers* and the ritual abuse scandals, *Rosemary's Baby* has also been blamed for the murder of Sharon Tate, Roman Polanski's wife, in 1965 by the Manson Family, because of a curse associated with the making of the film.[57] In 1976, Malachi Martin, a priest, penned a nonfiction account about real-life exorcisms called *Hostage to the Devil*.[58] The fact that these outrageous horror films have seemed somehow real is a product of their ability to conjoin horror with more realist aesthetics. It is also likely because they brought the viewer into a public space that overwhelmed the calm rationality cultivated in private that liberalism celebrated. The films puzzled a middle-class audience by showing how it could feel both terrifying and pleasurable to witness the cherished value of privacy being violated.

Stephen King's Working-Class Child Abuse

Much of Stephen King's fiction—*Carrie, Salem's Lot, The Shining, It, The Green Mile, 11/22/63*—has invoked child abuse or domestic violence in one form or another. But rather than participate in a spectacularized (though often nuanced) imagination of child abuse in middle- or upper-class spaces, many of King's early works anchor child abuse within the working class where King grew up. Like Blatty, his father abandoned him when he was young, and his mother worked a variety of jobs to make ends meet. Later in life, when King wrote *Carrie*, he was living in a trailer, teaching high school English for $6,400 annually, and working part-time at a laundry—like Carrie's mother.[59] Like Blatty, King says, "I didn't have a father to be abusive. He was just an absence." In his memoir *On Writing*, he chronicles some of the neglect that he experienced as a child while his mother was away; the family was evicted from their Wisconsin home when, with a supervising adult nowhere in sight, a neighbor saw his six-year-old brother standing on the roof.[60] As a two- or three-year-old, while staying with his aunt and uncle while his mother was at work and minimally supervised, he picked up a cement cinder block and stumbled into a wasp's nest before dropping the block on his toes.[61] He explained *The Shining* as his expression of feelings of anger he experienced toward his own children:

> I had feelings of anger about my kids that I never expected. I had never been led to believe by sitcom TV, or movies like *A Wonderful Life* that it was ever possible to think, "Won't this darned kid ever go to bed and let me write?" And Jack Torrance came out of that experience. An attempt to understand that experience.

In his 2003 National Book Award speech, King remembers calling writers of literary fiction an "old boy network" who had foundations and universities to support them. The rest of the speech is a paean to the unsung writers who languished in literary-critical obscurity as King had—Peter Straub, Jack Ketchum, Jodi Picoult, and others. King's early fiction suggests that he experienced powerful feelings of shame, rage, and resentment at his father, occasionally at his children, and at the literary field that excluded him. And, while he aspired to transcend his humble circumstances, he also felt ambivalent about his ambition. He gave voice to all those feelings in his novels.

Stephen King's works imagined child abuse differently than much of the horror of the period. While works like *Rosemary's Baby* and *The Exorcist* took up Mondale's assumption and represented the imagined abuse concealed by upper-class private spaces, King focused instead on child abuse that was known to exist within the working class. Compared to the demonic possession or satanic baby narratives like *Rosemary's Baby*, *The Exorcist*, *The Omen*, or *The Other*, King's early works represent the violence of abuse with minimal magical enchantment. Rather, in King, characters escape from child abuse by drawing on a magical power or anti-realist element, which destroys the privacy enabling their suffering. Through its association with modernist stream of consciousness, that power also enables King the author to imbue his mass market fiction with literary value.

In *Carrie*, child abuse is the province of the fundamentalist Christian, Margaret White, who works at a laundromat. The thematic absence of the nuclear family returns: she is also a single mother. Notably, even though he situates child abuse in the working class, in *Carrie*, King—like Mondale and like *Rosemary* or *The Exorcist*—still avoids imagining that abuse might be produced by the stresses of poverty. It is instead a problem not of income inequality per se but of culture and education—Margaret's evangelical values. Over the course of the novel, Carrie's mother Margaret slaps her, chokes her, kicks her, hits her, and locks her in a closet to pray. This closet scene is also taken from King's childhood when one in a parade of babysitters locks him in a closet while his mother is away at work.[62] When Carrie levitates a bottle as a baby, her mother tries to kill her and is stopped by her husband. Eventually, Margaret stabs and fatally wounds Carrie with a carving knife (and in return, Carrie stops her heart with her mind). While legislators of the period imagined that privacy shielded abuse in the middle class, King shows how privacy protects the child abuse taking place in the home of the fundamentalist Margaret White as much as the decadent Castevets and the negligent Chris MacNeil. Carrie's neighbors and teachers are aware that something is amiss in her household but are unable to do anything about it, and so she is beaten and locked in closets for her sin. Throughout the book, as in *The Exorcist*, the state remains ineffectual, first in preventing abuse and then in understanding her telekinesis. Struggling to understand Carrie's powers, Congress convenes the "White Commission," which concludes that Carrie's powers were a hoax or a fluke, burying the story "under the bureaucratic mat."[63]

The force that rescues Carrie from the confining space of privacy is not state agency but telekinesis. Carrie first manifests her telekinetic abilities when Margaret looks at her neighbor's daughter, Stella Horan, who is sunbathing in her bathing suit. Margaret complains to Stella's mother, and Stella's mother then buys her daughter a "little white bikini" and encourages her to sunbathe, citing "the privacy of our own back yard and all" (35). (In fact, privacy here ironically means the right to publicly display oneself.) When Margaret catches three-year-old Carrie admiring Stella's body, she screams, begins self-flagellating, and ushers Carrie back into the house, telling her to "get herself into her closet and pray" (40). In response, ice and stones begin falling on the Whites' house, summoned by three-year-old Carrie's telepathy. There is an irony in this punishment in that Margaret had called Stella "the Whore of Babylon" (34), who, in the Book of Revelation, causes Babylon to be engulfed in a shower of ice and stone because of her sin. While Margaret had tried to confine female sexuality within the private home, Carrie refuses to remain in private and instead repurposes a public shaming.

Throughout the novel, Carrie's telekinetic power obliterates spaces of privacy that would otherwise be confining and shameful. The book opens with Carrie wishing for her own privacy, for "individual—and thus private" showers (in the film, one of many allusions to *Psycho*), and this lack of privacy causes her humiliation when she has her first period (5). Carrie's telekinesis turns the exposed private space of the shower, the scene of her humiliation, into public shower-violence. She turns on "a shower" (231) in the gymnasium by activating the sprinklers. "*[T]hat'll* give them a shower" (204), she thinks, as she unscrews the nuts on the fire hydrants, and she brings down chunks of ice "in a shower" (41) on her own house. Her telekinetic powers enable her to reverse her private embarrassment of her sexuality and her family and instead to inflict suffering on targets of her choice in the public at large.

Carrie's power obliterates not only the privacy of the home but also the privacy of interiority. She cannot help but transmit her thoughts out to others; repeatedly, as they testify before Congress about her powers, witnesses are unable to explain how they knew what Carrie was thinking. King equates Carrie's power to remove privacy with literary modernism, since he represents it through stream-of-consciousness parentheticals.[64] For instance, when Carrie first realizes that she could knock the hinges off the closet door, she thinks to herself "(and i think i could i think i could yes i think i could)" (72). King thus aligns Carrie's telekinetic powers with Joyce and Faulkner, two authors who make private interiority legible to a reading public through modernist techniques. Carrie's feelings of shame, resentment, and rage against those who mock her are also King's feelings about the literary field in which he finds himself. While she turns to telekinesis for her revenge, he brings literary modernism into the space of mass market genre fiction.

In *The Shining*, King continues to anchor child abuse within the working class, but in that novel he imagines it more concretely as produced by economic pressures. Fired from his job as a high school English teacher (a profession he shared with King), Jack Torrance has to take a job as a caretaker of a hotel. Also like King, Jack suffers from alcoholism. When he thinks of leaving the hotel, he imagines to himself the potential working-class careers available to him, which he encases in mock euphemisms: "Custodial engineer—swamping out Greyhound buses. The automotive business—washing cars in a rubber suit. The culinary arts, diner. Or possibly a more responsible position, such as pumping gas."[65] This pressure ultimately leads him to abuse his child and wife. The novel's Overlook Hotel appears as a metaphor for the socioeconomic institutions that motivate Jack's abuse. Wendy tells Danny that "It's not your daddy talking, remember. It's the hotel" (378), and Danny tells his father, "You're the hotel" (429). Grady, the previous caretaker, had been put in the very same situation—and had ended up killing his daughters, suggesting that the institution, not the individual, is to blame. The hotel stokes Jack's careerist ambitions to transcend the working class. "He would show them that he was of managerial timber!" (383), Jack thinks to himself, not long before he turns homicidal. The ghost of Grady asks Jack to think how far he "could go in the Overlook's organizational structure. Perhaps . . . in time . . . to the very top" (354).

While Jack's worries about falling out of the middle class lead to his abuse of his family, his privacy conceals and enables that same abuse. Early in the novel, Wendy Torrance takes her son Danny to the doctor because he is stung after Jack places a wasp nest in his room (referring to the wasp incident from King's life). Jack thinks mistakenly that he has killed all the wasps with a bug bomb until Danny is attacked. At the physician's office, the doctor notices that Danny's arm had once been broken, but he tells the parents that aside from the incident with the wasps, "it's obvious that he's been in no way abused since then" (146). The doctor does not follow mandatory reporting laws and instead allows the Torrances their privacy. In the novel, Jack is even fired from his job as a teacher precisely because of child abuse; he brutally beats a student for slashing his tires. The fear and isolation created in *The Shining*—a family trapped in a hotel in the snow in the Colorado winter, unreachable by park rangers—is a metaphor for the privacy that sealed off the family from outside aid.

The Shining represents abuse as part of a working-class culture that can be passed down through the generations. Jack's ultimate descent into child abuse and domestic violence stems from his own father's abusiveness. Through flashbacks, we learn that Jack and his family had been violently abused in their childhood by their alcoholic father whom Jack increasingly comes to resemble over the course of the novel. Jack's father had brutally beaten his mother with his cane, and so Jack carries a roque mallet as "a crutch or a cane" (408). The mallet represents both the psychological factors causing child abuse—Jack's connection to his father—as well as the socioeconomic pressures; roque is a made-up pastime that is supposed to be even more posh than croquet. When Jack's mother is beaten by his father, we see the ills of privacy again; his mother goes to the hospital but insists that her injuries are from a fall, and the physician decides to let the family alone in their privacy. He repeatedly hears his father's voice in his head, encouraging him to abuse his children: "He's a goddam little pup. Cane him for it, Jacky, cane him within an inch of his life" (228). The Overlook Hotel even assimilates the psychological landscape of Jack's childhood, in addition to stoking his careerist aspirations. Just as Jack used to play "elevator" with his father, his father rides the elevator of the hotel, which spontaneously whirrs itself out of disrepair as he comes to find and hurt Danny. The Overlook stands for the social, socioeconomic, and psychological factors that impel Jack to hurt Danny.

The hotel also represents the forces that confine King in the literary field. The rage Jack feels toward his family isn't solely a reflection of his poverty: it also comes from his inability to produce a work of art. The careerist aspirations that Jack experiences are, like King's, specifically literary ones. Jack wants to align himself with literary fiction; he thinks of himself as a "man well qualified to teach that great mystery, creative writing" (36). In fact, the Overlook Hotel was even a creative writing program for one year, with two Pulitzer Prize winners attached to teach, until scandal ensued: a student either fell or jumped out of a window. But Jack, like King, finds the space of literary institutions to be imprisoning, not liberating. He is tormented by a hotel that, in its country clubbish, aristocratic connotations, reflects the old boy network that King decried in the National Book Award speech. While Jack tries to produce "the great American novel" in Thoreauvian isolation, he finds himself haunted instead by "The Masque of the Red Death," a tale from Poe, a writer who was enmeshed in the marketplace for fiction and whom Jack calls "the Great American Hack" (155). King reflects on Jack's (and, by extension, his own) desire for literary merit with a profound ambivalence—as a pretension to escape the working-class milieu from which he came. In fact, the ultimate difference between the character and author is that while Jack remains fixated on literariness, King figured out how to walk the line between literary prestige and broad appeal: to embed modernist techniques in a mass cultural environment.

To extricate his character from abuse and himself from marginalization in the literary field, King ultimately returns to the same technique he used in *Carrie*: privacy-dissolving stream of consciousness. Danny uses his gift, his "shining," to summon the hotel cook, Dick Hallorann, in Florida. As in *Carrie*, King uses stream-of-consciousness parentheticals to narrate characters' thoughts, the sensations of the house, and, most importantly, Danny's shining. The magical power King associates with the coincidence of literary modernism and mass culture enables the abused child to call for help across thousands of miles: "(!!! DICK PLEASE COME QUICK WE'RE IN BAD TROUBLE DICK WE NEED)" (337). It enables him to summon (one member of) a public. When his characters telecommunicate with others, King takes modernist techniques and makes them accessible to a mass public. Even as he renders Joyce and Faulkner readable by all, his allusion to modernism, because of its basis in syntax, also resists the possibility of adaptation into other media. In spite of his works' frequent adaptation into film, he has said that "I see them [the movies] as a lesser medium than fiction, than literature, and a more ephemeral medium."[66] Because it could not be perfectly adapted into film, television, or other visual media, King's allusion to modernism was stubbornly and residually literary.[67] While films like *The Exorcist* provided thrills and chills by exposing privacy in the space of the mass public, Danny's shining represents King's hope that his representation of child abuse might somehow find far-removed individuals who would appreciate his literariness.

King's literalization of the Overlook Hotel as an institution that produces child abuse points to the ways that individual privacy is not a wholly distinct realm; it is, rather, always inscribed within political, economic, and familial systems. In *DeShaney v. Winnebago County* (1989), a Supreme Court case where a child welfare organization was found not to be liable for failing to separate a child from his father after repeated signs of abuse, the majority noted that if the child, Joshua, had been harmed while in a public mental institution, a prison, or other state facility, he might have had legal recourse to sue. Chief Justice Rehnquist wrote that "the Due Process Clause does not 'requir[e] the State to protect the life, liberty, and property of its citizens against invasion by private actors.'"[68] By rendering the Overlook Hotel as an institution that infiltrates family life and represents capital more generally, *The Shining* suggests that, *pace* the law, there is no such thing as pure privacy, that a family as isolated as the Torrances is still circumscribed within socioeconomic institutions. Nevertheless, King still imagines the state as incapable of intervening—the rangers are miles away and unreachable, the doctors fail to follow the mandatory reporting laws. Reflecting the political reality Mondale faced, *The Shining* imagined government as ineffectual because its only possible tool was intervention in the private family. The best that King can hope for is that friends and neighbors might be capable of helping—and perhaps, too, those readers who feel horror and empathy upon their encounter with a written word that makes private horrors legible as public terrors.

Horror After the 1970s

While the specific panic about child abuse has subsided since the 1970s, images of middle-class child abuse remain prominent within the horror genre. Since the late 1970s, films like *Halloween, Friday the Thirteenth,* and *Nightmare on Elm Street* have imagined horrific figures as attacking the middle class, but they often seem to come more from outside the home than within (as in *Rosemary* or *The Shining*), even as some of these sociopaths faintly double fathers and boyfriends. Likewise, when a disheveled and hungry young girl wanders into a diner in Netflix's television series *Stranger Things*, the diner's owners conclude, "She's been abused or kidnapped or somethin'" and call social services.[69] The truth, as always, is, well, less quotidian and more strange. The girl has been abused, but not in any routine way; she has been kept in a laboratory for her whole life, her telekinetic powers the subject of scientific experiments. Her "Papa" is not really her father, but a researcher who abducted her from her mother at an early age. Throughout these works, the specter child abuse is summoned and then transformed into demonology external to the home, while the police, as agents of the state, remain terribly ineffectual.

M. Night Shyamalan's *The Sixth Sense* (1999), the most commercially successful horror film before the release of *It* (2017), combines elements of many of its predecessors. It features an absent father; horror emerging from the bathroom (*Psycho*, *Carrie*); photographs that show the shimmering presence of invisible ghosts (*The Omen*); a child who sees dead people (*The Other*); and a vomiting little girl who is the subject of abuse (*The Exorcist*). *The Sixth Sense* initially renders privacy a space of terror. "Do you know why you're afraid when you're alone?" asks Malcolm Crowe's troubled former patient, hauntingly, as he stands in the Crowes' bathroom (the private space associated with *Psycho* and *Carrie*), about to kill Malcolm.[70] The film's identification of privacy with danger later enfolds child abuse. The cuts found on Cole's arms are suggested as the result of potential domestic abuse. As in *The Exorcist*, the actual social problem of abuse is implied but then ascribed to phantasms. It turns out that Cole's cuts come, not from the abuse of an overworked mother and a broken family, but from otherwise well-intentioned ghosts who scratch at Cole as they ask him to do things for them. But there are representations of real abuse in the film. As in *The Shining*, a supernatural ability—Cole's capacity to see and talk to dead people—turns out to be useful for identifying violence against children. He uses his gift to find a VHS tape to reveal that a little girl was poisoned by her mother.

While its predecessors took privacy into the public space of the theater, *The Sixth Sense* imagines its public not just as in a theater but also in a living room watching it on VHS tape—a technology that was not yet widespread in the 1970s. In the film, watching and re-watching videotape enables the other characters to see dead people—thus echoing Cole's gift.[71] Malcolm's wife can be seen repeatedly re-watching her wedding video after her husband's death. The VHS tape that Cole unearths by talking to a dead girl enables him to reveal to her father how she was abused—cruelly murdered by her stepmother. VHS tapes can expose private secrets and moments (the girl's abuse, the wedding) for other private audiences; they can bridge boundaries, reveal truths, and transport viewers back into the past. In contrast to the books and films of the 1970s, the movie stresses the vital importance and enduring power of nurturing families. While the horror of the 1970s created terror and delight by dramatizing the horrors within the private family before mass publics, *The Sixth Sense*, which was given a "family-friendly" PG-13 rating, imagines itself as being watched in a living room on VHS tape, not a theater: the private scene of one family revealed before another private family. And it focuses on the way parental care and spousal love survive the grave rather than, in a work like *The Shining*, on the dissolution of the family because of class.

Whereas horror exposed scenes of white child abuse shielded by privacy, one might think of the literary, realist works of Toni Morrison and other female African American novelists as a countertradition—one that counterbalances the many images of white and upper-class children being afflicted by privacy by representing Black poverty. In *The Bluest Eye* (1970), the novel most contemporary with the films and books I discuss here, Morrison demonstrates that low-income Black people have never enjoyed privacy—a distinct prerogative of the white middle class. If horror took a middle-class audience and showed them the steady, delicious reveal of horrors in private spaces, Morrison shows how concepts of private and public have little purchase on a Black audience. In and out of prison and always drunk, Pecola's father Cholly seems to drift into the Breedloves' home as he pleases. The kitchen where he rapes his daughter presents a contrast to the kitchen of the white home where her mother Pauline works. The kitchen constitutes Pauline's own "private world," which she refuses to leave until it is immaculate, and she banishes Pecola and her friends from it, knocking Pecola to the ground.[72] Pecola is banished, also, from the middle-class home of Geraldine, the mother of a neighborhood boy. As opposed to the terrors of one little girl's bedroom on display in *The Exorcist*, little girls like Pecola have no privacy: they "slept six in a bed, all their pee mixing together in the night as they wet their beds each in his own candy-and-potato-chip dream" (90); Claudia and Frieda have, in their small quarters, "seen their own father naked," though they "didn't care to be reminded of it" (69). The MacTeer home has both a boarder and Pecola in it; the boarder molests Frieda. Rather than contrast private space with public, the narrators think about "indoors" as opposed to "outdoors" and homelessness (15). And while doors are open and people are outside, the town itself is ignored: "pedestrians, who are residents of the neighborhood, simply look away when they pass it" (31).

Though she attempted to show how a working-class Black child has no familial privacy, Morrison viewed the reception of her novel as unsatisfactory; she failed to lead readers "into an interrogation of themselves for the smashing" of Pecola; instead they took away only "the comfort of pitying her" (xii). While Morrison tried to effect political change and self-scrutiny in fiction, the horror and media of the same years had conditioned readers to see child abuse as a sensationalized problem affecting all classes equally, one of spectatorial intrigue and fear but not one that called for radical political change. Morrison takes a different tack in her most recent novel, *God Help the Child* (2015), which imagines two victims of the very abuse narratives whose sensationalization is co-extensive with genre fiction—one who falsely accuses her teacher of sexual abuse, resembling the satanic ritual abuse scandals of the 90s, and one whose brother was abducted and killed by a serial killer.[73] Rather than disown the spectacularized narratives of child abuse found in horror, *God Help the Child* renders them co-extensive with the more tragically quotidian kinds of abuse fleetingly depicted in the novel.

Morrison came to realize that she wrote in a literary field that was shaped by what Mark Seltzer has called "America's wound culture"—a desire to feel horror and pity at engrossing images of pain and suffering without necessarily taking political action.[74] If we include sexual abuse, physical abuse, and neglect, it is remarkable how many texts of the transatlantic postwar literary field are oriented around the imagination of child abuse, a list that would include not only the texts I have mentioned so far but also *The Woman Warrior* (1976); *Blood and Guts in High School* (1978/1984); *Housekeeping* (1980); *The Color Purple* (1982); *The Cider House Rules* (1985); *Beloved* (1987); *Atonement* (2001); and *Room* (2010). It is easy to condemn the horror output of the period as particularly meretricious, providing imagined resolutions to real social problems, substituting flattened fictional satanic bogeymen for real-life tragedy, and obscuring child abuse's correlation with class (though, indeed, as I have shown their relationships to child abuse were inevitably more complex). The literary works mentioned above would seem to be more restrained, more realistic, less sensational, more attuned to distinctions of race and class. But what all of these instances have in common nonetheless is that they are commodities. Whether it is narrated in terms of carnivalesque horror or tender, empathetic feeling, writing about child abuse is also a means of establishing oneself in the literary field. There can be a deep social value in the public narration of those private experiences, but horror novels and films show that the revelation of private spaces in fiction is never a strictly naïve encounter; reading, the horror writers of the 1970s discovered, takes place within a field structured around the desire to gape at the wounds of private life.

Bury Me Not on the Lone Prairie

IN 1997, Oregon enacted the Death with Dignity Act, the first assisted suicide law in the nation. Derek Humphry, founder of the Hemlock Society and one of the law's foremost advocates, describes its passage:

> Living among the vast forests and snowcapped mountains, the state's residents are famed for their independence of political spirit and social awareness. Attempts to pass laws that restrict their freedoms—ranging from how bears are hunted to what books can be read in public libraries—are always defeated.... Crucially, Oregonians resent outsiders, particularly those from the East Coast, trying to tell them how to think and act.[1]

He notes further that farmers and farmworkers were particularly accustomed to euthanasia because of the animals for which they care. In *The Oregonian*, debates about the bill were framed in the newspaper with a cartoon of the Grim Reaper on a horse.[2] Many of the early states to legalize the right have skewed west—Oregon, Montana, Washington, Colorado, California. In Humphry's telling, Oregonians imagined assisted suicide as the hardy prerogative of those living on the frontier who did not want to be told what to do and who were accustomed to the fact of death on the range. Their imaginations also likely drew on the many westerns of the period in which a cowboy contemplates suicide, assisted suicide, or euthanasia in the face of old age or a debilitating injury, a list that would include *Horseman, Pass By* (1961), *The Shootist* (1975; filmed 1976), *Lonesome Dove* (1985), *Streets of Laredo* (1993), and *No Country for Old Men* (2005), among others.

For decades before the passage of Oregon's act, euthanasia had not been imagined as the unique prerogative of the frontier-dweller. In the 1900s and 1910s, many thought it to be the demand of the effete intellectual who could not endure too much pain; between the 1930s and 1970s, it was associated with fascistic state planning. When euthanasia re-emerged as a topic of national conversation in the

FIGURE 5.1 Editorial cartoon from *The Oregonian* (April 13, 1986).
Source: Reprinted with permission.

mid-1970s, the western helped to reframe it as "voluntary euthanasia" or "assisted suicide." At that moment, the triumphant narrative of the right to privacy as a right to personal self-definition may seem to have been waning. In the previous chapter, we saw how horror represented the cultural backlash against the expanding right to privacy, limning the transformation of the 1960s celebration of personal autonomy into 1970s fears about the destruction of family values. The idea of privacy as a right to self-define was far from moribund, though it did become tinctured by the neoliberal suspicion of government involvement. Throughout the 1970s and into the 1990s and beyond, social activists and theorists tried to extend the boundaries of the right to privacy beyond the context of female reproduction and the home to encompass certain forms of euthanasia. Especially in an era that celebrated the atomistic individual, the imagery of the western—the lone cowboy's final act on the prairie—proved particularly effective in making their case for the right to die.[3]

The most influential formulation of the argument that euthanasia should be imagined as a privacy right did not invoke westerns, but it did imagine the right to privacy as a right to narrate one's life. In an amicus brief for two 1997 Supreme Court cases—*Washington v. Glucksberg* and *Vacco v. Quill*, the "philosophers' brief"—several prominent philosophers described physician-assisted suicide as a narrative conclusion. They were writing on behalf of physicians in Washington and New York who wanted to help their terminally ill patients end their lives. These philosophers (and one law professor)—Ronald Dworkin, Thomas Nagel, Robert Nozick, John Rawls, Thomas Scanlon, and Judith Jarvis Thomson—argued in their brief that "the final act of life's drama" is a moment that should "reflect our own convictions, those we have tried to live by, not the convictions of others forced on us in our most vulnerable moment."[4] In comparing life to a drama, they contended that its author should be able to structure its conclusion. They invoked the right to privacy formulated in *Planned Parenthood v. Casey*, "the right of people to make their own decisions about matters 'involving the most intimate and personal choices a person may make in a lifetime, choices central to personal dignity and autonomy.'"[5] When they wrote "dignity" and "autonomy," they were not referring to the ability to perform daily chores or exercise bodily functions without help. Rather, "dignity," "autonomy," and "privacy" meant the right to narrate one's life. This was even clearer in Dworkin's own writing, which marshals examples of literary form from Philip Roth, Tolstoy, and Shakespeare to argue that death is "a peculiarly significant event in the narrative of our lives, like the final scene of a play, with everything about it intensified, under a special spotlight."[6]

In representing acts of euthanasia as the cowboy's final determination on the frontier, the western provided perhaps the most popularly influential version of the philosophers' argument. Since James Fenimore Cooper, the western has long imagined a state of nature, a bygone world of moral codes (descended from the chivalric romance) that preceded the establishment of the liberal state. Placing euthanasia in that world could justify it as mutually agreed upon by all in the absence of state regulation. But the western was not the only genre to influentially represent euthanasia. The structure of this chapter will be somewhat different than previous ones. Whereas other chapters have largely focused on one legal issue and one genre, this chapter takes a longer view. To appreciate how the western intervened at a crucial moment in euthanasia discourse, removing *Griswold/*

Roe's right to privacy away from marital or female sexuality and reimagining it as the act of the cowboy on the range, it is helpful to have the earlier period in view. Not only has the literary story here largely been untold, but the longer history is also necessary to understand the curious paradox by which the culture leveraged a right so closely associated with female reproduction to dispel the imagination of euthanasia as effeminate.

The chapter begins at the turn of the century, with Edith Wharton's *Fruit of the Tree*, which imagined euthanasia as suited for the realist story of the female professional nurse who was able to balance the competing demands of professional duty and private sensitivity. It then shows how Charlotte Perkins Gilman's science fiction argued for euthanasia as a form of fascistic social planning. While debates about euthanasia were dormant for several decades after World War II, in the 1970s westerns intervened at a crucial moment in euthanasia discourse. They separated out involuntary from voluntary euthanasia and framed euthanasia as the right of the self-determining cowboy to die on the range. Finally, the chapter turns to Jodi Picoult's *Mercy* (1996) and argues that it imagines euthanasia as a romance: a right determined between two lovers.

While previous chapters imagined writers who did not or could not represent realistic people, the western and the romance come closest to realist, literary fiction, with characters closest to round of the works I treat in this book—especially when I consider a writer like Cormac McCarthy. However, we can still see in the conflict between literary realism and chivalric romance (the western's antecedent) a clash between the realist idea that life is a series of nonlinear accidents and the romantic one that life is a triumphant, self-determining narrative. While it would be hard to treat an author like McCarthy as marginalized in the literary field, a key part of the book's overall argument still holds here: that certain inherited anti-realist generic forms combined with aesthetic ambition made genre fiction particularly insightful when it came to questioning what it meant to be a private person.

By extending the focal length of analysis beyond the postwar era and by looking at representation of euthanasia in realism, science fiction, westerns, and romances, we can better understand how placing the controversial activity of euthanasia within a genre has helped writers contest whether it should be justified as a privacy right. While legal theorists have more recently relied on a relatively monolithic, Aristotelian idea of narrative (beginning, middle, end) to justify euthanasia, for over a century novelists have been examining what narrative means and what kinds of genres would be most appropriate in imagining euthanasia. Genre fiction and privacy evolved together: in trying to argue for or against euthanasia as an act of self-narrative, genre writers harked back to and rewrote older traditions and histories. Each genre brought with it a different set of conventions that, in turn, affected how its writers imagined the act of euthanasia.

From Female Professionalism to Social Collectivism

The debate about euthanasia would have been foreign to most Americans until the mid-nineteenth century. Before the nineteenth century, the term "euthanasia" meant simply a good or peaceful death—not one brought about by modern medicine. Debates about euthanasia, in the modern sense of ending the life of a person with a painful or terminal illness, arose first during the late nineteenth century with the advent of morphine. At that time, there was little distinction made between voluntary and involuntary forms of euthanasia. While most physicians and lawyers advocated for the use of morphine only to relieve pain, a few charged that doctors should use morphine to put patients out of their misery. This argument became possible only because of a shift in the way that many thought about death. While many eighteenth-century Christians believed death was a bridge between this world and the next, mid-nineteenth-century Methodists emphasized death and the ceremony of dying as a part of this life, a shift that would inadvertently lead to secular concerns about the painfulness of death.[7] Changing customs brought doctors and lawyers to the deathbed instead of priests, even when the patient was past hope of cure. With the advent of opioids, pain was pried apart from the more generalized condition of suffering—a mysterious and divine affliction—and reconceived as a medical condition that could be alleviated.[8]

One of the first attempts to describe euthanasia in fiction appeared in Edith Wharton's *The Fruit of the Tree* (1907). Wharton can often seem confused about which genre *Fruit of the Tree* belongs in, and several novels' worth of plotlines are contained within its pages. It begins as a realist-naturalist story about the social conditions of workers in a mill. John Amherst is a social reformer trying to better their lives, while Bessy Westmore is the widow of the mill owner. Amherst mistakes Bessy's romantic interest in him for a shared commitment to social improvement. The two marry, but their marriage devolves into a conflict over whether they will spend their money on quality-of-life improvements for the workers or high-society pursuits. Bessy and Amherst separate; when Amherst is away in South America studying cotton growing, Bessy falls into a coma after being thrown off her horse. Bessy's doctor, Dr. Stephen Wyant, tries to prolong her life while she is alternately insensate and racked with pain. Wyant is interested only in his own career advancement, not in his patient's quality of life, and so her friend and nurse Justine Brent must decide what, if anything, to do. She ultimately decides to euthanize Bessy by overdosing her on opium. With Bessy departed, Justine and Amherst fall in love and are married, while Wyant, who is addicted to opium, blackmails Justine by threatening to tell Bessy's family. Finally, Justine confesses to Amherst, who, despite his progressive ideals, is not as receptive as she had hoped. Lest she be blackmailed any further, Justine tells Bessy's family what she has done; they, in turn, demand that she separate herself from Amherst and from Bessy's daughter. Eventually, Justine and Amherst are reunited at the mill where they each work, but their romantic relationship is over.

If Wharton's novel seems like a chaotic salad of genre logics and conventions, part of the reason is that she found herself in the middle of a nascent debate about euthanasia. She saw that euthanasia could potentially belong in a number of genres, that it could be a story of social realism, a bona fide romance, or else the Gothic tale of a woman who murders her friend and takes her husband. Wharton's own indeterminacy about which genre euthanasia properly belonged to laid the groundwork for the rest of the century, in which different genres would attempt to annex the representation of euthanasia and represent it according to their own political allegiances.

But the novel's apparent incoherencies at least partially resolve into an underlying structure: Wharton saw euthanasia as the moral issue perfectly suited to illustrate the promises and travails of a new female, literate professional class. Amy Kaplan and Mark McGurl have argued that Wharton's fiction should be read in light of her own anxieties about her position as a professional female author.[9] She was the first in her patrician family to earn a living, which she did through writing bestsellers; Kaplan shows how she viewed realism as a "tenuous balancing act negating the idealism of genteel culture while resisting the sentimentalism of mass culture."[10] Euthanasia proved the ideal subject matter for her to carry out that balancing act, because she felt that elite, popular, and professional opinion about euthanasia were all lacking. She tried to establish a moral position that would recapitulate neither the hypocrisy of euthanasia's elitist supporters nor the error of its professional and clerical opponents. Instead, for Wharton, the morality of euthanasia could be seen only by Justine—the literate female nurse—whose perspicacious understanding of the issues involved justifies the value of female professionalism more generally.

To understand Wharton's position on euthanasia, it is worth reviewing some of the sources with which she was familiar. In 1904, Charles Eliot Norton, the famous Harvard humanist and a friend to both Wharton and Henry James, helped bring euthanasia debates into the public eye when he authored a public letter supporting euthanasia at the request of Anna Hill, a wealthy Cincinnati woman trying to pass the first euthanasia legislation in Ohio. For Norton, the idea that all human life should be considered sacred was a bygone superstition rooted in Christianity:

> There is no ground in reason to hold every human life as inviolably sacred, and to be preserved, no matter with what results to the individual or to others. On the contrary, there are lives to which every reasonable consideration urges that the end be put. Setting aside all doubtful cases, no right-thinking man would hesitate to give a dose of laudanum sufficient to end suffering and life together, to the victim of the accident, from the torturing effects of which recovery was impossible, however many hours of misery might be added to conscious life by stimulants or surgical operations.[11]

Norton's logic here is a utilitarian claim that religious tradition should not interfere with the prevention or cessation of pain or unhappiness. As the man who had established art history as an academic discipline in the United States and who was the leading voice in Dante studies, Norton's name was synonymous with secularized aesthetic appreciation as a replacement for Christian morality.[12] In his letter, he hints at those views in decrying the prohibition against euthanasia as rooted in "superstition" and hoping instead that liberal values—"the arguments of reason" and the "pleadings of compassion"—would win the day.[13] For Norton, the prohibition of euthanasia was an outmoded delusion, the kind that aesthetic training was designed to root out.

Wharton had also had a personal experience of a comatose life being medically prolonged. In 1905, just before Wharton began writing *Fruit of the Tree*, her friend, Ethel Cram, was kicked by a pony in the skull. Cram was unconscious for two months before dying. Upon Cram's death, Wharton wrote to her friend Sally Norton, Charles Eliot's daughter:

> I shudder to think of the effect that this two months' agony must have on Henrietta [Ethel's sister] and the future of her child—How often I have thought of that article of Dr. Baldwin's these terrible weeks! I am sure I should have the "triste courage," in such a case, to let life ebb out quietly—should not you?[14]

The article she referred to, by Simeon E. Baldwin, a professor at Yale Law School, argued that it was a great irony that suffering was linked to wealth and status: "the higher the station or the greater the means of the sufferer by a mortal malady, the less he can hope for a natural death." Baldwin felt that euthanasia, by which he meant the refusal of medical treatment, was a mark of civilization and that civilization should accord to its citizens the same privilege enjoyed by "savages and brutes." Like Dworkin, writing many years later, he compared life itself to a drama, describing "the tragedy which ends in death, and which nature, if left unthwarted, will limit itself to a single scene, and that of the shortest."[15] For Baldwin, thinking of life as a controlled drama and deploying a rhetoric of civilization and culture allowed him to abandon the idea that life should be prolonged to the utmost.

Wharton's close friend Gaillard Lapsley had also given her an article by G. Lowes Dickinson, a British intellectual, entitled "Euthanasia: From the Note-book of an Alpinist."[16] Dickinson imagined a scene of euthanasia from the perspective of a man in a mountain hut who was planning his death, watching the dawn. Blurring the two meanings of "a good death" and "a mercy killing," Dickinson equated euthanasia with a Neoplatonist ascension into "Truth" and immortality. Dickinson began the article with

> My sensations and thoughts point beyond themselves. The boundary between perception and imagination, between thought and intuition, is blurred. Things are become symbols, ideas realities; and all forms of matter or mind are but a metaphor of the Truth I begin more directly to apprehend.[17]

Dickinson's logic was something like this: the exquisite facility for recording sensory impressions is capable of leading us upward to the divine forms. For as long as this facility remains, we should be able to commit suicide, an act closer to apotheosis than flouting the divine law. The moment of death is narrated: "All I can do, in this prison of the flesh, I have done; I have learnt what I can learn, I have felt what I can feel."[18] Dickinson's article did not mention a speaker who was explicitly in pain or aging; rather, he thought of euthanasia as a discarding of the weakened corporeal body. We see the beginnings of the idea that euthanasia is an act of narrative: imposing one's own value system onto the scope of one's life.

The aesthetic presuppositions of the pro-euthanasia camp are almost clearer when seen from their detractors' point of view. In response to his letter, the *New York Times* criticized Charles Eliot Norton for "a morbid sensitiveness at the sight of what is or seems to be uselessly prolonged suffering." His views belonged to the "literary dilettante and the neurotic 'intellectuals.'" The newspaper claimed that Norton was letting a "moral and religious principle [be] supplanted by sentimental and aesthetic considerations."[19] Norton's opponents thought that euthanasia's main proponent, an effete professor of literature, had cultivated tastes that were simply too sensitive, an overly refined sense of art and beauty, accompanied by an abhorrence of pain. Many felt that those on the deathbed would not experience pain, as Dr. Henry S. Stearns insisted in response to Norton's letter:

> In most desperate cases, my experience is that pain already suffered or effects of high temperature or presence of toxins in the circulation, or the certainty of the near approach of death have so dulled the capacity to suffer pain that it would be imposing a needless hardship on my profession to saddle it with the responsibility of willfully shortening the patient's life.[20]

While Stearns believed that the man on his deathbed often did not experience pain, James H. Hamilton, head worker at the University Settlement, a nonprofit community center for immigrants, gave voice to the still-popular religious belief that pain was redemptive:

> The agonies of death purify the soul, not only of the dying, but of the living, and perhaps nothing does so much to purge people of low and unworthy thoughts and lift them to a higher plane of living as the inspiration of the deathbed. At such times the ministrations of a physician are more valuable than those of a priest in the keeping and cherishing of the sacred spark to the last possible moment.[21]

Others insisted that euthanasia advocates like Anna Hill and Norton "have had no medical training" and lacked a firsthand understanding of the physician's duty and the impossibility of knowing which cases were truly terminal.

Wharton thus confronted two different sides of the euthanasia debate. The anti-euthanasia camp claimed that euthanasia violated God's will and the professional duties of a physician and that those who demanded it were overly effete. This camp sometimes seemed indifferent to patients' suffering, and they held to a picture of divine order that no longer seemed compelling to Wharton and other secularized intellectuals. The pro-euthanasia camp suggested that there was no point to needless suffering; they grounded their logic in a secular, liberal tradition, elevating private reason and sentiment above custom. This camp often approached the ideas that sympathy and rationality were the highest faculties to which one could appeal in moral adjudication and that aesthetics helped cultivate those faculties. But there were a number of problems with this view too: like Baldwin, these people concerned themselves almost exclusively with euthanasia as it pertained to wealthy, educated elites, not, as it was often problematically urged, for the benighted, poor, and disabled. Dickinson even framed euthanasia as a kind of ascent into the realm of the Neoplatonic Forms, completely neglecting the pain of those desiring it.

Wharton framed Justine's decision as one of deliberate iconoclasm; she decides to kill Bessy before encountering a commonplace of classical quotes in Amherst's hand: "We perish because we follow other men's examples" (Seneca) and "Socrates used to call the opinions of the many the Lamiae—bugbears to frighten children" (Marcus Aurelius).[22] She acts in defiance of the recommendations of clerical, legal, and medical professionals. The clergyman claims that Bessy must be kept alive "for the sake of the spiritual life that may be mysteriously wrung out of" her (407), ignoring that she is barely conscious; the lawyer believes that Bessy is kept alive as "the result of the world's accumulated experience" (418). The doctor sees Bessy as "no longer a suffering, agonizing creature" but as "a case" (419). Justine is the only character able to perceive Bessy's suffering and to act upon that perception, and her decision comes as a combination of natural sentiment and literary and professional training.

Wharton's novel repeatedly refers to the moral importance of cultivated sentiment as opposed to naked intuition. Earlier in the novel, when he tries to awaken Bessy to the plight of the workers of the mills, Amherst realizes that "the swift apprehension of suffering in others is as much the result of training as the immediate perception of beauty" (59). While Bessy is unable to apprehend that suffering, Justine is keenly aware of it, just as she notices, when none of the professionals do, how Bessy has been reduced "to a mere instrument on which pain played its incessant variations" (423). And she is able to notice, when no one else is, Bessy mumbling at the end of her life, "I want to die" (424).

Justine cultivates her heightened professional sensitivity by reading novels. Whereas Bessy has no books in her house, Amherst and Justine are passionate readers. When Bessy does allude to books, she reveals that she has a taste for mawkish novels of domestic bliss, telling Justine about a novel she read of a nurse who married a rich man and started a hospital: "All the nurses and doctors that the heroine had worked with were there to receive her . . . and her little boy went about and gave toys to the crippled children . . ." (232). Early in their marriage, Amherst tries to lead a kind of salon to educate Bessy, but he finds that "her outward signs of attention never ripened into any expression of opinion" and "that Justine Brent was his only listener" (320). Because Amherst's commonplacing inspires Justine to euthanize Bessy, we know that she does so out of a particular sensibility that is shaped by reading. When she encounters Amherst's commonplacing, Justine feels "herself in the presence of great thoughts—to know that in this room, among these books, another restless baffled mind has sought escape from the 'dusty answer' of life" (399). She arrives at her decision after considering the value that she and Amherst share in the reading of great books.

Justine's decision initially appears to be framed as elevating private sensibility—literary cultivation and female sentiment—over the claims of professionalism. Justine claims that her career as a nurse dictates that she cannot perform euthanasia: "the professional instinct to save would always come first" (15). Throughout the novel, Justine's emotions are alive beneath a thin veneer of professional distance. Amherst muses that she is "as cool as a drum-major till she took off her uniform—and then!" (27). Justine thinks about herself as a sentimentalist who is a keen dissembler: "She always sympathized too much with her patients . . . . Her quick-gushing pity lay too near that professional exterior which she had managed to endue with such a bright glaze of insensibility" (388). When Bessy is injured, she wonders if she will be able "to perform a nurse's duties, steadily, expertly, unflinchingly, while every fibre was torn with inward anguish" (388–389). She repeatedly finds herself torn between the calls of sentiment and of profession.

But while it may initially appear that Justine's private feminine sentiment overwhelms her professionalism, the novel actually aims to redefine professionalism so as to imbue it with both female sentiment and literary training. The cultivated female nurse was the only person capable of determining when private sympathy should override public professional duty. When Bessy is brought in after her accident, Justine understands the violation of the private space in a way that others do not:

> To stand there, knowing, with each tick of the clock, what was being said and done within—how the great luxurious room, with its pale draperies and scented cushions, and the hundred pretty trifles strewing the lace toilet-table and the delicate old furniture, was being swept bare, cleared for action like a ship's deck, drearily garnished with rows of instruments, rolls of medicated cotton, oiled silk, bottles, bandages, water-pillows—all the grim paraphernalia of the awful rites of pain: to know this, and to be able to call up with torturing vividness that poor pale face on the pillows, vague-eyed, expressionless, perhaps, as she had last seen it, or—worse yet—stirred already with the first creeping pangs of consciousness: to have these images slowly, deliberately burn themselves into her brain, and to be aware, at the same time, of that underlying moral disaster, of which the accident seemed the monstrous outward symbol—ah, this was worse than anything she had ever dreamed! (389)

When Bessy's bedroom is invaded by impassive, professional men, it is remade "like a ship's deck," where there is no privacy at all. If doctors see professionalism as wholly impersonal, the mechanical exercise of duty, Justine betters them by combining her professional knowledge with intuitive sentiment. She is uniquely suited to the sickbed, which is located at the confluence of public and private realms. The fact that this scene occurs entirely in Justine's imagination, "burned into her brain," emphasizes her capacity for feeling and imagination, as well as her professional experience—she is aware of what will happen without actually being present. She knows also the "underlying moral disaster" of Bessy and Amherst's marriage, in which Bessy, despite Amherst's warning, rides a horse ominously titled "Impulse." Wharton's case for euthanasia becomes rooted in a figure who combines cultivated sentiment, professional know-how, and a background knowledge of the patient.

Gender plays a role in her decision as well. Amherst shares Justine's keen interest in social betterment, her cultivated aesthetic sense, her professional training, and an iconoclastic personality, and yet he is unable to approve of

Bessy's euthanasia. In the opening pages of the novel, Amherst had suggested that an injured factory worker should be euthanized: "I know what I should do if I could get anywhere near Dillon—give him an overdose of morphine, and let the widow collect his life-insurance, and make a fresh start" (15). Still, he cannot bring himself to condone Justine's decision to euthanize Bessy, precisely because he lacks sentimental pliability. His progressive opinions belie an intuitive conservatism: "like many men of emancipated thought, he had remained subject to the old conventions of feeling" (525). As Mrs. Ansell—the only other character, also a woman, to understand the need for euthanasia—says: "man's code of honour is such a clumsy cast-iron thing. But a woman's, luckily, can be cut over—if she's clever—to fit any new occasion; and in this case I should be willing to reduce mine to tatters if necessary" (602). While Amherst knows intellectually that Justine did the right thing, only the women in the novel are able to muster the appropriate moral sentiment to condone euthanasia. Wharton makes the case for Justine's unique qualifications as a literate female professional, while she also argues for her own interrelated literary female professionalism; literature, as we have seen, helps to produce Justine's enlightened morality.

The Fruit of the Tree's reception history reveals that the novel disturbed many because it overturned conventional representations of private female sensibility. The novel's critics believed that euthanasia was impossible for anyone working in the medical professions, much less for a woman. The *New York Medical Journal* concluded that, "With a character as strong, as sane, and as well poised as that of Justine it is hardly conceivable that a woman could have deliberately and solely for the purpose of relieving the sufferer have administered a poison to her patient."[23] Likewise, the *New York Times* wrote that the act was inconceivable for "any young woman, above all a woman of Justine Brent's intellect and temperament."[24] Because it defied traditional notions of female sentiment and capability, the novel triggered a minor storm of controversy in a way that *Ethan Frome*, the story of a failed suicide, and *House of Mirth*, the story of a potentially deliberate drug overdose, did not.

Wharton tried to argue instead that a woman of Justine's refinement and sensibility would be particularly able to adjudicate the suitability of euthanasia, to navigate the murky boundary between public duty and private conscience. A different writer for the *New York Sun*, in a clipping saved in Wharton's archive, suggested that in contrasting male and female reactions to euthanasia, she may have "slyly tried to demonstrate the contrast between the masculine and the feminine attitude toward abstract questions of right and wrong."[25] In contrast to Norton, who refers to abstract faculties like reason in justifying euthanasia, Wharton dramatizes how abstract principles are thwarted when they confront personal and feminine emotions. Justine ultimately realizes that "life is not a matter of abstract principles, but a succession of pitiful compromises with fate, of concessions to old tradition, old beliefs, old charities and frailties" (624). The absolutism and impersonality of Christian moralizing, the certain knowledge of good and evil—the eponymous fruit of the tree—interferes with Justine's justified decision to euthanize her friend. (The title may also refer to the Christian diminishment of women in the person of Eve and to the birth of a private shame that conflicts with public morality.)

Even as *The Fruit of the Tree* makes the case for the professional value of the female nurse, in its juxtaposition of Justine against Bessy, the novel demonstrates the difficulty for women in balancing public and private happiness—a dilemma to which Wharton's fiction was particularly attuned. Bessy seeks happiness only in the private sphere; she imagines finding "a life of your own" by being a wife and a mother (232). Her retreat into the private realm ruins her marriage to Amherst; she wants only to entertain guests and to build a personal gymnasium, and she is irritated that he spends all their money on helping the mill-hands her family employs. Bessy sustains only a private life, the restlessness of which ultimately consumes and destroys her; she goes riding when she knows she should not. Justine, married to the same man, finds that her attempt to follow her conscience and professional duty to euthanize Bessy ultimately destroys her private life. She and Amherst publicly help the mill workers, and draw on Bessy's income, but they have no romantic intimacy. When Amherst and Justine are first reunited, they kiss, but then a nurse comes to get Justine: "Miss Brent—the doctor wants you to come right up and give the morphine" (619). This interruption serves as an unpleasant reminder of her professional responsibilities, and it also extinguishes their rekindling inner life; after she leaves, "their lips met again, but not in the same kiss" (619). The novel concludes with Justine being incapable of sustaining both her professional commitment to nursing and her private love for Amherst, and she ultimately chooses the former.

While contemporary advocates like Dworkin often think of euthanasia as taking deliberate control of one's life narrative, Wharton casts doubt on the idea that a life narrative can be determined so easily. Especially for the women of her time, who struggled to balance public and private roles, it was not so easy to live a life "structured by a theme."[26] Bessy's life ends not in triumphant control of her own circumstances, but prematurely as she is reduced to a shriveling bundle of reflexes. Justine, in her pursuit of what she believed to be morally right, concludes the novel with professional happiness but with an unsatisfying private life. Wharton's discussion of narrative form appears at the end of the novel when Justine and Amherst recall a conversation that they had had earlier about the best moment in life:

> ". . . one never says, *This is the moment!* because, however good it is, it always seems the door to a better one beyond. Faust never said it till the end, when he'd nothing left of all he began by thinking worthwhile; and then, with what a difference it was said!" (304)

As in Henry James, narrative patterns only seem to emerge at the story's conclusion and after much suffering; it is impossible to live life according to a theme while it goes along. Wharton does not believe in narrative as the triumphant assertion of fate and of personal value in the face of chance. Rather, her narrative suggests that lives are characterized by repeated capitulations and compromises with social restrictions in the pursuit of personal ideals. Wharton thus saw the narrative of euthanasia as a topos to establish the value of female, literate professionalism as well as the social challenges circumscribing it. The female professional would be uniquely able to discern the boundary between private conscience and professional duty—but would also face tremendous social challenges when she exercised that conscience.

While Wharton's imaginations of euthanasia drew on a version of the private individual of classical liberalism autonomously using reason and sympathy, Charlotte Perkins Gilman instead justified euthanasia in the terms of social collectivism. Gilman was an advocate of both voluntary and involuntary euthanasia for much of her career. She was diagnosed with terminal breast cancer and committed suicide in 1935, writing in a widely published suicide note, "I have preferred chloroform to cancer."[27] In 1911, Gilman began editing a magazine called *The Forerunner*, which first published many of her essays and fiction. Gilman wanted her inexpensive, political, and eclectic magazine to contrast with the aesthetic, unified, and apolitical aspiration of the art-novel. In her inaugural issue, she published an article mocking the pretensions of what was putatively "pure, high, legitimate literature." While some decried "the Novel With a Purpose" as lacking aesthetic value, she criticized the aimlessness of the "Novel Without a Purpose." If the art-novel seemed rarefied and stuffy, the inexpensive and new magazine could redefine what counted as literature, and it could reach a larger audience, presenting "the fresh current and feeling of knowledge belonging to our times."[28]

Most importantly, though, it could dramatize positions that the mainstream presses studiously avoided—topics like euthanasia:

> Suppose someone comes along with a story advocating euthanasia, showing with all the force of the art of fiction the slow, hideous suffering of some helpless cancer patient or the like, the blessed release that might be humanly given; showing it so as to make an indelible impression—this story is refused as "controversial," as being written with a purpose.[29]

Gilman seems to have been unaware of Wharton's novel and believed that realist, artistic representation was stymied by a kind of conservatism: it normalized certain activities by casting them as a part of everyday life, while it neglected to represent ones like euthanasia.

Though *The Forerunner* never exactly published a fictional narrative of euthanasia, Gilman did print a nonfictional article entitled "Euthanasia Again," about a New York woman who had been quadriplegic for three years and had finally asked to die. Gilman tried to combat the idea that pain was inherently redemptive:

> Some few rare souls have remained sweet and strong in spite of pain; there are not too many such even among the healthy. But most invalids are *not* improved by it. Sickness is a morbid condition, an evil condition. It generates a miserable self-consciousness and irritability. A sick body is a heavy strain on the mind and injures its working.[30]

For Gilman, the condition of "sickness," which could potentially include both pain and disability, was a drain on the individual, her family, and the rest of society—and should be rooted out.

As her description of sickness as "morbid" and "evil" suggests, *The Forerunner* served as a platform to advocate eugenics as often as euthanasia; Gilman failed to see a difference. In an essay entitled "Euthanasia for Incurables," Gilman linked the two: "Of course I believe 'that the state should be permitted to give a painless death to incurables' who desire it and also to incurables incapable of asking for release through mental incapacity."[31] She saw euthanasia as merely one measure alongside of eugenics, education, and social welfare programs, all of which could be used in the name of a better society:

> Our love, our care, our vivid sympathy with human life should be applied most strongly at the other end. With eugenics and euthenics, care and education from infancy, better conditions for everyone, all that can be done to safeguard and improve human life we should do as a matter of course.[32]

Gilman believed in the progressive, reformist idea that care and sympathy could lead to better social measures, even as these measures also included eugenics. Nowhere was this vision more clearly realized than in the world of the feminist utopia of *Herland* (1915), which deviated from the incremental change of realism to imagine a futuristic, wholly reformed society.

In *Herland*, which she published in *The Forerunner*, Gilman imagines a planet of women reproducing through parthenogenesis and a place that has eliminated disease. In the sequel, *With Her in Ourland* (1915), a woman from Herland, Ellador, returns with her new astronaut husband to Earth. Ellador sees disease largely as a social problem, curable within twenty years. She exclaims: "Look at these girls who do not even know enough about motherhood to demand a healthy father. Why, a—a—sheep would know better than to mate with such creatures as some of your women marry." Ellador is appalled by "the degradation of women, the corruption of the body and mind through these wholly unnecessary diseases, and the miserable misborn children."[33] She insists that if women chose better mates, they could eliminate not only venereal disease but disease altogether. Sharing much with the social hygiene movement, Gilman suggested that by breeding out and euthanizing those members of society who bore diseases, they could build a better world.

Gilman's language can sometimes seem to be rooted in liberalism, but it quickly veers toward collectivism. Gilman was among the first to claim euthanasia as a "right," and yet her justification of that right is always in terms of the larger social good: "Human life consists in mutual service." She claims that it is only "when all usefulness is over" that society could exercise euthanasia.[34] In her posthumously published op-ed "The Right to Die," she groups together both those who insist on their own death with those who cannot make the request: "the hopeless idiot, lunatic, or helpless paretic." She claims that the greatest obstacle to euthanasia is our failure to think about society as a larger unit: "our outdated sense of individuality, our failure to recognize social responsibility." Part of her motivation for euthanasia is clearly grounded in ableist sentiment: "One does not either 'forgive' or 'punish' an inflamed appendix, but one does cut it out. The same position may be taken with regard to the incurable idiot or maniac." While she speaks in effusive terms toward the "practical Germany" of the 1930s, her language toward the disabled is that of disgust; she describes a man who had become "a gross baby, a huge, brainless baby lying like a log in an unclean bed, while nurse and doctor wait for him—for it—to die."[35] Perhaps because euthanasia was condemned as overly effete, Gilman tries to channel a discourse of disgust and cleanliness rather than of sentiment.

Contrasting Wharton with Gilman suggests that imagining euthanasia's morality was a question, in part, of imagining its genre. Edith Wharton saw her realist euthanasia novel as a means to emphasize the moral importance of the private sentiment of a professional, literate woman afflicted with the suffering of another, even as that novel also suggested some uncertainty about to which genre euthanasia belonged. By contrast, Charlotte Perkins Gilman looked at her science fiction as a way of realizing a collective unit of social organization greater than the individual. As time went on, these two competing perspectives on euthanasia—the realist story of individual privacy or the SF one of collectivist social engineering—would persist.

The Retirement Home on the Range:
The Euthanasia Western

Euthanasia advocacy remained quiet between 1945 and the 1970s. Tainted by its association with Nazi Germany, euthanasia became a deeply unpopular position. Debates about euthanasia returned to national consciousness in the 1970s as people became aware of persistent vegetative states and protracted deaths in hospitals. Whereas Gilman imagined science fictional utopias as giving voice to a pro-euthanasia position, more contemporary science fiction has imagined similar worlds as dystopian: the state has arrogated the power to determine the conditions of death. Modern incarnations of this vision hark back to Anthony Trollope's *The Fixed Period* (1882), a novel in which a society does not allow people to live past the age of sixty-seven. More recent works like *Soylent Green* (based on the 1966 book *Make Room! Make Room!*; filmed 1973) and *Logan's Run* (written 1967; filmed 1976) imagine societies where people are killed prematurely or else encouraged and assisted in committing suicide. The public imagery surrounding Dr. Kevorkian often channeled the affect of dystopian science fiction or horror; "Dr. Death," in Neil Gorsuch's words, "regularly used a machine in the back of his van to kill patients who were neither terminally ill, nor suffering intolerable pain."[36] An anonymous article published in the *Journal of the American Medical Association* in 1988 titled "It's Over Debbie" seemed to borrow from the psychopathic serial killer narrative, telling the possibly fictional, first-person story of a physician who abruptly overdosed a twenty-year-old woman on morphine to whom he had never spoken; the narrator frames it as all in a day's work.[37] Like Wharton's novel, the article implied that this practice was routine—and thus triggered an outrage.

With euthanasia contaminated by ideas of social collectivism gone wrong, the western intervened at a crucial moment in euthanasia discourse. It insisted on the distinction between the involuntary euthanasia of *Soylent Green* and voluntary euthanasia/suicide, which it framed as a privacy right—the unique prerogative of the self-determining liberal subject. When the subject was a white man like John Wayne, criticisms of euthanasia as an effete position became far less prevalent, even though representing the subject of assisted suicide as a tough white man also occluded the idea that different groups might perceive euthanasia differently.[38] With Wayne as its exemplar, suicide in the face of terminal illness was framed as a hardy, implicitly white masculine stoicism and recalcitrance.

As slow, invisible deaths in hospitals and dependency on machines became more common, the western genre dramatized a sense that death was ubiquitous, that it could come for anyone and at any time. In the same years that euthanasia was returning to national consciousness, books like Ernest Becker's bestselling and prizewinning book *Denial of Death* (1973) claimed that people had lost touch with the ubiquity of death. As a character in Larry McMurtry's *Lonesome Dove* (1985) exclaims, "I guess in New York there are so many people you don't notice the dying so much."[39] In its dime novel form, the western could sometimes be the genre most resistant to the ineluctability of personal death, as the hero, repeatedly and against all odds, cheats fate, evades villains, and leaves an ever-mounting toll of corpses in his wake. But in its ballad forms, which emphasize instead the perils of the frontier, the western seems far more attuned to death's omnipresence. Perhaps the two most famous cowboy ballads of all time, "Streets of Laredo" and "Bury Me Not on the Lone Prairie," which date back to the early nineteenth century, concern protagonists who die too early. The former features a young man who, while lying shot, asks for a drink of water but dies before the narrator can return—it became the title for one of McMurtry's novels. The latter is sung by a young man who laments that he will have to die alone on the prairie away from his home.

Aging cowboys had been dotting the landscape of the western film as early as *The Man Who Shot Liberty Valance* (1962), a trope that continues into *True Grit* (1969), *The Shootist* (1976) and other late Wayne films, as well as in movies like *Unforgiven* (1992) and *No Country for Old Men* (2007). The narrative prevalence of aging cowboys would create parts for older actors like Wayne, and it would appeal to graying audiences who were familiar with westerns from their youth. Western novels, too, took up questions of old age or disability in Wallace Stegner's *Angle of Repose* (1971), McMurtry's *Lonesome Dove* (1985), and Annie Proulx's "The Half-Skinned Steer" (1997) and "Tits-Up in a Ditch" (2008).

The western was a natural fit for tropes of euthanasia, because, since its inception in dime novel form, the western has dramatized threats to American liberalism. In older and pulpier westerns, those threats have often taken the form of figures like Native Americans and Chicanos/as—racialized Others who might have a precedent and better claim on land and property—and bandits—social outlaws who do not comply with the rule of law enforced by the liberal social order.[40] In the novels of James Fenimore Cooper and the folktales of Daniel Boone, the western has been an elegiac form, one coming to terms with what it imagines as the vanishing of the halcyon frontier days—hence the frequent appearance of old frontiersmen and ancient Native Americans. Though famine and illness have been staples of the genre from its inception, in the twentieth century, perhaps the greatest threat to the autonomy of the heroes of the western has been old age—with enfeeblement and disability. The western further alleged that mercy-killing was far more common in the past, providing a historical precedent for contemporary euthanasia rights. In the HBO series *Deadwood* (set in the nineteenth century), for instance, when the reverend is dying of a brain tumor, the local pimp and saloon owner decides to kill him when the doctor will not.[41]

By representing questions of the right to die, these westerns were also becoming more literary. Though the popular western would continue to thrive well into the late twentieth century under the guidance of Louis L'Amour, fictional westerns had been approaching more "literary fiction" ever since Walter Van Tilburg Clark's *The Ox-Bow Incident* (1940). A staggering number of established authors have attempted to write a literary or semi-literary western—E. L. Doctorow, John Williams, Stegner, McCarthy, McMurtry, Proulx, among others (not to mention directors like John Ford or Sergio Leone, who elevated the western film to "serious" art). As early as 1960, a reviewer of Doctorow's *Welcome to Hard Times* noted that the "serious western' has established itself firmly as a subgenre of fiction."[42] In practice, being literary has meant that the western approaches "serious" moral questions, blurs the boundary between right and wrong, and incorporates lyrical description. The serious western also includes rounder interiorities, temporal reflection, introspection, and characters who are victimized by accident and circumstance. Westerns have traditionally been a teleological genre, descended from romance, celebrating the triumphant thumping of "evil" interests by the good liberal agents of economic development and family life.[43]

But the question for the western as it entered the twentieth century and became a more literary genre has been how to reconcile the telos of the romance with the inevitabilities of realism and naturalism—accident, circumstance, misfortune. Importing the realist novel into their genre sixty years after Wharton helped define it, western writers, like Wharton, saw euthanasia as the ideal issue on which to brand their versions of realism. For them as for her, euthanasia lies at the confluence of two opposing strands of idealistic self-determination and brute material luck. But for Wharton, privacy had largely referred to the domestic realm of the home, in which Justine was uniquely equipped to discern the role of private sentiment. In contrast, the 1970s western took up privacy in its more modern form—as the right of the self-determining, self-creating individual. In its treatment of euthanasia, the western thus comes quite close to the liberal philosophical terrain imagined by Dworkin and others. Westerns juxtapose the individual's triumphant life narrative—the romantic cowboy story—against the accident—the terminal illness, the sudden disability. The western has also been what might be called a quasi-governmental space, with heroes who are sheriffs or marshals or shootists, but who serve voluntarily. They are not representative of official, organized government, which is far to the east; framing end-of-life choices in the absence of official state bureaucracy helps to counter the "death panel" imaginary that often surrounds the topic.

Perhaps the most explicit early engagement with euthanasia in the western appears in Glendon Swarthout's *The Shootist* (1975; film 1976), which was adapted into John Wayne's last film. In January 1976, Wayne was dying of cancer. He was playing a cowboy who was also dying of cancer. "Sometimes," he told a reporter, "the irony of this film gets to me."[44] He starred, alongside Jimmy Stewart and Lauren Bacall, in a film that told the story of J. B. Books, a cowboy who refuses a protracted death from prostate cancer. Instead, Books decides to go out with guns blazing, in a duel with some of the best shooters in town (who also happen to be men of dubious moral character). As Wayne shot the film, he required oxygen assistance, a round-the-clock nurse, and a two-week-long hospitalization.[45] During the making of *The Shootist*, the case of Karen Ann Quinlan was sweeping the nation. Quinlan was a twenty-one-year-old who, in April 1975, took alcohol with sedatives and lapsed into an irreversible coma, but doctors refused to disconnect her from her respirator. She was featured on the cover of *Newsweek* with the phrase, "A Right to Die?" and her story appeared in the *New York Times*, *Time*, and other major periodicals.[46]

As a novel and a film, *The Shootist* complemented *True Grit*, the novel by Charles Portis that became one of Wayne's last films; in that film, old, drunk, fat, and one-eyed though he may have been, Wayne could still shoot his way to victory by sheer "grit." If *True Grit* was a heroic fantasy about old age, *The Shootist* is a fantasy about the good death—one that avoids the thorniest of moral issues provoked by Quinlan and subsequent cases. Books is able to shoot his way to his final moments; he does not need a doctor or a family member to help him end his life, nor does he need to take a drug. Books is a cipher for the liberal individual of social contract theory who exists in the state of nature, and whose moral code is the basis for the establishment of the government. He announces his credo: "I won't be wronged, I won't be insulted, and I won't be laid a hand on. I don't do these things to other people, and I require the same from them."[47] The novel provides an imagined historical space where the right to die could be justified in terms of liberal social contract theory, overcoming objections like conservative bioethicist Leon Kass's that liberalism has historically been devoted to securing the rights as forms of "self-preservation."[48] *The Shootist* also helped to alleviate the paradox that the right to end one's life, a right of self-destruction, could be defined as a right of self-creation. Books's final act is not solely self-destructive; it serves an identifiable social purpose: he takes the bad guys to hell with him (or so one might imagine).

The novel further represents voluntary euthanasia as private self-creation insofar as it intertwines Books's decision to commit suicide with the cultivation of his literary and aesthetic sensibility. Books's name, of course, conjures literature, and like the novel itself, he is torn between the claims of romance and realism. In its treatment of euthanasia, *The Shootist* initially opposes the realism and masculinity of Books and his world to aestheticism and Romanticism. When Books's doctor gives him opium for the first time, the doctor quotes the last four lines of Coleridge's "Kubla Khan": "'Weave a circle round him thrice / And close your eyes with holy dread / For he on honey-dew hath fed / And drunk the milk of Paradise.'" Books has never heard the poem before, and initially, Romanticism and opium seem to represent the vision that Books rejects. The effeminate vision of Kubla Khan drinking the "milk of Paradise" is juxtaposed against Books's hardscrabble decision to die in a gunfight. In contrast to the opulence of Coleridge, Swarthout embraces gross realism: "He got out the chamber pot and tried for several minutes to use it, but in vain. His bladder was distended; it hung in his guts like a great rock." Euthanasia and suicide, it is suggested, are routine in the life of a cowboy. Early in the novel Books reads the obituary of another cowboy: "It is supposed that he killed himself because he was suffering with the grippe."

And yet, rather than reject Romanticism, *The Shootist* hopes to dialectically absorb it. As Books struggles to remember the lines throughout the novel, they become prophetic of his final duel. The men weaving "a circle round him thrice" correspond to the three shooters he faces. The "honey-dew" refers, in Books's memory, to the happy moments he recollects of frontier life. He muses to himself: "Oh, I have fed on honey-dew. On wine and whiskey and champagne and the tender white meat of women and fine clothes . . ." The "holy dread" initially refers to his fear of death; before he recalls that line, he thinks, "Oh my god I am afraid to die," but his fear is transmuted into the dread he inspires in his opponents. The "milk of Paradise" alludes to the opium that he has drunk before the final duel. Books turns to and rewrites "Kubla Khan" as he prepares to die, because he reads the final lines as referring to his triumphant self-determining death.

The duel takes place in a saloon that resembles the poem's Xanadu. The saloon is entitled "The Constantinople," and though the historical Kublai Khan never visited there, the doctor identifies Xanadu as "Some strange and oriental sphere of the imagination. Probably in the Near East." The saloon itself is carved with exotic murals:

> It was the murals, however, the scope and subject matter of the murals, which stunned. They covered the walls, that over the bar, over the archway, and the full wall to the left. They depicted, in colors that whooped, in perspective that was fantastically out of whack, exotic scenes on the far side of exotic seas. There were domes and mosques and caravans of camels and pyramids and horsemen waving scimitars and minarets and palm trees and Sphinxes and tombs and dancing girls with navels as big as the tops of tin cans and boobs as pendant as hams hung on hooks and tents and oases on burning sands and dhows on rivers and dusty battles. The Constantinople had class, all right, but Books was in some doubt about the murals. They appeared to be the masterwork of a frontier genius who had been paid in alcohol or opium and who, by the time he had slap-dashed his visions and laid down his brush, had become either an addict or an irredeemable drunk. They spit in the rational eye. They kicked art in the ass.

The murals are carved through the ecstatic vision of a kind of frontier Coleridge, an opium addict, who—striving for an "exotic" "perspective that was fantastically out of whack"— depicted a decadent scene of implied fornication, Orientalism, and Egyptology. Like Coleridge's Romanticism, they embody a principle of art that spits "in the rational eye." They represent the exotic scene of a Xanadu-like place, migrated to the frontier—the perfect, ecstatic backdrop for Books's decision to refuse to succumb to a slow and painful death and for a western that transposes realist unpleasantries into Romantic triumph.

The Shootist is a fanciful rewriting of "Kubla Khan," transposing a realist-naturalist story of accidental, meaningless death into a Romanticist narrative of triumphant self-determination. The final scene further underscores the ultimate triumph of dramatic liberal self-determination in a world in which no narratives are prewritten:

> They were like actors on an empty stage, the five. The curtain had risen, the hour come. But they had no audience, save for one another, and even more bewildering, they had no play. They were assembled to take roles for which no lines had yet been written, to participate in a tragedy behind which there was no clear creative intent, to impose upon senselessness some sort of deadly order.

In the world of *The Shootist*, comparing life to a dramatic narrative is not derided as the effeminate position of an elite artistic and intellectual class. Rather, imposing order on senselessness, ending one's life instead of succumbing to pain and dependence, is the masculine prerogative of the gun-slinging cowboy practicing his aesthetic sense and shaping his life into narrative form.

As a metanarrative about Wayne's life, the film version of *The Shootist* also suggests how generic narratives serve to obscure the realities of dying. The film begins with a montage of Wayne firing a gun in past films, creating a sense that the real-life Wayne had been the same cowboy he played over and over again on the big screen. The movie suggests that he had shaped his life as a work of art and was now bidding goodbye. And yet, a few years after *The Shootist*, Wayne would not have the same options; he would die of stomach cancer in a hospital at UCLA; he would be emaciated, sedated on morphine, after surgery, radiation, and experimental treatments. He would avoid telling the country until a few weeks before his death, having claimed earlier in his life "I licked the Big C," as if cancer were a monikered adversary who lost in a shoot-out.[49] While Dworkin argues aspirationally for narrative form as a model for self-actualization in the face of death, in practice, fictions of dying can also serve as forms of public self-delusion—even advancing a form of ableism. They enable the public to avoid the pain and disability that precedes death. Wayne was able to achieve in fiction what he could not realize in life—a quick and heroic death.

In *Lonesome Dove*, Larry McMurtry continues to represent voluntary euthanasia as the property of a self-determining cowboy committing suicide. Toward the end of the novel, the aging cowboy Augustus (Gus) McCrae has been ambushed, and when he makes it to the nearest town, he finds that both of his legs have become gangrenous. Rather than have them amputated and live out his days in a wheelchair, he chooses to die from the gangrene. Gus feels that unless he has two legs, he will not be himself anymore: "I've walked the earth in my pride all these years. If that's lost, then let the rest be lost with it. There's certain things my vanity won't abide."[50] As in *The Shootist*, McMurtry prevents Gus from having to commit suicide: Gus does not have to choose to kill himself after finding himself disabled; he only has to refuse surgical treatment. McMurtry narrates the situation that the Supreme Court and Congress at the time would feel most comfortable authorizing: the individual who can quickly die by refusing care, not the individual who wants his life to be actively terminated. Gus's situation is nonetheless the one that troubles disability rights advocates the most: Gus is not terminally ill, or even facing chronic pain; he chooses to end his life solely to avoid becoming a disabled old man.

McMurtry links Gus's situation to that of another character, Bob, a comatose man who has no chance of recovery. Bob is the husband of Gus's long-lost love Clara; he has been kicked in the head by a horse, causing him to lose control over his bowels and bladder. Catatonic, he is kept alive by drinking chicken broth, but his family must do everything else for him. After several months of this catatonia, he finally dies in the middle of the night. The family is miserable beforehand. "I wanted Daddy to die," his daughter says. Taking care of Bob is, for Clara, "as hard as anything she had had to do in her marriage . . . at times she wished Bob would go on and die, if he couldn't get well" (829). By juxtaposing the two cases of Bob and Gus, McMurtry represents euthanasia as a question of agency, of which actions are permissible at the end of life. On the frontier, in the absence of government, McMurtry imagines the morality of euthanasia roughly as the way the law would in the past and ensuing decades: a person can actively refuse medical treatment (Gus), but food cannot be withheld from an unconscious person (Bob).[51] The imagined space of the frontier naturalizes the modern legal prohibitions surrounding death, which persist in moral form even without the active presence of law.

As if regretting the ableism of his previous novel, McMurtry decided in *Streets of Laredo*, the sequel to *Lonesome Dove*, to narrate the scenario of a disabled individual who chooses to live. Call, Gus's closest friend, loses an arm and a leg—and Call wishes that he could commit suicide, but he has no knife and does not think he "could have made a clean job of it with only his right hand to use."[52] Call laments that disability fractures his self: "he could remember the person he had been, but he could not become that person again" (485). And yet, he ultimately chooses to go on, because he finds a craft in sharpening tools. In some of the last pages of the novel, others comment about Call: "Life's but a knife edge, anyway. Sooner or later people slip and get cut" (498). Call, sharpening knives and other tools, may have decided to live, but in refusing euthanasia, he becomes less a human than a living embodiment of life's fatalism—a kind of Grim Reaper figure, endlessly preparing the tool of death.

McMurtry wants to portray both Call's and Gus's decisions as deliberately irrational, anti-normative behavior; they are private choices. (This is why Gus refers to "vanity" rather than the liberal category of "dignity.") In both novels, he casts an imagined scene of public opinion as a counterpoint to his protagonist's decision. In *Lonesome Dove*, Gus's friends sit around a bar puzzling over his decision. "I knew a spry little fellow from Virginia who could go nearly as fast on crutches as I can on my own legs," says one (887). In *Streets of Laredo*, another exclaims about Call: "Well, but now look . . . what's he doing? Sharpening sickles in a dern barn!" (498). Whether one chooses to live or die, McMurtry sees life as a romantic quest that flies in the face of rationality. Call and Gus both give up comfortable lives in Texas to herd "skinny cattle" to Montana, where cattle-selling opportunities are questionable; they are interested, rather, in the adventure (242). Throughout, Gus throws off bon mots like, "A man is foolish to give up the stable pleasure of life just to follow a bunch of shitting cattle" (524). In his memoir about aging, *Walter Benjamin at the Dairy Queen*, McMurtry calls *Lonesome Dove*, a buddy narrative that blends romance and realism, about "as close as I could get to Sancho and the Don."[53] Like Quixote's invocation of the disappearing values of the chivalric romance, the two are on a quest to bring back the romance of the frontier, which they see as losing ground to industrial capitalism. And yet, they are repeatedly confronted with the difficult consequences of this aspiration: accident, misfortune, and death. Each novel ends with one having to make the choice of whether to live or die with a disability.[54]

The romance of Gus and Call's quest through the plains is also connected to the romance of collecting antique and used books. McMurtry spent almost fifty years as an antiquarian bookseller, collecting nearly half a million books at his store Booked Up in Archer City, Texas. He writes about Don Quixote: "The old Don was clearly a bibliomaniac, the first in literature, collecting those romances of chivalry. He seemed crazy in the way many book collectors are crazy."[55] Because of McMurtry's fondness for book collecting and his lack of literary pretention, the materiality of the text in *Lonesome Dove* often outweighs its actual meaning.

A repeated motif in *Lonesome Dove* is meaningful illiteracy or misreading. Gus is unable to read the Latin that he proudly places on the sign outside his store, which he writes just below "We don't rent pigs." The words "UVA UVAM VIVENDO VARIA FIT" turn out to mean (though they are never translated) "A grape turns red when it sees another grape," alluding to his own longstanding homosocial bromance with Call (90–91). Call brings the sign for the store to mark Gus's grave, but with no other inscription, the words force their readers into a similarly irrational quest: "People might be inconvenienced for days, wandering through the limestone hills, trying to find a company who were mostly ghosts" (558). Wilbarger carries around Milton and Virgil on his trip through the plains, explaining why he reads Milton in the morning: "At night I'm apt to be in a stampede, and you cannot read Mr. Milton during a stampede" (434). He ultimately reveals that he can't read the Virgil—and he gives it to Gus, who also can't read it. Finally, at the end of the novel, Gus pens a letter to his sweetheart, a prostitute, who is illiterate, but she prefers not to have her rival read it to her, thinking "It was hers from Gus. What the words were didn't matter" (930).

McMurtry's fiction may support suicide and even perhaps euthanasia for paraplegics, but it also suggests that the ultimate meaning of life narratives is less determined by final exits, the intentional choice to die or not to die, than by the way a person's presence is diffused throughout the world: one's effects on other people. Thus, the materiality of the text, the way it can be gifted or transferred from one person to another, turns out to be more important than the author's intention or the meaning of the words.

While McMurtry and Swarthout imagine the cowboy committing forms of voluntary euthanasia, involuntary euthanasia lingers in the background of Cormac McCarthy's *No Country for Old Men* (2005). *No Country* initially began as a screenplay about drug smuggling, in which Anton Chigurh, the villain (then named Milo), is a henchman who has killed the daughter of the sheriff, Ed Tom. At the end of the screenplay, Ed Tom gets his revenge in a standoff with Milo and his boss and then uses the recovered drug money to start a medical clinic for the ailing rural town. As his western became more literary, *No Country* became less a shoot-'em-up, cowboy-against-drug-smuggler tale and more a metaphysical questioning of the stakes of life and death. Chigurh becomes the main villain instead of a henchman and delivers monologues about the nature of fate and luck. He is a representation of cosmic evil; Chigurh has no personal connection to Ed Tom.

In one of McCarthy's final revisions, he added a line about euthanasia and abortion—the final step in a transformation of the novel from typical genre entry to metaphysical questioning of what it meant to narrate one's life.[56] Ed Tom sits next to a woman at a conference who complains about "the right wing" and insists that she wants her daughter to have an abortion, to which he responds: "The way I see it goin I dont have much doubt but what she'll be able to have an abortion. I'm goin to say that not only will she be able to have an abortion, she'll be able to have you put to sleep. Which pretty much ended the conversation."[57] Ed Tom is a figure who believes in strong, unified, and self-determined life narratives—and likely sees euthanasia and abortion as artificial interruptions to those narratives. But he is thwarted in his attempts to unify his life into a single narrative; he reveals his failures: "It's a life's work to see yourself for what you really are and even then you might be wrong" (295). Ed Tom wants his own heroic western narrative, the defeat of evil, to be perfectly aligned with the narrative of national success. He wants to be in the type of story that McCarthy envisioned for *No Country*—a cinematic genre screenplay. But Ed Tom fails to live out this strong, unified narrative. He retires having witnessed the decline of the country over the preceding forty years: the rise in violent crime, the growing drug trade, and the young people with "green hair and nosebones" (305). His secret, revealed to his uncle, is that he received a Bronze Star in the Second World War for shooting Germans, but his troop lost their position, and he actually abandoned his comrades when they were dying. At the end of the novel, rather than catch the villain Chigurh, Ed Tom retires from the sheriff's office with Chigurh still at large.

Instead of a climactic final face-off with Chigurh as in the screenplay, Ed Tom confronts old age and retirement. "Where do they find somebody like you? Have they got you in diapers yet?" jeers an inmate on whose behalf Ed Tom has testified (297). Toward the end of the novel, Ed Tom encounters his uncle Ellis, an image of his future; Ellis, who has been thrown by a horse, sits in a wheelchair and has only one eye. His home smells of urine that "wasn't just [from] cats" (263). His sink is covered in dirty dishes; his television is gone; he is unable to leave the house; and he spends his days reminiscing about people who died long ago. With the exception of Ellis's Rangers badge, which he sends to a museum, the heroic relics that remain of his pioneering family seem destined for the dustbin. Because Ellis is also a retired sheriff, his decrepitude is, the novel implies, the future for Ed Tom. For Ellis, who describes aging as an unstoppable injury, life entails a gradual ratcheting down of capacities and repeated incidents of loss: "You wear out, Ed Tom. All the time you spend tryin to get back what's been took from you there's more goin out the door. After a while you just try and get your tourniquet on it" (267). The scene reveals the frontier as less a place of triumphant heroism as one of abrupt, unsatisfying narrative endings.

While Ed Tom confronts the way the slow and unsatisfying attrition of old age troubles his desire for strong life narratives, his double, Chigurh, believes that nothing is an accident. For Chigurh, life is structured by a master narrative of fate. Before he kills one of his victims, he tells her that her life takes the form of an Aristotelian plot:

> "When I came into your life your life was over. It had a beginning, a middle, and an end. This is the end. You can say that things could have turned out differently. That they could have been some other way. But what does that mean? They are not some other way. They are this way." (260)

To Chigurh, the flip of the coin indicates not chance but destiny. What seems to him like a final triumphant ending seems to everyone else like mere dumb luck. He dispatches a man at the beginning of the novel with a pneumatic "stungun like they use at the slaughterhouse," which comes with "one of them oxygen tanks they use for emphysema" (5). McCarthy's original screenplay began with the Chigurh character using the cattle gun on cows at a slaughterhouse.[58] The reference to emphysema emphasizes Chigurh's visits to his victims as representing bodily infirmity, and captive bolt guns are most notably used in slaughterhouses, to give cattle a quick and painless death—what Temple Grandin and others call "cattle euthanasia."[59]

McCarthy offers a choice between, on the one hand, an episodic life narrative that trickles off into the oblivion of old age, one that seems aimless and disunified, and, on the other hand, a strongly unified life narrative that ends suddenly and decisively but without consent. McCarthy's answer to Dworkin's argument—that the right to die should be grounded in a strong life narrative and thus a right of privacy—is Chigurh, who shows that to euthanize people is to treat them like cattle even while he thinks of them as fulfilling their life narratives. Even if Kant himself decried suicide, Dworkin's intellectual framework is neo-Kantian, deriving morality from universal concepts of dignity and autonomy that the individual subject wills. Chigurh is a kind of Kantian bad dream, precisely because he patterns his own decisions on God's: "Even a nonbeliever might find it useful to pattern himself off God" (256). He gives himself his own law: binding himself by his promises to spare his victim's lives if they win the coin flip.

McCarthy's conflictedness about euthanasia appears in his titular allusion to Yeats's poem about old age, "Sailing to Byzantium." In the Yeats poem, the speaker is notoriously ambivalent about his two imagined alternatives: Either he can stay in the land of the living, a land where he will grow old and be ignored, or else he can sail to the eternal aesthetic realm of Byzantium, where, having shed his human form, he sings only "to keep a drowsy emperor awake."[60] If we were to read Yeats's poem as an ambivalent story about euthanasia, it would frame the choice as one between growing decrepit or else taking one's own life and hoping for a disembodied refuge in the immortality of one's art. In other words, as an old man, one can choose to be sick and dying or else eternal—detached and formless. This reading of the poem is transposed onto the two characters of *No Country*. If Yeats saw the choice in his poem as one between transient mortality and mystical, aesthetic immortality, McCarthy does not see the possibility of mystical immortality that Yeats does. Rather, he sees the choice of his novel as between transient, realist mortality and the machine-like plots of genre. Thus, Chigurh, the mechanical murderer, reads as a stock genre character—reminding us of the predetermined plotline, the man of action and no reflection—whereas Ed Tom, who takes virtually no action that affects the events of the novel itself, represents realism, accident, and consciousness. The novel emerges as the fusion of these two equally unsatisfying perspectives of old age. It offers the choice of an abrupt and final conclusion, in which the self becomes instrumentalized in someone else's narrative, or a life of dwindling capacity and little consequence.

Chigurh believes that his life is wholly determined; on a diegetic level, his belief seems dubious at best—he uses fate to justify murder. On an extradiegetic level, however, he is absolutely correct: his life is determined by an author named Cormac McCarthy. The reverse is true for Ed Tom: he perceives life as totally chaotic and meaningless, and yet his life as a fictional character is explicitly patterned. For McCarthy, at the heart of authorship is a kind of crisis: how can one shape a narrative in language without knowing the ultimate pattern that one's life takes? In his essay on the Kekulé problem, he explores the fundamental arbitrariness of narrative patterning: "The facts of the world do not for the most part come in narrative form. We have to do that." The prelinguistic unconscious potentially corresponds to inherited biological knowledge with a purpose that we do not understand: "the unconscious is a machine for operating an animal."[61] For McCarthy, to hold up narrative as a model for euthanasia seems particularly inept, because narrative, unlike life, has a much clearer relationship between creator and created. A person who, like Chigurh, insists that he fulfills a fundamental pattern and order may be blithely unaware of what the real pattern and order is.

While one understanding of the western describes the genre as narrating individual liberal self-determination, another would treat the modern western, as practiced by McCarthy and Sergio Leone, as a genre that emphasizes the unknowability and immensity of all things. The landscape of the western reveals, in Mark Goble's words, the "world that moves too slowly for any product of human thought or making to apprehend."[62] The western can justify euthanasia as the cowboy's last radical act of self-making on the range. But it can also lead to a consciousness that there may be more to life than one individual human narrative can contain—a perspective that would invalidate the triumphalism of the private person creating herself and her life's narrative in the final act of choosing death.

Kiss Me Deadly: The Euthanasia Romance

Even as the western began in Swarthout's treatment by framing voluntary euthanasia as the act of radical self-determination, we saw emerging, in McMurtry's representation of euthanasia, a tension between the self-determining individual cowboy who kills himself and the embedded social world in which he persists. For McCarthy, another, different tension emerged: between the cowboy contemplating euthanasia and the vast, omnipresent forces of nature that he cannot understand. The first of these tensions—between the social and the individual—is the subject of the euthanasia romance. (While the premature death of a lover has established itself as its own subgenre in romance, Derek Humphry's memoir *Jean's Way: A Love Story* (1978)—about how he helped his wife end her life— did catalyze awareness of the right to die.) Jodi Picoult's *Mercy* (1996), a novel that incorporates tropes from romance, imagines euthanasia as an act of co-determination, as carried out between two lovers.

The central question of *Mercy* is: could euthanasia ever be an act of love? *Mercy* describes a character called Jamie, who kills his wife Maggie, who has terminal breast cancer. Jamie's defense attorney explains that Jamie and Maggie had a unique bond:

> It's unsettling to hear about a man who loved his wife so much that he'd be capable of doing this. It makes us all feel a little guilty, because we probably wouldn't go to such an extreme. Admitting that Jamie had the courage to do such a thing

also forces us to admit that we wouldn't. That we don't have the same kind of strength, or the same depth of emotion for our husbands and wives and lovers.[63]

Euthanasia is not here the act of radical individual agency that we saw in westerns, nor is it the decision of the collective as we witnessed in SF. It is still personal: in the *Mercy* quote above, the lawyer emphasizes that "we" would not make the same choice that Jamie did. But it also stems from the emotion between lovers, not from a single individual's triumphant decision.

Picoult's is nonetheless a classically liberal imagination of family life: there is a special bond between Jamie and Maggie that neither the jury nor the reader can inhabit and that the state needs to respect. Picoult's particular relationship to liberal thought stresses not the radically self-determining individual, but rather the miniature social collective of the family. We can see this vision through the title of her novel, which is permuted in different combinations throughout the book. The other story of *Mercy* is that of Cam, the police chief, who cheats on his wife Allie, with her assistant Mia. Allie eventually decides to forgive him. The word "mercy" structures the three major actions of the story: Jamie's decision to give mercy to his wife by euthanizing her; the jury's decision to have mercy on Jamie; and finally Allie's decision to forgive Cam for his infidelity.

Picoult imagines law and morality as opposed to mercy: she opens one section with an epigraph from *Timon of Athens*: "Nothing emboldens sin so much as mercy."[64] But in her final epigraph, she quotes from middlebrow novelist James Hilton: "If you forgive people enough, you belong to them, and they to you, whether either person likes it or not—squatter's rights of the heart."[65] The squatter's right is a way of imagining communal property but within the liberal tradition: the value of mercy suggests that individuals' lives do not belong to themselves alone—any more than does an epigraph, another author's words adapted for one's own purposes.

And yet, even when recast within the romance, it may still be ableist to argue for euthanasia as part of the right to privacy reimagined as a right to narrate one's own life. Writing from within disability studies, David Mitchell and Sharon Snyder argue that narrative form often functions as a kind of "prosthesis," as an attempt to reinscribe disability within a normative framework.[66] We might understand arguments for assisted suicide in narrative form as ableist attempts to take what seems uncomfortable—disability and dependence—and resolve them within familiar-seeming narratives: the cowboy riding off into the sunset or the star-crossed lovers parting ways. Much of the backlash against the romance film *Me Before You* (2016), in which Will Traynor, an aristocratic paraplegic, falls in love with his working-class caretaker before choosing suicide, stemmed from precisely the idea that popular narratives most often tend to do away with the disabled or infirm in the end. As one disabled viewer put it, "I'm not a thing to be pitied or killed off to make the audience cry."[67]

While Mitchell and Snyder make their claim as one about narrative in general (since Oedipus), it is also possible that although we are aware of one generic trope (the paraplegic whose life ends in euthanasia) we have a paucity of others. What would it mean to think about the dying person as a cowboy? A lover? A gynotopianist? A nurse? We tend to think about genres as particularly formulaic and law-like, but when viewed in aggregate, genres have a remarkably myriad imagination of who and what might count as a private person—and what it might mean to be self-defining. What if we thought about the decision of euthanasia not as narrating one's life in terms of choosing a determinant beginning, middle, and end but as finding the appropriate genre? That would open up a clearer possibility that there could be a multiplicity of ways to determine the self.

Putting a few different genres together in this chapter has enabled us to see some of the heterogeneity of what can be meant by narrative form. Perhaps one day in the future narrative "self-creation" will encompass people with a broader variety of illnesses and conditions than terminal ones. Perhaps, as *Mercy* has suggested, we will view "self-creation" as a more collaborative process than we do now, such that we are more willing to accept forms of nonvoluntary euthanasia as well as voluntary ones. Perhaps we will conclude that, as disability rights advocate Felicia Ackerman argues: "True privacy and autonomy would allow each person to determine for himself what conditions would justify suicide," regardless of disability or illness.[68] Perhaps there will simply be more cultural narratives of disabled people choosing not to die and instead living fulfilling lives. It may be that narrative form in general relies on a logic that renormalizes disability, or it may be that, more than a hundred years after Wharton wrote, we are still groping toward a full expression of the appropriate narrative genres to understand how to think about euthanasia.

CONCLUSION

THE NOVELS OF THIS BOOK responded to the idea, stretching from Lionel Trilling to David Foster Wallace, that reading literary fiction went hand in hand with the cultivation of individual privacy. Reading would enhance an individual's ability to deliberate or self-reflect in private by exposing the person to other private lives or points of view. That exposure would thereby enable the individual to enter public life and to better reason about the public/private split that is fundamental to liberal society. Many critics and authors of literary fiction believed the danger of mass culture (of which genre fiction was a part) was that it was too seductive, immersive; it didn't cultivate the capacity for sustained reflection that was the hallmark of liberalism. It robbed people of unique individual identity; it taught everyone to be an unthinking consumer; it spoke to base urges, not higher ideals. It destroyed privacy.

Between 1945 and 2001 or so, a certain type of genre fiction stood on the borders of literary fiction. Few imagined that these writers would help shape the rich private lives of readers. But as a result of their aesthetic ambitions, their unique situation in the literary field, and the illiberal generic forms they inherited, these authors showed that privacy was broader and more complex than the liberalism of the period that had framed it: as the right to define oneself. They latched onto particular tensions in the idea of privacy, sometimes years if not decades before they were explicitly regulated by law. What about the privacy of the body? Did privacy include the right to an abortion, the right to die, the right to hit one's children? How was privacy mediated through race and class and sexuality? They used their works as a way of transmuting private struggles and sorrows into forms that would be culturally resonant.

Today the literary field looks quite different: it can seem as if nearly all writers are genre writers. We need to point only to the staggering number of transatlantic "literary" authors—Jonathan Lethem, Michael Chabon, Colson Whitehead, Viet Thanh Nguyen, Junot Díaz, Carmen Maria Machado, Kelly Link, Gish Jen, Marlon James, Charles Yu, Ling Ma, Chang-rae Lee—who adapt generic plotlines and tropes, or at the very least borrow elements from crime fiction, superhero comics, fairy tale, suspense, or myth. This is more than an American story, as authors like Ian McEwan, Kazuo Ishiguro, or Haruki Murakami suggest. And, while one strand of literary fiction becomes more genre-like, authors like Jeff VanderMeer, Ted Chiang, N. K. Jemisin, Kim Stanley Robinson, and William Gibson began their careers writing hard science fiction but are increasingly welcome in the pages of the *New York Times* or on academic syllabi. Of course, it is still true that there is a difference between these authors and John Grisham and James Patterson at the level of plot and style. But what I had referred to as the upper middlebrow, or writers of genre fiction with aesthetic ambitions, has expanded: its boundaries have become more porous.[1]

From a theoretical perspective, the recent turn to genre may have happened because life-as-we-know-it is less amenable to being narrated in the terms of classical realism. If realism was suited to the representation of a particular nineteenth-century middle-class subjectivity, one that depicted the inexorability of bourgeois life, it seems inadequate to a world riven by technological change, inequality, digital media, and new awarenesses of class, gender, and racial struggles.[2] Perhaps the nineteenth-century novel, with its emphasis on private consciousness, cannot adequately represent postcolonialism, structural racism, patriarchy, or climate change—for which the nearer analogy is the superhero or zombie novel or fairy tale or post-apocalyptic wasteland. Generic forms, as we have seen, carry with them an inherited anti-liberalism that they modify and reshape to address the moment of their writing, and we can read the plethora of new literary-genre hybrids as reflecting the increasing complexity and fragility of liberalism in contemporary life.

But another possibility is that, from a sociological perspective, authors of literary fiction are turning to genre because fewer can convincingly claim insulation from the marketplace. As Dan Sinykin points out, smaller margins and more consolidation have meant that literary fiction has had to defend its value in economic terms, and writing a novel that fits in an existing genre with an existing readership is one way of making a case for the market value of one's fiction. With the social institutions (like the welfare state and the public university) that had propped up postwar liberalism in decline and with publishing overtaken by corporate conglomerates, it seems harder than ever to believe that realist, literary fiction can bear the non-market ideal of liberal personhood as enshrined by writers like Faulkner.[3] One of the major effects that the emergence of Amazon has had on contemporary fiction is the doubling down on genre: genres allow fiction to be classified and targeted to customers in the Everything Store.[4]

While the market has nearly swallowed fiction, it has also arguably engulfed privacy. Whereas 1970s anxieties about privacy mostly revolved around government surveillance, our own moment is characterized by unprecedented hand-wringing about the way that corporate technology is tracking our every move, by a fear that businesses might start to know us better than we know ourselves. Even the way we speak about defending privacy from those corporations involves an understanding of privacy as a marketplace commodity. "Surveillance capitalism," writes Shoshana Zuboff, one of its most notable critics, "unilaterally claims human experience as free raw material for translation into behavioral data."[5] To writers like Zuboff, privacy is a matter of data and information flow—the dimensions on which it can most easily be commercially exchanged—and to the exclusion of the ideas of personal autonomy that this book contemplates.

What might genre's engagement with privacy look like today now that privacy, like fiction, is most often imagined in terms of the marketplace? For one case study, we might turn to Gish Jen, who in 2017, at the age of sixty-two, decided to write her first work of dystopian surveillance fiction. Jen is an Iowa MFA program graduate whose previous four novels about Asian American immigrants have looked like "Exhibit A" in Mark McGurl's description of "high cultural pluralism."[6] Contemplating climate change, the Internet of Things, and the Trump presidency, Jen produced *The Resisters* (2020), which imagines a future America (retitled AutoAmerica to refer to ubiquitous automation) in which privacy invasion has become commonplace. With the country of ChinRussia adapting Total Persuasion Architectures to monitor their citizens, Americans destroyed privacy protections and bioethics laws and adapted their own version of those architectures, installing an Aunt Nettie—an Amazon Alexa-type smart-home device to monitor inhabitants—in each house. In the world of the novel, "Surplus" people, who are often of color, find that their occupations have been rendered obsolete. Seas have risen, and the Surplus live on the margins of the cities in houseboats and swampland, while the wealthier, employed, fairer-skinned "Netted" live in the city's center. Surplus are watched by SwarmDrones and NanoCams; they are tracked through RegiChips installed at birth; the disobedient are controlled with BioNet brain implants. The story follows Eleanor, a civil rights lawyer who chooses to live among and defend the Surplus, and Gwen, her daughter, who is preternaturally gifted at baseball and is pressured to represent AutoAmerica as a pitcher against ChinRussia at the Olympic Games.

In contrast to many authors considered in this book who felt marginalized because they were genre writers, Jen has found writing genre liberating. "Genre fiction," she told me, "does represent an area of freedom."[7] When writing novels like *World and Town* (2010), which featured Cambodian immigrants, excruciating faithfulness mattered. When writing genre fiction, Jen could afford to be more speculative, more playful, combining baseball and knitting with her anxieties about privacy in a story about multicultural characters. For her, writing genre stood for a self that was more liberated, more experimental. In her nonfiction book *The Girl at the Baggage Claim* (2017), Jen contrasts the strong, unchanging, American hyperindividualist self (what she calls "the avocado pit self") in which identity is fixed to the more flexible "interdependent self" of Asia.[8] When I spoke with her, she compared her ability to cross genres to the Taiwanese American director Ang Lee's serial experimentation with martial arts (*Crouching Tiger, Hidden Dragon*), Jane Austen (*Sense and Sensibility*), and the superhero film (*The Hulk*), reflecting what she calls in her book "ambidependence"—an imagination of the self as both independent of and interdependent on its context.[9] Moving in and out of genres represented a flexible self, one capable of remaining constant even as it takes on new forms. Genre fiction, for Jen as for many of the authors of this study, reflects both the desire to "make it new" and the desire to pay homage to an inherited form.

The freedom Jen found in genre may also have been a freedom to be able to write a book that would sell. *The Resisters* did not make the bestseller list, but it outsold any of her previous books. It was the first of Jen's books to accompany a blurb from Stephen King, which notes "I wouldn't mind a sequel" (which would make the book even more genre-like).[10] Jen's attitude toward King's support is not snobbery but gratitude. "Hey," she said, "if Stephen King wants to help us [literary writers], we're grateful. We need all the help we can get."[11] If Jen's veneration for King is any indication, it may be difficult in our age of neoliberalism for literary writers to imagine themselves as free from the market. If anything, writers of literary fiction can seem marginalized in favor of those writers able to command larger sales and blockbuster adaptations.

At the same time, *The Resisters* is also a story of resistance to the market—the Surplus featured in the novel are those who have been left behind by market values. Aunt Nettie's regime initially began with the consumer technology we use today: "DroneDeliverers and FridgeStockers, KidTrackers and RoboSitters, ElderHelpers and YardBots."[12] The novel might appear as market-oriented genre fiction, but it reads also as high cultural pluralism renovated. All of Jen's novels navigate the balance between Asian and American cultural traditions, no less *The Resisters*. Gwen is a Blasian American baseball player who sparks a riot against the Total Persuasion Architecture imported from ChinRussia, where genetic modification and state surveillance have run amok. The baseball theme running through the novel partakes of the aspects of the best version of America Jen imagines in describing "the flexi-self": it is at once meritocratic and individualistic but also team oriented, played by a multicultural team.[13] And it ends up being the site of a collective resistance against the market-derived technologies that threaten to dissolve private life.

Jen further claims in interviews that her interest in genre fiction lies in her desire "to return the human to the foreground."[14] The science fictional privacy-invading tropes—the Total Persuasion Architecture, the SwarmDrones, the AutoHouses, the PermaDerms—are the technologies to be resisted by human individuals. Gwen refuses her final pitch and the Olympic Games descends into a riot against AutoAmerica's authoritarianism. In the aftermath, Gwen joins her deceased mother's legal team and continues a lawsuit alleging that the mall truck food feeding the Surplus is being poisoned to thin their ranks. *The Resisters* ultimately finds and celebrates liberal proceduralism amidst a science fictional dystopia. "For all the changes wrought by AI and Automation . . . we did still have a Constitution," the narrator reminds us.[15] While many authors of this study imagined their semi-persons—murderers or cops or androids or telekinetic children—as allegories for their marginalized genres, Jen focuses on the way un-typed, rounder characters like Gwen and Eleanor struggle for freedom from the tropes of science fictional dystopia. Jen thus imagines her novel as rediscovering humanistic, literary values amid dystopian tropes of the market gone awry. Ironically, though, she cannot help but be encircled, if not captured by, the very forces of the commercial market from which she imagines an escape.

In 2021, Jen released the multimedia sequel *I, AutoHouse* on Audible Originals, told from the perspective of Aunt Nettie.

While a writer of a literary-genre hybrid like Jen may use genre to try to recover more traditional values of literary fiction and privacy as inner thought, other writers today continue to stand at the confluence of the three factors that most of the authors of this study shared: aesthetic ambition, a semi-marginalized status in the literary field, and inherited anti-realist form. Take, as another case study, the science fiction writer N. K. Jemisin. Jemisin has repeatedly suggested that her work should be read in light of her position in the publishing industry.[16] Jemisin wrote her first novel, *The Hundred Thousand Kingdoms*, about Yeine—a woman who discovers she is a mixed-race heiress to the vicious Arameri kingdom and vies with her nasty relatives—in response to publishers telling her when she shopped her first novel that they could not imagine a market for Black characters of science fiction. "I am going to write something full of white people," she decided, "but it is going to be all about how evil those white people are."[17]

Jemisin continues to give voice to feelings of anger and oppression in her award-winning series *The Broken Earth*, which she says "derives from my feelings about science fiction."[18] The trilogy is set in a world with one continent called the Stillness, which will periodically experience an extinction-level event, known as a Fifth Season, triggered by seismic activity. A certain class of people, those known as orogenes, are able to manipulate thermal, kinetic, and other types of energy to address these seismic events; they can both cause or remediate earthquakes and other geological occurrences. The orogenes are feared and killed by the "stills" in society and are rounded up by Guardians who enslave and use them to prevent geological disasters. The trilogy follows the orogene Essun as she attempts to find her abducted daughter and to ultimately restore the moon in orbit around the planet, thereby ending Fifth Seasons altogether. The unjust society that fears and harnesses the creative abilities of the orogenes mirrors Jemisin's account of the industry in which she wrote, and Essun's anger at those who try to oppress her can be understood as a version of Jemisin's own.

Jemisin's trilogy, like the works of this book, can be read as a double allegory—not just of publishing but of political liberalism: it covers each of the topics of privacy taken up in the chapters of this book. There is child abuse: the series begins with a scene of Essun's husband Jija killing their son Uche after discovering that he is an orogene and then abducting their daughter Nassun. There is queer sexuality and reproductive freedom. In the first book, Essun (then known as Syenite) escapes from the Fulcrum, the orogenes' training ground, to an island where she has sex with Alabaster and Innon (both men) and makes a case for reproductive choice. "Freedom," she tells Alabaster while contemplating her "pessary," "means *we* get to control what we do now. No one else."[19] Then there is racist police surveillance when the Guardians locate, round up, enslave, and kill orogenes. There is something like euthanasia—Essun kills her fellow orogene Alabaster when he is in a state where he cannot feed himself or control his bowels and seems to want to die. There is even a scene of abortion: at the end of *The Stone Sky*, Essun is pregnant but gives up her child when she is turned to stone in the course of saving her other child Nassun.

If Jemisin's fiction is any indication, the forces that had marginalized her in the literary field were, in part, planetary (her ancestors had grown up in a part of the world where they would appear darker), historical (they had been kidnapped, brought to America, and enslaved), and sociological (humans did not want to read about or think about people different from themselves). By changing the conditions of the planet and society she wrote about, Jemisin could show how seemingly private, individual stories were affected by the larger social and geological forces surrounding them. Jemisin showed how each of these private actions was influenced by the geology and culture of the planet of *The Broken Earth*: Jija abuses his children because he discovers they are orogenes; Essun discovers freedom in her sexuality once she leaves the forcible breeding grounds of the Fulcrum; and the Guardians surveil, kill, and enslave orogenes to ensure the success of their society. Abortion and euthanasia are imagined as more personal choices: Essun gives up her fetus in order to save her daughter Nassun's life; Alabaster sacrifices himself while dying in order to prevent Essun from destruction. At the same time, it is impossible to deny that each of these "private" choices, which all result from the struggle associated with being born an orogene, are also at least partly the result of planetary conditions.

In writing fiction, Jemisin starts with worlds (or characters alongside worlds—she has said *The Fifth Season* was inspired by a dream of a furious Black woman levitating a pyramid with her mind).[20] In leading world-building exercises for admiring fans and would-be SF authors, she first considers the planet (whether it's habitable, its geology and continents, its climate, and its flora and fauna), she then moves to a people who have physically and socially evolved to contend with that environment, and then moves on to imagine her world's art, architecture, and culture.[21] Jemisin's fictional imagination, then, is an answer to the liberal thought experiment in which people are imagined to exist as private individuals in the state of nature who therein determine the moral or natural law. Her novels emphasize how much nature, and then a society that evolves in accordance with that nature, determine what seems politically natural. The private individual, the character, is the last to emerge: formed by minerals, weather patterns, geological formations, and inequalities that shape culture and humanity.

Whether Jen's attempt to recover literary fiction and privacy as interiority, as a freedom to be let alone, or Jemisin's representation of privacy as bodily autonomy that is, in turn, influenced by planetary circumstances, few authors today are willing to take for granted realist characters and settings and their implications about the meaning of private life. What had been the dominant idea for the postwar authors of this book—that the value of fiction is in its ability to provide a representation of private life that is independent of the work's value as a commodity—is now, I would argue, a residual one. Instead, we have an unprecedented number of anti-realist experiments in representing private life as it becomes enmeshed with the novel and strange realities of the present day.

At the same time, the fuller sense of privacy I have contemplated in this book, one more aligned with individual autonomy, often seems eclipsed in discussions about privacy today. For right-leaning originalists who now occupy most of the Supreme Court, the privacy right has always been ahistorical. "I can find neither in the Bill of Rights nor any other part of the Constitution a general right to privacy," Justice Clarence Thomas has written.[22] For those on the Left, the privacy right has often been thought inadequate compared to a truly robust idea of equality. The late Justice Ruth Bader Ginsburg criticized *Roe* for relying on privacy instead of "a constitutionally based sex-equality perspective."[23]

What I hope this book has shown is that, for the past seventy years or so, the protean concept of privacy has had a powerful hold on the American imagination of a just society. It has been a cultural construct as much as a legal one, and genre fiction has played a crucial role in its definition. Not long ago, even a nominal originalist like Neil Gorsuch found himself quoting from science fiction to justify Fourth Amendment protections. "Ours is not supposed to be the government of *The Hunger Games* with power centralized in one district, but a government of diffused and divided power, the better to prevent its abuse," he wrote, referring to the centralized surveillance of Suzanne Collins's dystopian world.[24] In the coming years, we may find the conservative Court reluctant to extend privacy rights, which are not explicitly written in the Constitution, but it is quite likely that that cultural experimentation that informs and is informed by our understanding of those rights will continue. And while science fiction authors are better at imagining the future than literary critics, it seems reasonable to expect that writers experimenting with genre, continually revising their anti-realist forms, will remain at the vanguard of imagining the limitations, the boundaries, the possibilities of what privacy could mean.

Acknowledgments

Writing is seldom the product of a private individual, and I am grateful to acknowledge many who helped make this book exist in the world. *Genres of Privacy* began at Yale University, where Amy Hungerford showed me how to craft a sharp argument and inspired me to think about the postwar period, Michael Warner sparked my engagement with privacy, and R. John Williams taught me how to navigate academia. Caleb Smith and David Scott Kastan each helped me understand aspects of my argument before I did. Among my graduate school colleagues, I am especially grateful to my friend and former roommate Jordan Brower, who made sense of much of this material when it was in drafty stages and has continued to support the project in the years after Yale. Margaret Deli provided invaluable edits and responses to several of the chapters herein. In Amy's working group, I found a supportive community of scholars who helped make me a better thinker—special thanks go to Merve Emre, Dave Gorin, Len Gutkin, Sam Huber, Shaj Mathew, Anna Shechtman, Ayten Tartici, and Arthur Wang. Also at Yale, Paul Franz, Angus Ledingham, and Rebecca Rush provided excellent sounding boards for various ideas. Jacqueline Goldsby, Joseph North, and Marta Figlerowicz read this whole project, and the book has benefited from their generous intellectual engagement with it.

I have been very lucky to be involved with the Post45 collective, and I am keenly grateful to Sean McCann for his generous reading of the entire project, as well as for his earlier input. Annie McClanahan, Theodore Martin, and Rachel Greenwald Smith also provided valuable feedback and encouragement along the way. Working with Stanford University Press has been wonderful, and I very much appreciate the support of Kate Marshall, Loren Glass, Erica Wetter, Faith Wilson Stein, and Caroline McKusick, the generous, thoughtful response from my anonymous reader, and Jennifer Gordon's superb copy editing.

Acknowledgments

A fellowship from the American Academy of Arts and Sciences gave me what many authors in this area do not have: the freedom and time to craft a book. Many thanks go to Paul Erickson and Tania Munz for overseeing the program and to Jeannette Estruth, Ben Holtzman, and Gabriel Winant for their intellectual companionship. Lawrence Buell inspired me to go to graduate school and helped me create a book proposal in this project's later stages, and I am indebted to Gordon Teskey for sparking an interest in allegory that he hopefully recognizes in these pages. Audiences at Harvard, Yale, ACLA, and Oxford also provided helpful feedback on my ideas here.

Kenneth Parris, John Thomas, and John Silvers, whom I met over the course of my research, helped me understand more about Jess Kimbrough's life and uncover lost documents; I deeply appreciate their help and kindness.

I am eternally grateful to my parents who supported and inspired this project in a multitude of ways—financially, emotionally, intellectually, and even helping with proofreading. They always believed that my work was valuable and coherent scholarship, when even I had my doubts, and if sales of this book end up in the black, it will likely be because they have purchased more copies than any single individual or institution, for which I thank them in advance.

Finally, my wife Kelly Diep has had to devote many of our private moments to a discussion of genre fiction and privacy over the past eight years; her influence can be found throughout these pages.

Notes

Introduction

1. See Andrew Liptak, "How *The Handmaid's Tale* Inspired a Protest Movement: Turning Cosplay into a Political Act," *The Verge* (October 31, 2017): https://www.theverge.com/2017/10/31/15799882/handmaids-tale-costumes-cosplay-protest; Christine Hauser, "A Handmaid's Tale of Protest," *New York Times* (June 30, 2018): https://www.nytimes.com/2017/06/30/us/handmaids-protests-abortion.html; Laura Bradley, "Under Their Eye: The Rise of Handmaid's Tale-Inspired Protests," *Vanity Fair* (October 9, 2018): https://www.vanityfair.com/hollywood/photos/2018/10/handmaids-tale-protests-kavanaugh-healthcare-womens-march

2. Margaret Atwood, *The Handmaid's Tale* (Boston: Houghton Mifflin, 1986), 156, 11. The television show's costume designer has called the outfits "walking wombs." Ane Crabtree, quoted in E. Alex Jung, "From the Handmaids to the Marthas, How Each Handmaid's Tale Costume Came Together," *Vulture* (April 28, 2017): https://www.vulture.com/2017/04/handmaids-tale-costumes-how-they-came-together.html

3. Atwood, *Handmaid's Tale*, 11.

4. Quoted in David Barnett, "Science Fiction: The Genre That Dare Not Speak Its Name," *The Guardian* (January 28, 2009): http://www.theguardian.com/books/booksblog/2009/jan/28/science-fiction-genre

5. Margaret Atwood, *In Other Worlds: SF and the Human Imagination* (New York: Anchor Books, 2011), 6.

6. See Jed Rubenfeld, "The Right of Privacy," *Harvard Law Review*, vol. 102, no. 4 (1989): 737–807.

7. Samuel D. Warren and Louis D. Brandeis, *Harvard Law Review*, vol. 4, no. 5 (1890): 195, 193, 205.

8. William L. Prosser, "Privacy," *California Law Review*, vol. 48, no. 3 (August 1960): 383–423.

9. Charles R. Epp, *The Rights Revolution: Lawyers, Activists, and Supreme Courts in Comparative Perspective* (Chicago: University of Chicago Press, 1998), 27. See also Mary

Ann Glendon, *Rights Talk: The Impoverishment of Political Discourse* (New York: Free Press, 1991).

10. Epp, *Rights Revolution*, especially 1–70.

11. Kermit L. Hall and John J. Patrick, *The Pursuit of Justice: Supreme Court Decisions That Shaped America* (New York: Oxford University Press, 2006), 156.

12. Sarah Igo, *The Known Citizen: A History of Privacy in Modern America* (Cambridge, MA: Harvard University Press, 2018), 152.

13. *Griswold v. Connecticut* 381 U.S. 479 (1965), 485.

14. Ibid., 483.

15. *Katz v. United States* 389 U.S. 347 (1967), 352.

16. *Eisenstadt v. Baird* 405 U.S. 438 (1972), 405.

17. *Roe v. Wade* 410 U.S. 113 (1973), 154.

18. Mary Ziegler, *Beyond Abortion:* Roe v. Wade *and the Battle for Privacy* (Cambridge, MA: Harvard University Press, 2018).

19. *Thornburgh v. American College of Obstetricians and Gynecologists* 476 U.S. 747 (1986) (Stevens, J. P., concurring). Stevens quotes from Charles Fried, "Correspondence," *Philosophy & Public Affairs*, vol. 6, no. 3 (Spring 1977): 288–289.

20. *Planned Parenthood of Southeastern Pa. v. Casey* 505 U.S. 833 (1992), 861.

21. Ironically, even as its rhetoric about privacy grew more expansive, *Casey* actually limited abortion rights; it upheld 24-hour waiting periods and informed consent as failing to impose an "undue burden" on women seeking to terminate a pregnancy.

22. Daniel Solove, *Understanding Privacy* (Cambridge, MA: Harvard University Press, 2008), 1–2.

23. See Catharine A. MacKinnon, "Privacy v. Equality: Beyond *Roe v. Wade* (1983)," in *Feminism Unmodified: Discourses on Life and Law* (Cambridge, MA: Harvard University Press, 1988).

24. See Lauren Berlant and Michael Warner, "Sex in Public," *Critical Inquiry*, vol. 42, no. 2 (Winter 1998): 547–556.

25. See, for instance, Patricia Ann Boling, *Privacy and the Politics of Intimate Life* (Ithaca, NY: Cornell University Press, 1996).

26. See Kristin Luker, *Abortion and the Politics of Motherhood* (Berkeley: University of California Press, 1985).

27. See Robert H. Bork, *The Tempting of America: The Political Seduction of the Law* (New York: Free Press, 1990), 95–100.

28. John Rawls, *Theory of Justice*, rev. ed. (Cambridge, MA: Harvard University Press, 1991), 3. On the link between Rawls and privacy, see Charles Fried, "Privacy," *Yale Law Journal*, vol. 77, no. 3 (1968): 475–493.

29. On Rawls as stemming from the midcentury moment and insulated from the

1960s social movements, see Katrina Forrester, *In the Shadow of Justice: Postwar Liberalism and the Remaking of Political Philosophy* (Princeton: Princeton University Press, 2019).

30. Betty Friedan, "Abortion: A Woman's Civil Right" (1969), in *Before Roe v. Wade*, eds. Linda Greenhouse and Reva Siegel (New York: Kaplan Publishing, 2010), 39, available at https://documents.law.yale.edu/sites/default/files/beforeroe2nded_1.pdf

31. Ziegler, *Beyond Abortion*, 40–81.

32. Dorothy E. Roberts, "Punishing Drug Addicts Who Have Babies: Women of Color and the Right to Privacy," *Harvard Law Review*, vol. 104, no. 7 (May 1991): 1419–1482. See also Imani Perry, *More Beautiful and More Terrible: The Embrace and Transcendence of Racial Equality in the United States* (New York: NYU Press, 2011), 85–126, who tries "To articulate the demand for a more robust privacy right for people of color in the United States" (88); and Anita L. Allen, "Coercing Privacy," *William & Mary Law Review*, vol. 40, no. 3 (March 1999), who argues that privacy could be consistent "both with liberalism and with the egalitarian aspirations of feminism" (729).

33. Glendon, *Rights Talk*, x.

34. See Elaine Tyler May, *Homeward Bound: American Families in the Cold War Era*, rev. ed. ([1988] New York: Basic Books, 2008); Alan Nadel, *Containment Culture: American Narratives, Postmodernism, and the Atomic Age* (Durham: Duke University Press, 1995); Deborah Nelson, *Pursuing Privacy in Cold War America* (New York: Columbia University Press, 2002), 1–42.

35. Igo, *The Known Citizen*, 99–144.

36. See my "Privacy Cultures," *Public Books* (July 25, 2018): https://www.publicbooks.org/privacy-cultures/

37. Lionel Trilling, *The Liberal Imagination* ([1950] New York: NYRB Classics, 2012); Ian Watt, *The Rise of the Novel: Studies in Defoe, Richardson, and Fielding* ([1957] Berkeley: University of California Press, 1962); Jürgen Habermas, *The Structural Transformation of the Public Sphere: An Inquiry into a Category of Bourgeois Society*, trans. Thomas Burger and Frederick Lawrence (Cambridge, MA: MIT Press, 1989); Martha C. Nussbaum, *Love's Knowledge: Essays in Philosophy and Literature* (New York: Oxford University Press, 1992); Lynn Hunt, *Inventing Human Rights: A History* (New York: Norton, 2007).

38. William Faulkner, "On Privacy: The American Dream: What Happened to It," *Harper's Magazine*, vol. 211, no. 1262 (July 1955): 36.

39. Larry McCaffery, "A Conversation with David Foster Wallace," *The Review of Contemporary Fiction*, vol. 13, no. 2 (Summer 1993), available at https://www.dalkeyarchive.com/a-conversation-with-david-foster-wallace-by-larry-mccaffery/. I have used Wallace's quote for its epigrammatic verve, but, to be fair, his bugaboo was more television than genre fiction. Indeed, he assigned works by writers like Stephen King and Larry

McMurtry in his class at Illinois State. See "Teaching Materials from the David Foster Wallace Archive," Harry Ransom Center, University of Texas, Austin: http://www.hrc.utexas.edu/press/releases/2010/dfw/teaching/

40. David Foster Wallace, "E Unibus Pluram: Television and U.S. Fiction," in *A Supposedly Fun Thing I'll Never Do Again: Essays and Arguments* (New York: Little Brown, 1997), 24.

41. Richard Powers, "Losing Our Souls, Bit by Bit," *New York Times* (July 15, 1998): A19; Jonathan Franzen, "Imperial Bedroom," *New Yorker* (October 12, 1998): 48–53.

42. Michael Wreszin, *Interviews with Dwight Macdonald* (Jackson: University Press of Mississippi, 2003), 38.

43. Mark McGurl, *The Program Era: Postwar Fiction and the Rise of Creative Writing* (Cambridge, MA: Harvard University Press, 2011), 26. Even as the mantra of the creative writing program shifted from the liberal emphasis on experience ("Write what you know") to one that better reflected the New Left celebration of authenticity ("Find your voice"), both were undergirded by an imagination of good fiction as an expression of the private self.

44. Edmund Wilson, "Why Do People Read Detective Stories?" *New Yorker* (October 14, 1944): 78–84.

45. Andrew Hoberek, "Cormac McCarthy and the Aesthetics of Exhaustion," *American Literary History*, vol. 23, no. 3 (Fall 2011): 483–499; and Nicholas Brown, *Autonomy: The Social Ontology of Art Under Capitalism* (Durham: Duke University Press, 2019), 79–115.

46. For a small sampling of this literature, see, on Shelley, Mary Poovey, *The Proper Lady and the Woman Writer: Ideology as Style in the Works of Mary Wollstonecraft, Mary Shelley, and Jane Austen* (Chicago: University of Chicago Press, 1984), 114–142; on Poe, Sean McCann, *Gumshoe America: Hard-Boiled Crime Fiction and the Rise and Fall of New Deal Liberalism* (Durham: Duke University Press, 2000); on Cooper, Jeffrey Insko, "The Logic of Left Alone: *The Pioneers* and the Conditions of U.S. Privacy," *American Literature*, vol. 81, no. 4 (December 2009): 659–685. If, as Rosen and Santesso have argued, the legal imagination of privacy, as most influentially formulated by Louis Brandeis, drew on Wordsworth, writers of genre fiction wrote in a lineage critical of that very strain of Romanticism. See David Rosen and Aaron Santesso, *The Watchman in Pieces: Surveillance, Literature, and Liberal Personhood* (New Haven: Yale University Press, 2013), 105–157.

47. Theodore Martin, *Contemporary Drift: Genre Historicism and the Problem of the Present* (New York: Columbia University Press, 2017).

48. See Ellen Moers, "Female Gothic: The Monster's Mother," *New York Review of Books* (March 21, 1974).

49. E. M. Forster, *Aspects of the Novel* (New York: Harcourt, Brace, 1927), 103, 104.

50. See, for this view on realism, Franco Moretti, *The Bourgeois: Between History and*

Literature (London: Verso, 2013), 67–101. On the relationship between allegory and genre fiction and privacy, see Rosen and Santesso, *The Watchman in Pieces*, 157–223.

51. For the former, see Ellen Moers, "Female Gothic: The Monster's Mother," *New York Review of Books* (March 21, 1974): http://www.nybooks.com/articles/1974/03/21/female-gothic-the-monsters-mother/. For the latter, see Sandra M. Gilbert and Susan Gubar, *The Madwoman in the Attic: The Woman Writer and the Nineteenth- Century Imagination*, 2nd ed. (New Haven and London: Yale University Press, 2000), 213–247. See also Mary Poovey, "'My Hideous Progeny': The Lady and the Monster," in *The Proper Lady and the Woman Writer*, 114–143.

52. For the former view, see Walter Benn Michaels, "Romance and Real Estate," in *The Gold Standard and the Logic of Naturalism: American Literature at the Turn of the Century* (Berkeley: University of California Press, 1987); for the latter, see Meredith L. McGill, *American Literature and the Culture of Reprinting, 1834–1853* (Philadelphia: University of Pennsylvania Press, 2013), 218–269.

53. For authors who endorse this viewpoint, see Hunt, *Inventing Human Rights*; Nussbaum, *Love's Knowledge*; and Richard Rorty, *Contingency, Irony, and Solidarity* (Cambridge, UK: Cambridge University Press, 1989). For those who critique it as ideology, see Nancy Armstrong, *Desire and Domestic Fiction: A Political History of the Novel* (Oxford: Oxford University Press, 1987); Gillian Brown, *Domestic Individualism: Imagining Self in Nineteenth Century America* (Berkeley: University of California Press, 1990); Lauren Berlant, "The Subject of True Feeling: Pain, Privacy and Politics," in *Cultural Pluralism, Identity Politics, and the Law* (Ann Arbor: University of Michigan Press, 1999), 49–84; and Rachel Greenwald Smith, *Affect and American Literature in the Age of Neoliberalism* (Cambridge, UK: Cambridge University Press, 2015).

54. On the importance of James and on the term "New Ethics," see Dorothy Hale, *The Novel and the New Ethics* (Stanford: Stanford University Press, 2020).

55. As C. Namwali Serpell writes in *Seven Modes of Uncertainty* (Cambridge, MA: Harvard University Press, 2014), "after decades of imperatives to honor the Other, every text seems to give back the same old Otherness" (297). For some notable critiques of the discourse of sentiment, see Suzanne Keen, *Empathy and the Novel* (Oxford: Oxford University Press, 2010) and Berlant, "The Subject of True Feeling."

56. Charlotte Perkins Gilman, "The Right to Die—I," *Forum and Century*, vol. 94 (November 1935): 299.

57. For the traditional view, with respect to horror, see, for instance, Franco Moretti, "The Dialectic of Fear," *New Left Review*, 136 (November–December 1982): 67–85, and Robin Wood, "The American Nightmare: Horror in the 1970s," *Hollywood from Vietnam to Reagan* (New York: Columbia University Press, 1986), 70–94. For science fiction, consider N. Katherine Hayles, *How We Became Posthuman: Virtual Bodies in Cybernetics,*

Literature, and Informatics (Chicago: University of Chicago Press, 1999); Donna Haraway, "The Cyborg Manifesto," in *The Cybercultures Reader*, eds. David Bell and Barbara M. Kennedy (New York: Routledge, 2000), 291–323; and Fredric Jameson, *Archaeologies of the Future: The Desire Called Utopia and Other Science Fictions* (New York: Verso, 2005). For a notable and early exception, which sees horror as "craft art," see Ann Douglas, "The Dream of the Wise Child: Freud's 'Family Romance' Revisited in Contemporary Narratives of Horror," *Prospects*, vol. 9 (October 1984): 293–348. For more recent accounts, see Martin, *Contemporary Drift*; and Annie McClanahan, *Dead Pledges: Debt, Crisis, and Twenty-First Century Culture* (Stanford: Stanford University Press, 2017), 143–185.

58. For recent, insightful attempts in literary studies to rehabilitate the value of privacy independent of genre fiction, see Katie Fitzpatrick, "Love Actuarially: Privacy, Intimacy, and Information in The Apartment," *Post45* (February 3, 2016): http://post45.research.yale.edu/2016/02/love-actuarially-privacy-intimacy-and-information-in-the-apartment/; Scott Selisker, "The Novel and WikiLeaks: Transparency and the Social Life of Privacy," *American Literary History*, vol. 30, no. 4 (2018): 756–776; and Rosen and Santesso, *The Watchman in Pieces*, though Rosen and Santesso ultimately reproduce the empathy argument I critique here.

59. Shoshana Zuboff, *The Age of Surveillance Capitalism: The Fight for a Human Future at the New Frontier of Power* (New York: Hachette, 2020), 7.

Chapter 1

1. Patricia Highsmith, Cahier 26 (February 9, 1961), Patricia Highsmith Papers, Swiss Literary Archives, Bern.

2. Patricia Highsmith, "First-Person Novel" (1961), 6, Patricia Highsmith Papers, Swiss Literary Archives, Bern.

3. Andrew Wilson, *Beautiful Shadow: A Life of Patricia Highsmith* (New York: Bloomsbury, 2003), 157.

4. On the association between psychopathy and homosexuality, see Lionel Trilling, *The Liberal Imagination* ([1950] New York: NYRB Classics, 2012), 240.

5. On the relationship between the confessional form and privacy, see Deborah Nelson, *Pursuing Privacy in Cold War America* (New York: Columbia University Press, 2002).

6. Patricia Highsmith, Cahier 19 (May 17, 1950), Patricia Highsmith Papers, Swiss Literary Archives, Bern.

7. Patricia Highsmith, Cahier 17 (April 25, 1948), Patricia Highsmith Papers, Swiss Literary Archives, Bern.

8. On Highsmith as embracing the fantasy of the closet, see Michael Trask, *Camp Sites: Sex, Politics, and Academic Style in Postwar America* (Stanford: Stanford University Press, 2013), 119–149,

9. A number of critics have insightfully pointed out how crime or detective fiction constructed the idea of white heterosexual masculinity, which often depended on its opposite terms—queer culture and femininity. These critics tend to focus on male-authored novels, but viewing these three female practitioners in the same chapter reveals how this masculine-oriented space was the perfect vessel for the three female practitioners considered here to secrete ideas about femininity and queer sexuality. On the culture of masculinity within noir novels, see Erin Smith, *Hard-Boiled: Working-Class Readers and Pulp Magazines* (Philadelphia: Temple University Press, 2000); Megan Abbott, *The Street Was Mine: White Masculinity in Hardboiled Fiction and Film Noir* (New York: Palgrave Macmillan, 2002); and Leonard Cassuto, *Hard-Boiled Sentimentality: The Secret History of American Crime Stories* (New York: Columbia University Press, 2009). On straight characters as unstably defined against queer ones in the detective novel, see Richard Dyer, "Homosexuality in Film Noir," *Jump Cut*, no. 16 (1977), 18–21; Robert Corbier, *Homosexuality in Cold War America: Resistance and the Crisis of Masculinity* (Durham: Duke University Press, 1997), 12; and Len Gutkin, *Dandyism: Forming Fiction from Modernism to the Present* (University of Virginia Press, 2000).

10. Sean McCann, *Gumshoe America: Hard-Boiled Crime Fiction and the Fall of New Deal Liberalism* (Durham: Duke University Press, 2000), 1–39.

11. David Riesman, with Nathan Glazer and Reuel Denney, *The Lonely Crowd: A Study of the Changing American Character*, abridged and rev. ed. (New Haven: Yale University Press, 1961), 43.

12. William H. Whyte, Jr., *The Organization Man* (Philadelphia: University of Pennsylvania Press, 2000), 352.

13. C. Wright Mills, *The Sociological Imagination* (Oxford: Oxford University Press, 1959), 3.

14. Vance Packard, *The Naked Society* (New York: Ig Publishing, 1964).

15. *Griswold v. Connecticut* 381 U.S. 479 (1965), 484, 479, 494.

16. *Eisenstadt v. Baird* 405 U.S. 438 (1972), 454.

17. *Griswold v. Connecticut*, 485–486.

18. See Elaine Tyler May, *Homeward Bound: American Families in the Cold War Era* (New York: Basic Books, 1988), 89–129.

19. David K. Johnson, *The Lavender Scare: The Cold War Persecution of Gays and Lesbians in the Federal Government* (Chicago: University of Chicago Press, 2004), 41–65.

20. On privacy as defending spousal rape, see Michael Gary Hilf, "Marital Privacy and Spousal Rape," *New England Law Review*. vol. 16, no. 31 (1980): 31–44; on excluding homosexuality, see *Bowers v. Hardwick* 478 U.S. 186 (1986).

21. Betty Friedan, *The Feminine Mystique* ([1963] New York: Norton, 2001), 349, 479.

22. Laud Humphries, *Tearoom Trade* (New Brunswick, NJ: AldineTransaction, 1970), enlarged ed., 12.

23. Trilling, *Liberal Imagination*, 222.

24. Ibid., xix.

25. On Trilling, see Amanda Anderson, *Bleak Liberalism* (Chicago: University of Chicago Press, 2016), 99–115.

26. W. K. Wimsatt, *The Verbal Icon: Studies in the Meaning of Poetry* (Lexington: University Press of Kentucky, 1954), 95.

27. Wayne Booth, *Rhetoric of Fiction* ([1961] Chicago: University of Chicago Press, 1983), 378.

28. Harold C. Gardiner, *Norms for the Novel*, rev. ed. (Garden City, NY: Hanover House, 1960), 22.

29. See Trilling, *Liberal Imagination*, 58–93, and Booth, *Rhetoric of Fiction*, 339–377.

30. Ian Watt, *The Rise of the Novel: Studies in Defoe, Richardson, and Fielding* ([1957] Berkeley: University of California Press, 1962), 201, 199.

31. Jürgen Habermas, *The Structural Transformation of the Public Sphere: An Inquiry into a Category of Bourgeois Society*, trans. Thomas Burger and Frederick Lawrence (Cambridge, MA: MIT Press, 1989), 49–50, 172.

32. Lionel Trilling, *Sincerity and Authenticity* (Cambridge, MA: Harvard University Press, 1971), 25, 74.

33. Booth, *Rhetoric of Fiction*, 395.

34. Dwight Macdonald, "Masscult & Midcult," *Against the American Grain* (New York: DaCapo, 1962), 5.

35. Henry James, "The Art of Fiction," *Longman's Magazine* (September 1884): 520. On the persistence of James, see Dorothy Hale, "Aesthetics and the New Ethics: Theorizing the Novel in the Twenty-First Century," *PMLA*, vol. 124, no. 3 (2009): 896–905. On James and the art-novel, see Mark McGurl, *The Novel Art* (Princeton: Princeton University Press, 2001).

36. Of course, another reading of James has him deeply invested in mass culture and commodity form; it was perhaps this James to whom Highsmith turned in her own writing. See Jean-Christophe Agnew, "The Consuming Vision of Henry James," in *The Culture of Consumption: Critical Essays in American History, 1880–1890*, eds. Richard Wightman Fox and T. J. Jackson Lears (New York: Pantheon Books, 1983), 67–100.

37. Irving Howe, "Notes on Mass Culture," in *Mass Culture: The Popular Arts in America*, eds. Bernard Rosenberg and David Manning White (London: The Free Press of Glencoe, 1957), 497, 503.

38. Edmund Wilson, "Why Do People Read Detective Stories?" *New Yorker*

(October 14, 1944): http://www.newyorker.com/magazine/1944/10/14/why-do-people-read-detective-stories

39. Crime fiction had defenders in the period as well. See, for instance, W. H. Auden, "The Guilty Vicarage," *Harper's Magazine* (May 1948): 406–412; or Louise Bogan, "The Time of the Assassins," in *Selected Criticism: Prose, Poetry* (New York: Noonday Press, 1955); or for genre fiction more broadly, Leslie Fiedler, contribution to "Our Country and Our Culture," *Partisan Review*, vol. 19, no. 3 (May–June 1952): 296. Even Auden, though, was not prepared to defend the villain-focused noir novel and treated detective fiction as a form of escape.

40. See Trilling's review of *Lolita*: Lionel Trilling, "The Last Lover," *Encounter* (October 1958): 14.

41. Trilling, *Liberal Imagination*, 241.

42. See Jeff Solomon, "Capote and the Trillings: Homophobia and Literary Culture at Midcentury," *Twentieth Century Literature*, vol. 54, no. 2 (Summer 2008): 129–165.

43. See Karen Halttunen, *Murder Most Foul: The Killer and the American Gothic Imagination* (Cambridge, MA: Harvard University Press, 2000), 1–90.

44. McCann, *Gumshoe America*, 1–39.

45. See Trilling, "The Last Lover," 14.

46. Dorothy Belle Flanagan, "Circe," in *Dark Certainty* (New Haven: Yale University Press, 1931), 62.

47. Ibid., 65, 19.

48. Dorothy B. Hughes, Interview by Rose Diaz (March 1989), El Paso, Texas, CD 6, Box 1, Oral History Interview with Dorothy B. Hughes, Special Collections and Center for Southwest Research, University of New Mexico Libraries. By permission of Gagency LLC.

49. Ibid.

50. Dorothy B. Hughes, *In a Lonely Place* (New York: Duell, Sloan and Pierce, 1947); republished in *Women Crime Writers: Four Suspense Novels of the 1940s*, ed. Sarah Weinman (New York: Library of America, 2015), 411, 395, 460–461, 477, 466. Hereafter cited from *Women Crime Writers: 1940s* parenthetically in the text.

51. On Laurel and Sylvia as female detectives, see Megan Abbott, "Dorothy B. Hughes and the Birth of American Noir," *The Paris Review* (August 1, 2017): https://www.theparisreview.org/blog/2017/08/01/origins-american-noir-2/

52. E. H. Mikhail, *J. M. Synge: Interviews and Recollections* (London: Macmillan, 1977), 22–30.

53. Quoted in Tom Nolan, *Ross Macdonald: A Biography* (New York: Simon & Schuster, 1999), Kindle Edition.

54. Sally Ogle Davis, "Through Illness, Millar Writes, Lives with Vigor," *Los Angeles Times* (September 12, 1983): F5.

55. Margaret Millar, *Beast in View* (New York: Random House, 1955); republished in *Women Crime Writers: Four Suspense Novels of the 1950s*, ed. Sarah Weinman (New York: Library of America, 2015), 397, 515. Hereafter cited from *Women Crime Writers: 1950s* parenthetically in the text.

56. *Katz v. United States* 389 U.S. 347 (1967), 361.

57. Muriel Rukeyser, *Beast in View* (Garden City, NY: Doubleday, 1944), 53.

58. Joan Schenkar, *The Talented Miss Highsmith: The Secret Life and Serious Art of Patricia Highsmith* (New York: St. Martin's Press, 2009), 133.

59. Wilson, *Beautiful Shadow*, 94.

60. Ibid.; Schenkar, *Talented Miss Highsmith*, 126.

61. Quoted in Schenkar, *Talented Miss Highsmith*, 13.

62. Wilson, *Beautiful Shadow*, 137.

63. Patricia Highsmith, Letter to Kate "Kingsley" Skattebol (June 14, 1952), Patricia Highsmith Papers, Swiss Literary Archives, Bern.

64. Patricia Highsmith, Cahier 22 (October 29, 1953), Patricia Highsmith Papers, Swiss Literary Archives, Bern.

65. Patricia Highsmith, Cahier 20, undated, Patricia Highsmith Papers, Swiss Literary Archives, Bern; William Faulkner's Nobel Prize speech, delivered December 10, 1950, in Stockholm, is available at https://www.nobelprize.org/prizes/literature/1949/faulkner/speech/ On Faulkner and the crisis of "man," see Mark Greif, *The Age of the Crisis of Man: Thought and Fiction in America, 1933–1973* (Princeton: Princeton University Press, 2015), 103–143.

66. Schenkar, *Talented Miss Highsmith*, 261.

67. Patricia Highsmith, *The Price of Salt* ([1952] New York: Dover, 2015), 240.

68. See Tom Perrin, "Rebuilding *Bildung*: The Middlebrow Novel of Aesthetic Education in the Mid-Twentieth-Century United States," *Novel*, vol. 44, no. 3 (2011): 382–401.

69. Highsmith, *Price of Salt*, 248–249.

70. Quoted in Schenkar, *Talented Miss Highsmith*, 282.

71. Ibid., 252.

72. Patricia Highsmith, "The Snail-Watcher," in *Eleven* ([1970] New York: Grove Press, 2011), 2.

73. Patricia Highsmith, Cahier 19 (June 30, 1950), Patricia Highsmith Papers, Swiss Literary Archives, Bern.

74. Highsmith, "The Snail-Watcher," 1.

75. Ibid., 3.

76. Ibid., 4.

77. Ibid., 7.

78. Susan Sontag, *Against Interpretation and Other Essays* (New York: Picador, 1961), 275–293; Trask, *Camp Sites*, 7.

79. Patricia Highsmith, *The Talented Mr. Ripley* ([1955] New York: Norton, 2008), 175. Hereafter cited parenthetically in the text.

80. On Highsmith and middlebrow culture, see Perrin, "Rebuilding *Bildung*," 381–401; and "Coward-McCann, Inc.," *Open Library*: https://openlibrary.org/publishers/Coward-McCann,_inc.

81. As Frank Rich commented about the film version of *Ripley*: "Ripley is an unmistakable descendant of Gatsby, that 'penniless young man without a past' who will stop at nothing to will his romantic idol, Daisy, into believing he is of her class." Frank Rich, "The Talented Mr. Minghella," *The Guardian* (January 23, 2000): http://www.theguardian.com/film/2000/jan/23/1

82. David Halperin, *How to Be Gay* (Cambridge, MA: Harvard University Press, 2012), 140.

83. Eve Kosofsky Sedgwick, *Touching Feeling: Affect, Pedagogy, Performativity* (Durham: Duke University Press, 2003), 150–151.

84. Wilson, *Beautiful Shadow*, 165.

85. Yvonne Keller, "'Was It Right to Love Her Brother's Wife So Passionately?': Lesbian Pulp Novels and U.S. Lesbian Identity, 1950–1965," *American Quarterly*, vol. 57, no. 2 (June 2005): 385–410.

86. On the urinals and G-strings, see Trask, *Camp Sites*, 148.

87. See Loren Glass, "Redeeming Value: Obscenity and Anglo-American Modernism," *Critical Inquiry*, vol. 32, no. 2 (Winter 2006): 341–361.

88. McGurl, *Novel Art*, 12; Quoted in Perrin, "Rebuilding *Bildung*," 386.

89. Patricia Highsmith, *Ripley Under Ground* (New York: Norton, 2008), 78.

90. Quoted in Schenkar, *Talented Miss Highsmith*, 344.

91. Highsmith, *Ripley Under Ground*, 71.

92. Trilling, *Liberal Imagination*, 222.

93. Truman Capote, *In Cold Blood* (New York: Vintage, 1965), 91.

94. Ibid., 343.

95. Trask, *Camp Sites*, 147.

96. As Fredric Jameson observes, in the modernist, Jamesian art-novel, "we are so fully sealed into the protagonist's consciousness that we can scarcely see them from the outside." Fredric Jameson, *The Antinomies of Realism* (New York: Verso, 2013), 183.

97. Patricia Highsmith, *The Animal-Lover's Book of Beastly Murder* ([1975] New York: Norton, 2002), 157.

98. See McGurl, *Novel Art*, 4.

99. Eve Kosofsky Sedgwick, *Epistemology of the Closet* (Berkeley: University of California Press, 1990), 182–213.

Chapter 2

1. Chester Himes, Letter to Henry Lee Moon (June 27, 1941), Schomburg Center for Research in Black Culture, Box 3, Folder 342. Used with the permission of the estate of Chester B. Himes.

2. Chester Himes, Letter to Carl Van Vechten (December 16, 1954), Carl Van Vechten Papers, Box 13, Folder 325, Beinecke Library, Yale University, New Haven, CT. Used with the permission of the estate of Chester B. Himes.

3. Langston Hughes, Letter to Maurice Murphy (October 11, 1941), Loren Miller Papers, Box 3, Folder 6, Huntington Library, San Marino, CA.

4. Chester Himes, Letter to Henry Lee and Mollie Moon (May 25, 1942), Henry Lee and Mollie Moon Archive, Schomberg Center for Research in Black Culture, New York Public Library, Box 3, Folder 342. Used with the permission of the estate of Chester B. Himes.

5. Chester Himes, Interview with Michael Mok, in *Conversations with Chester Himes*, eds. Michael Fabre and Robert Skinner (Jackson: University of Mississippi Press, 1995), 107. Himes would sometimes misremember if the real-life Coffin Ed and Grave Digger were in Chicago or L.A., but he claimed that Kimbrough and his partner were "the most brutal cops I ever heard of." He saw his achievement as humanizing Kimbrough: "I took two people who would be anti-black in real life, and made them sympathetic." "Most black cops," he claimed, "are brutal and reactionary." Chester Himes, Interview with Michael Fabre, 1970, in *Conversations*, 85. In some ways, I read Himes's cops differently than his statements here: the historical record suggests that Kimbrough was less reactionary than Himes claimed.

6. This connection was recently unearthed in Lawrence P. Jackson, *Chester B. Himes: A Biography* (New York: Norton, 2017), 149, 158, 376. Himes claims that one of the cops shot and killed his partner in a duel over a woman, but both Kimbrough and his long-time partner Charles Broady survived well past Kimbrough's retirement in 1939. See Himes, *Conversations*, 27, 104, 107, 143. R. J. Smith argues that the real-life cops were Charles Broady and Carl Kimbro, but Kimbro too survived past his retirement (he was convicted of racketeering in the 1940s). See R. J. Smith, *The Great Black Way: L.A. in the 1940s and the Lost African-American Renaissance* (New York: Perseus, 2006), 114. In light of Himes's mention of brutality, a more remote possibility might be the notorious African American officers Maceo Sheffield and Frank Randolph. Sheffield did shoot Randolph in the arm in 1927, while drunk during a liquor raid in which he killed Samuel Faulkner. See Kelly Lytle Hernandez, *City of Inmates: Conquest, Caging, and Rebellion* (Chapel Hill: University of North Carolina Press, 2017), 158–194.

7. On race and privacy, see Simone Browne, *Dark Matters: On the Surveillance of Blackness* (Durham: Duke University Press, 2015).

8. Sarah Igo, *The Known Citizen: A History of Privacy in Modern America* (Cambridge, MA: Harvard University Press, 2018), 178–179.

9. For more, see Dorothy Roberts, *Killing the Black Body* (New York: Pantheon, 1997).

10. *Terry v. Ohio* 392 U.S. 1 (1968); see Michelle Alexander, *The New Jim Crow: Mass Incarceration in the Age of Colorblindness* (New York: The New Press, 2010), 59–97.

11. On the relationship between the War on Poverty and the War on Crime, see Naomi Murakawa, *The First Civil Right: How Liberals Built Prison America* (Oxford: Oxford University Press, 2014), and Elizabeth Hinton, *From the War on Poverty to the War on Crime* (Cambridge, MA: Harvard University Press, 2016). On the curtailment of the Fourth Amendment after 1968, see Alexander, *The New Jim Crow*, 61–75.

12. James Forman, Jr., *Locking Up Our Own: Crime and Punishment in Black America* (New York: Farrar, Straus, and Giroux, 2017), 78–119.

13. See Hernandez, *City of Inmates*, 186–188.

14. An interesting and mostly forgotten exception to the trend would be Christopher St. John's *Top of the Heap* (1972). These representations of Black cops were taken up by 1980s rappers like N.W.A. and KRS-One, who attacked the violence of Black cops and glorified drug dealers and users in songs like "Fuck the Police" and "Black Cop."

15. Sean McCann, *Gumshoe America: Hard-Boiled Crime Fiction and the Fall of New Deal Liberalism* (Durham: Duke University Press, 2000), 282.

16. Hilton Als, "In Black and White," *New Yorker* (June 4, 2001): https://www.newyorker.com/magazine/2001/06/04/in-black-and-white

17. Michael Denning argues that Himes's police officers allow him to dramatize the absurdity and pointlessness of everyday violence and state-sponsored law enforcement. Sean McCann contends that Himes's officers represent his confidence in the visions of solidarity of the New Deal state, which erodes as time goes on. Most recently, Margaret Gram argues that Himes participated in the civil rights–era strategy of "selective statism," a provisional alliance with the government to achieve certain race-centered policies, without completely embracing it. Michael Denning, "Topographies of Violence: Chester Himes' Harlem Domestic Novels," *Critical Texts: A Review of Theory and Criticism*, Special Issue on Popular Culture, ed. Eric Lott, vol. 1 (1988): 10–18. McCann, *Gumshoe America*, 251–305. Margaret Gram, "Chester Himes and the Capacities of State," *Studies in American Fiction*, vol. 39, no. 2 (Fall 2012): 243–268. On surrealism, see Jonathan Eburne, "The Transatlantic Mysteries of Paris: Chester Himes, Surrealism, and the Série Noire," *PMLA*, vol. 120, no. 3 (May 2005): 806–821.

18. Khalil Gibran Muhammad, *The Condemnation of Blackness: Race, Crime, and the Making of Modern Urban America* (Cambridge, MA: Harvard University Press, 2010).

Likewise, Paula Massood describes how visual imagery of Harlem in the 1950s further linked race and crime: "The problem for African Americans at this time may have been the white man, but for the nation as a whole, the problem of the inner city—-and the color line more broadly—was most often embodied by black male youth engaged in criminal activity." Paula J. Massood, *Making a Promised Land: Harlem in Twentieth-Century Photography and Film* (New Brunswick, NJ: Rutgers University Press, 2013), 124–125. Jean-Christophe Cloutier has also chronicled how both Ralph Ellison and Frantz Fanon complained about the representation of Black characters as villains in the comic books of the period. Jean-Christophe Cloutier, *Shadow Archives: The Lifecycles of African American Literature* (New York: Columbia University Press, 2019), 253.

19. Theodore Martin, "Crime Fiction and Black Criminality," *American Literary History*, vol. 30, no. 4 (Winter 2018): 705.

20. Gunnar Myrdal, *An American Dilemma: The Negro Problem and Modern Democracy*, vol. 2 ([1944] New Brunswick, NJ: Transaction, 1996), 763. As Naomi Murakawa has shown, the cultural conjunction of race and criminality as epitomized by the Myrdal reading of Bigger also had a profound effect on the anti-crime legislation that would lead up to mass incarceration. Murakawa, *The First Civil Right*, 13.

21. Myrdal, *An American Dilemma*, 969.

22. Daryl Michael Scott, *Contempt and Pity: Social Policy and the Image of the Damaged Black Psyche, 1880–1996* (Chapel Hill: University of North Carolina Press, 1997).

23. Ralph Ellison, "Going to the Territory," in *The Collected Essays of Ralph Ellison* (New York: Modern Library, 1995), 710.

24. Hughes Allison, "Corollary," *Ellery Queen's Mystery Magazine* (July 1948): 92.

25. Quoted in Sarah Weinman, "The Case of the Disappearing Black Detective Novel," *New Republic* (December 8, 2015): https://newrepublic.com/article/124468/case-disappearing-black-detective-novel

26. Chester Himes, *If He Hollers Let Him Go* ([1945] New York: Thunder's Mouth Press, 1986), 87–88.

27. Lloyd L. Brown, "'White Flag,' Review of *The Lonely Crusade*," *New Masses* (September 9, 1947): 18–20.

28. Chester Himes, "The Dilemma of the Negro Novelist in the U.S.," in *Beyond the Angry Black*, ed. John A. Williams (New York: Cooper Square Publishers, 1966), 53–54.

29. Chester Himes, *The End of a Primitive* (New York: Norton, 1997), 62.

30. While Jonathan Eburne reads the moment of one of reciprocal influence (Himes had already contemplated a crime novel of sorts, and Duhamel was familiar with Himes's work), I argue that his contemporary letter to Carl Van Vechten is probably the most accurate account of the exchange rather than the later accounts on which Eburne relies. See Himes, Letter to Van Vechten (December 16, 1954).

31. Richard Marsten, *Runaway Black* (New York: Gold Medal, 1954), 4.

32. Ibid., 77.

33. Gertrude Martin, "Book Reviews by Gertrude Martin," *Chicago Defender* (July 31, 1954): 7.

34. "First Novel Has Harlem for Locale," *Philadelphia Tribune* (September 11, 1954): 4

35. Marsten, *Runaway Black,* 94.

36. Ibid., 96.

37. Jackson, *Himes: A Biography*, 346.

38. Chester Himes, Letter to William Targ (September 13, 1965), Chester Himes Papers, Box 22, Folder 232, Beinecke Library, Yale University, New Haven, CT. Used with the permission of the estate of Chester B. Himes.

39. William Faulkner, Preface to *Sanctuary* (New York: Modern Library, 1932), v. On *Sanctuary* as a barbed modernist indictment of mass culture, see Peter Lurie, *Vision's Immanence* (Baltimore: Johns Hopkins University Press, 2004), 25–68.

40. Himes, *Conversations*, 137.

41. William Faulkner, *Sanctuary: The Corrected Text* ([1931] New York: Vintage, 1993), 3.

42. Chester Himes, *The Crazy Kill* (New York: Vintage, 1959), 78.

43. Faulkner, *Sanctuary,* 112 (1993 edition).

44. Ibid., 113.

45. Ibid.

46. Ibid.

47. Chester Himes, "He Knew," *Abbott's Weekly and Illustrated News* (December 2, 1933): 15.

48. Grave Digger tells his boss Lieutenant Anderson that there are only three ways to solve crime: "Make the criminals pay for it—you don't want to do that; pay the people enough to live decently—you ain't going to do that; so all that's left is let 'em eat one another up." See Chester Himes, *Cotton Comes to Harlem* ([1964] New York: Knopf, 2011), 14.

49. Jess L. Kimbrough, Interview with Joseph Woods (March 21, 1972), Donated Oral Histories Collection, Box 22, Folder 5, UCLA Library Special Collections, Los Angeles. See also, for Kimbrough's life, Sgt. John Thomas, "Defender of the Angels: Jesse L. Kimbrough," *The Link,* vol. 5, no. 1 (February 1998): 3–12. I gratefully acknowledge Kenneth Parris for granting permission to quote from this and other unpublished Kimbrough excerpts in this chapter.

50. Jess Kimbrough, Letter to T. Rokotov (February 11, 1938), Fund 1397, inv. 1, doc. 847—22 folios, Russian State Archive of Literature and Art, Moscow.

51. Kimbrough, Interview with Woods.

52. See Ernest Fredrick Anderson, *The Development of Leadership and Organization Building in the Black Community of Los Angeles from 1900 Through World War II* (PhD

dissertation, University of Southern California, June 1976), 136. Jess Kimbrough, "Convention Night," *The Clipper* (November 1940): 19–21.

53. See Gerald Woods, *The Police in Los Angeles: Reform and Professionalization* (New York: Garland, 1993), 41.

54. Daniel Widener, *Black Arts West* (Durham: Duke University Press, 2010), 36.

55. On the league and its relation to the Communist Party, see Judy Kutulas, "Becoming 'More Liberal': The League of American Writers, the Communist Party, and the Literary People's Front," *Journal of American Culture* (1990): 71–80. On Kimbrough's involvement, see Franklin Folsom, *Days of Anger, Days of Hope: A Memoir of the League of American Writers, 1937-1942* (Niwot: University Press of Colorado, 1994), 299.

56. See Lawrence De Graaf, "The City of Black Angels: Emergence of the Los Angeles Ghetto, 1890–1930," *Pacific History Review* (January 1970): 323–352; Regina Freer, "L.A. Race Woman: Charlotta Bass and the Complexities of Black Political Development in Los Angeles," *American Quarterly*, vol. 56, no. 3 (September 2004): 607–632; Douglas Flamming, *Bound for Freedom: Black Los Angeles in Jim Crow America* (Berkeley: University of California Press, 2005), 259–295.

57. In the culminating scene of his novel *Defender of the Angels* (which I discuss in the following), Kimbrough realizes that a local crime boss has more power than the police.

58. Chester Himes, *A Rage in Harlem* ([1957] New York: Vintage, 1991), Kindle Edition.

59. See Thomas, "Defender of the Angels."

60. Issues of the *California Eagle* can be found at https://archive.org/details/caleagle.

61. "Bank Bandit Capture After Long Chase," *California Eagle* (February 26, 1926).

62. "Patrolmen Save Embalmer from Would-be Robbers," *California Eagle* (November 23, 1938).

63. "Fiend Attacks Young Girl with Knife," *California Eagle* (May 23, 1930).

64. Himes, *A Rage in Harlem*, Kindle Edition.

65. Chester Himes, *The Crazy Kill* (New York: Vintage, 1959), Kindle Edition.

66. Himes, *Conversations*, 47.

67. Ibid., 144.

68. Homer F. Broome, *LAPD's Black History, 1886–1976* (Broome, 1978), 77.

69. "Bring No Proof: Delegation Complain About Conduct of a Policeman," *Los Angeles Times* (February 20, 1916); "Vindication for Negro Policeman: Police Commission Says He Saw Duty and Did It," *California Eagle* (March 28, 1916).

70. Quoted in David P. Wolcott, *Cops and Kids: Policing Juvenile Delinquency in Urban America, 1890–1940* (Columbus: Ohio State University Press, 2005), 147; Kimbrough, Interview with Woods.

71. Jesse Kimbrough, "The Psychology of the Negro Criminal," *Municipal Employee* (March–April 1925): 23–24, 50–51.

72. Jess Kimbrough, "The Lure of the Black Belt," *Flash*, vol. 2, no. 33 (December 31, 1929): 30–31.

73. Jess Kimbrough, Letter to T. Rokotov (October 4, 1937).

74. Ibid.; Jess Kimbrough, Letter to T. Rokotov (August 6, 1938). These novels turned out to be too didactic even for the Soviet realists. Timofei Rokotov, editor of *International Literature*, noted in his rejection letter for his second novel that his work was insufficiently "literary," that there were too many "monologues" of "moral-instructive character," and that there was too much gratuitous sex, appealing to an American audience but not to a Soviet one.

75. Jess Kimbrough, "Humpy," *The Clipper* (January 1941): 21–23.

76. J. Kimbrough, *Georgia Sundown: A Drama in One Act* (Los Angeles: Theatre Journal Publishing, 1940), 36, 38.

77. Jess Kimbrough, *Enoch Dawson*, unpublished manuscript, private collection of Kenneth Parris, Lemon Grove, CA; Jess Kimbrough, *A Kitchen in Sandton*, unpublished manuscript, private collection of Kenneth Parris, Lemon Grove, CA.

78. Alan Rinzler, Interview with author, by telephone (October 11, 2019). Quotation used with permission of Alan Rinzler, consulting editor: https://alanrinzler.com/

79. Charles Champlin, "Ernest Tidyman Lifts the Curse," *Los Angeles Times* (January 21, 1972): H1.

80. See Aya de Leon, "The Black Detective in the White Mind," *Armchair Detective*, vol. 26, no. 4 (Fall 1993): 34–39.

81. Adina Williamson, Letter to Jess Kimbrough (August 16, 1986), private collection of Kenneth Parris, Lemon Grove, CA.

82. Kimbrough, Interview with Woods.

83. Ibid.

84. Jess Kimbrough, *Defender of the Angels: A Black Policeman in Old Los Angeles* (New York: Macmillan, 1969), 7.

85. For contemporary views of LAPD officers on race, see *Law Enforcement in Los Angeles Police Department* (August Vollmer, Chief), Annual Report, 1924 (New York: Arno Press, 1974), 23, 162, 174.

86. Kimbrough, *Defender of the Angels*, viii–ix.

87. Ibid., 257.

88. Ibid., 52.

89. Ibid., 267.

90. Eburne, "The Transatlantic Mysteries of Paris," 813.

91. Chester Himes, *The Real Cool Killers* ([1959] New York: Vintage, 1988), 19.

92. Chester Himes, *Cotton Comes to Harlem* (New York: Random House, 1965), 83, 146.

93. Himes, *Real Cool Killers*, 13.

94. Ibid., 135.

95. Chester Himes, *The Heat's On* (New York: Vintage, 1966), 101.

96. Ibid., 25.

97. Chester Himes, *The Quality of Hurt: The Autobiography of Chester Himes*, vol. 1 (New York: Thunder's Mouth Press, 1971), 11.

98. Himes, "Dilemma of the Negro Novelist," 55.

99. Chester Himes, *My Life of Absurdity: The Autobiography of Chester Himes*, vol. 2 (New York: Doubleday, 1976), 102.

100. Chester Himes, Letter to Carl Van Vechten (July 29, 1961), Carl Van Vechten Papers, Box 13, Folder 325, Beinecke Library, Yale University, New Haven, CT. Used with the permission of the estate of Chester B. Himes.

101. Jackson, *Himes: A Biography*, 394.

102. Himes, Letter to Van Vechten (July 29, 1961).

103. Chester Himes, Letter to William Targ (December 17, 1967), Chester Himes Papers, Box 232, Folder 232, Beinecke Library, Yale University, New Haven, CT. Used with the permission of the estate of Chester B. Himes.

104. Jackson, *Himes: A Biography*, 443, 375.

105. Himes, *Cotton Comes to Harlem*, 7.

106. Ibid., 26.

Chapter 3

1. Ronald Reagan, "Abortion and the Conscience of the Nation," *Human Life Review* (Spring 1983), republished at the *Patriot Post*: http://patriotpost.us/documents/84

2. Abraham Lincoln, *The Language of Liberty: The Political Speeches and Writings of Abraham Lincoln*, ed. Joseph R. Fornieri (New York: Regneri, 2009), 224.

3. See Thomas W. Hilgers, Marjory Mecklenburg, and Gayle Riordan, "Is Abortion the Best We Have to Offer? A Challenge to the Abortive Society," in *Abortion and Social Justice*, eds. Thomas W. Hilgers and Dennis J. Horan (New York: Sheed & Ward, 1972); also found in Linda Greenhouse and Reva B. Siegel, eds., *Before Roe v. Wade*, 2nd ed. (2012): http://documents.law.yale.edu/sites/default/files/BeforeRoe2ndEd_1.pdf; and Vanessa Williams, "Ben Carson Likens Abortion to Slavery, Wants to See Roe v. Wade Overturned," *Washington Post* (October 25, 2015): https://www.washingtonpost.com/news/post-politics/wp/2015/10/25/ben-carson-likens-abortion-to-slavery-wants-to-see-roe-v-wade-overturned/

4. Philip K. Dick, *Do Androids Dream of Electric Sheep?* ([1968] New York: Ballantine Books, 1996), 17.

5. For Dick's views on abortion, see the Philip K. Dick biography by Lawrence Sutin, *Divine Invasions: A Life of Philip K. Dick* (New York: Da Capo Press, 2009), 108, 109, 124, and 253. To my knowledge, the only previous critic to note "The Pre-Persons" and Dick's stance on abortion is Christopher Palmer in *Philip K. Dick: Exhilaration and Terror of the Postmodern* (Liverpool: Liverpool University Press, 2003); but while admirable for considering Dick's uncomfortable politics, Palmer's argument does not trace Dick's engagement with abortion through his fiction beyond "The Pre-Persons" and his realist novel, *The Man Whose Teeth Were All Exactly Alike* (written in 1960, published in 1984).

6. Philip K. Dick, "The Pre-Persons," in *The Eye of The Sibyl and Other Classic Stories* (New York: Citadel, 2000), 277, 290–291.

7. The Voigt-Kampff empathy test involves outlining a series of social situations for a subject and measuring bodily reactions like eye muscle movements and capillaries so as to determine whether or not they are a human.

8. Mark McGurl, *The Program Era: Postwar Fiction and the Rise of Creative Writing* (Cambridge, MA: Harvard University Press, 2011), 26.

9. Michael Wreszin, *Interviews with Dwight Macdonald* (Jackson: University Press of Mississippi, 2003), 38.

10. Quoted in David Barnett, "Science Fiction: The Genre That Dare Not Speak Its Name," *The Guardian* (January 28, 2009): http://www.theguardian.com/books/booksblog/2009/jan/28/science-fiction-genre

11. See Ellen Moers, "Female Gothic: The Monster's Mother," *New York Review of Books* (March 21, 1974): http://www.nybooks.com/articles/1974/03/21/female-gothic-the-monsters-mother/; Mary Poovey, *The Proper Lady and the Woman Writer: Ideology as Style in the Works of Mary Wollstonecraft, Mary Shelley, and Jane Austen* (Chicago: University of Chicago Press, 1984), 114–142.

12. See Octavia E. Butler, "Bloodchild," *Isaac Asimov's Science Fiction Magazine* (1984), reprinted in *Bloodchild and Other Stories*, 2nd ed. (New York: Seven Stories, 1996) and *Lilith's Brood* (New York: Open Road, 2012), originally published as a trilogy: *Dawn* (1987), *Adulthood Rites* (1988), and *Imago* (1989) (New York: Warner Books); Ursula K. Le Guin, "Standing Ground," *Ms.* (1992), reprinted in *Ms.* (Summer 2002): 82–88, and "The Princess" (1982), in *Dancing at the Edge of the World: Thoughts on Words, Women, Places* (New York: Grove Press, 1989), 75–79; Harlan Ellison, "Croatoan," in *Strange Wine* ([1978] New York: Open Road, 2014), Kindle Edition; Kurt Vonnegut, "The Big Space Fuck," in *Again, Dangerous Visions*, ed. Harlan Ellison ([1972] New York: Open Road, 2014), Kindle Edition; James Tiptree, Jr., "Morality Meat," in *Crown of Stars* (New York: Tom Doherty Associates, 1988), 69–95; Margaret Atwood, *A Handmaid's Tale* ([1986] New York: Anchor Books, 1998).

13. For SF, Dick, and posthumanism, see N. Katherine Hayles, *How We Became Posthuman: Virtual Bodies in Cybernetics, Literature, and Informatics* (Chicago: University of Chicago Press, 1999), 5, 160–192. See also Donna Haraway, "The Cyborg Manifesto," in *The Cybercultures Reader*, eds. David Bell and Barbara M. Kennedy (New York: Routledge, 2000), 291–323, which famously treats the cyborg or android as "an ironic political myth faithful to feminism, socialism, and materialism" (291), citing *Blade Runner* but also ignoring Dick's influential pro-life vision of the android. Haraway has been qualified by scholars who note that the fluidity of the cyborg can be used to make the "fetal cyborg" seem like a naturalized person—a process in which Dick participates. See Marilyn Maness Mehaffy, "Fetal Attractions: The Limits of Cyborg Theory," *Women's Studies* 29 (2000): 177–194.

14. Barbara Johnson, "Apostrophe, Animation, and Abortion," *Diacritics*, vol. 16, no. 1 (1986): 34. For Johnson, female poets tend to be particularly sensitive to this rhetorical problem; their poems about abortion reveal a conflictedness about apostrophe, which constructs a fetal addressee as both a person and not-a-person at the same time. Jonathan Crewe responds to Johnson by arguing that historical discourse, as much as gender, mediates responses to abortion. For Crewe, poems and accounts by Ben Jonson and John Donne suggest that two seventeenth-century male poets experienced what Johnson treats as exclusive to twentieth-century female poets: anxiety about the connection between cultural and biological parenthood. Jonathan Crewe, "Baby Killers," *Differences: A Journal of Feminist Cultural Studies*, vol. 7, no. 3 (1995): 1–23

15. Rosalind Pollack Petchesky, "Fetal Images: The Power of Visual Culture in the Politics of Reproduction," *Feminist Studies* 13 (1987): 263–292; Barbara Duden, *Disembodying Women: Perspectives on Pregnancy and the Unborn*, trans. Lee Hoinacki (Cambridge, MA: Harvard University Press, 1993); Lauren Berlant, "America, 'Fat,' the Fetus," *boundary 2*, vol. 21, no. 3 (1994): 145–195; Valerie Hartouni, *Cultural Conceptions: On Reproductive Technologies and the Making of Life* (Minneapolis: University of Minnesota Press, 2008). For further feminist engagement with fetal personhood, see also the essays in the volume *Fetal Subjects, Feminist Positions*, eds. Lynn M. Morgan and Meredith W. Michaels (Philadelphia: University of Pennsylvania Press, 1999). See also, for more recent work, Christina Hauck, "Abortion and the Individual Talent," *ELH*, vol. 70 (2003): 223–266, which interprets T. S. Eliot's *The Waste Land* as drawing upon historical anxieties about abortion and female reproductive failure in order to suggest modernism's broader failure to narrate "wholeness . . . at the level of the individual male subject or at the level of history." In *Abortion in the American Imagination: Before Life and Choice, 1880–1940* (New Brunswick, NJ: Rutgers University Press, 2014), Karen Weingarten contends that by studying early twentieth-century literature, film, and popular culture, we can understand how the abortion debate came to be framed in the liberal language of life, choice, and rights. See also Heather Latimer, *Reproductive Acts: Sexual Politics in North American Fiction and*

Film (Montreal: McGill-Queen's Press, 2013), which shows that these liberal frames, and resistance to them, are visible in more recent American and Canadian fiction and film.

16. The classic account of science fiction's function as a genre remains Darko Suvin's "cognitive estrangement," which suggests that SF conjures worlds that are unfamiliar but also recognizable as reflections of our own—and which promotes intellectual comparison between the two. See Darko Suvin, "On the Poetics of the Science Fiction Genre," *College English*, vol. 34 (1972): 372–382. More recently, Seo-Young Chu has argued persuasively that SF is better able to represent cognitively estranging aspects of the world than traditional realism. See Seo-Young Chu, *Do Metaphors Dream of Literal Sleep?* (Cambridge, MA: Harvard University Press, 2011). These are both essentially ahistorical accounts. Whereas Chu seems to take for granted that some referents are inherently estranging, I would argue that one important reason why abortion is cognitively estranging is that the law, conceived as a liberal system of distinct persons, struggles to represent pregnancy. SF thus evolved to compensate for a deficient legal system.

17. Petchesky, "Fetal Images," 263–292.

18. Johnson, "Apostrophe, Animation, and Abortion," 29–47.

19. Deborah Nelson, *Pursuing Privacy in Cold War America* (New York: Columbia University Press, 2002), 112–114.

20. Judith Wilt, *Abortion, Choice, and Contemporary Fiction: The Armageddon of the Maternal Instinct* (Chicago: University of Chicago Press, 1990), 8–9.

21. On the literary field, see Pierre Bourdieu, "The Field of Cultural Production, or: the Economic World Reversed," in *The Field of Cultural Production: Essays on Art and Literature*, ed. and introduced by Randal Johnson (New York: Columbia University Press, 1993), 29–73, quotation on 30.

22. Moers, "Female Gothic."

23. For *Frankenstein* and nineteenth-century obstetrics, see, in particular, Alan Bewell, "'An Issue of Monstrous Desire': *Frankenstein* and Obstetrics," *Yale Journal of Criticism*, vol. 2, no. 1 (1988): 105–128.

24. John Keown, "The First Statutory Prohibition of Abortion: Lord Ellenborough's Act 1803," in *Abortion, Doctors, and the Law: Some Aspects of the Legal Regulation of Abortion in England from 1803 to 1982* (Cambridge, UK: Cambridge University Press, 1988), 3–25.

25. Mary (with Percy) Shelley, *The Original Frankenstein*, ed. Charles E. Robinson (New York: Vintage, 2008), 193, 378, 243.

26. On the history of abortion in the United States pre–*Roe v. Wade* (1973), see Kristin Luker, *Abortion and the Politics of Motherhood* (Berkeley: University of California Press, 1985), 11–126; and Leslie J. Regan, *When Abortion Was a Crime: Women, Medicine, and the Law in the United States, 1867-1973* (Berkeley: University of California Press, 1997).

27. Ibid.

28. Those cases were, respectively, *Griswold v. Connecticut* (1965), *Loving v. Virginia* (1967), *Stanley v. Georgia* (1969), *Skinner v. Oklahoma* (1942), and *Meyer v. Nebraska* (1923).

29. *Roe v. Wade* 410 U.S. 113 (1973).

30. Judith Jarvis Thomson, "A Defense of Abortion," *Philosophy & Public Affairs*, vol. 1, no. 1 (October 1, 1971): 47–66. For a similar argument from a political theorist characterizing pregnancy as invasion, see Eileen McDonagh, *Breaking the Abortion Deadlock: From Choice to Consent* (Oxford: Oxford University Press, 1996), particularly 84–107.

31. See, in order, Catharine A. MacKinnon, "Reflections on Sex Equality Under Law," *Yale Law Journal*, vol. 100 (1991): 1314; Donald H. Regan, "Rewriting Roe v. Wade," *Michigan Law Review*, vol. 77 (1979): 1569; Derek Parfit, *Reasons and Persons* (Oxford: Oxford University Press, 1986), 322; John Hart Ely, "The Wages of Crying Wolf: A Comment on *Roe v. Wade*," *Yale Law Journal*, vol. 82 (1973): 926; Jed Rubenfeld, "The Right of Privacy," *Harvard Law Review*, vol. 102 (1989): 794.

32. For the pro-choice allusion to slavery, Joan Bradford and California Committee to Legalize Abortion; South Bay Chapter of the National Organization for Women; Zero Population Growth, Inc.; California Committee to Legalize Abortion, et al., "Amicus Curiae Brief in Support of Jane Roe," in Greenhouse and Siegel, *Before Roe v. Wade*, 341–348.

33. Dr. and Mrs. J. C. Wilke, "Handbook on Abortion," in Greenhouse and Siegel, *Before Roe v. Wade*, 103.

34. Adrienne Rich, *Of Woman Born: Motherhood as Experience and Institution* (New York: Norton, 1976), 64. See A. Robin Hoffman, "How to See the Horror: The Hostile Fetus in *Rosemary's Baby* and *Alien*," in *The 'Evil Child' in Literature, Film and Popular Culture*, ed. Karen J. Renner (New York: Routledge, 2013), 150–172.

35. Lynn M. Paltrow, "Amicus Brief: *Richard Thornburgh v. American College of Obstetricians and Gynecologists*," *Women's Rights Law Reporter*, vol. 9, no. 1 (Winter 1986): 3–24, quotation on 16, 23.

36. Jane Doe, "There Just Wasn't Room in Our Lives Now for Another Baby," *New York Times* (May 14, 1976): 21. Jane Doe was later revealed to be Linda Bird Francke, who republished the testimonial in *The Ambivalence of Abortion* (New York: Random House, 1978).

37. For the first scholar to speak of a "right to personhood," see Paul Freund, *American Law Institute*, 52nd Annual Meeting (1975), 42–43, quoted in J. Braxton Craven, Jr., "Personhood: The Right to Be Let Alone," *Duke Law Journal*, vol. 699 (1976): 706. Of course, the connection between "an inviolate personality" and a right to privacy extends back as far as Louis Brandeis in 1890. Samuel D. Warren and Louis D. Brandeis, *Harvard Law Review*, vol. 4 (1890): 205. See Rubenfeld, "The Right of Privacy," 737–807.

38. Laurence H. Tribe, *American Constitutional Law* (Mineola, NY: Foundation Press, 1988), 1304.

39. Rubenfeld, "The Right of Privacy," 782. As many feminist scholars have pointed out, privacy law was implicitly gendered male. See, for instance, Catharine A. MacKinnon, "Privacy v. Equality: Beyond *Roe v. Wade* (1983)," in *Feminism Unmodified: Discourses on Life and Law* (Cambridge, MA: Harvard University Press, 1988), 93–102.

40. *Bowers v. Hardwick* 478 U.S. 205 (Blackmun, J., dissenting). See also Rubenfeld, "The Right of Privacy," 753.

41. For a pro-life appraisal of Dick, see, for instance, Stephanie Pacheco, "'The Pre-Persons' Saw the Horrors of Abortion in 1974," *Truth and Charity Forum* (March 31, 2014): https://web.archive.org/web/20190828093153/http://www.truthandcharityforum.org/the-pre-persons-saw-the-horrors-of-abortion-in-1974/ In literary criticism, Dick has been praised for his leftist politics, beginning with some of the most influential early Marxist appraisals. See Fredric Jameson, "After Armageddon: Character Systems in 'Dr. Bloodmoney,'" *Science Fiction Studies*, vol. 2 (1975): 31–42, republished in *Archaeologies of the Future: The Desire Called Utopia and Other Science Fictions* (New York: Verso, 2005). See also Carl Freedman, "Towards a Theory of Paranoia: The Science Fiction of Philip K. Dick," *Science Fiction Studies,* vol. 11 (1984): 15–24; and most recently, Bill Brown, *Other Things* (Chicago: University of Chicago Press, 2015), 125–155. David Golumbia and N. Katherine Hayles provide accounts that enlist Dick on behalf of their favored poststructuralist theories—anti-realism and posthumanism, respectively. David Golumbia, "Resisting 'The World': Philip K. Dick, Cultural Studies, and Metaphysical Realism," *Science Fiction Studies,* vol. 23 (1996): 83–102; and Hayles, *How We Became Posthuman*. Andrew Hoberek stands as a corrective to leftist and poststructuralist readings insofar as he argues that these accounts of labor occlude Dick's masculinism. See Andrew P. Hoberek, "The 'Work' of Science Fiction: Philip K. Dick and Occupational Masculinity in the Post-World War II United States," *Modern Fiction Studies,* vol. 43, no. 2 (Summer 1997): 374–404. More recent scholarship has charted Dick's oscillations between humanism and postmodernism. See Lejla Kucukalic, *Philip K. Dick: Canonical Writer of the Digital Age* (New York: Routledge, 2009); Christopher Palmer, *Philip K. Dick: Exhilaration and Terror of the Postmodern* (Liverpool: Liverpool University Press, 2003); Jason Vest, *The Postmodern Humanism of Philip K. Dick* (Lanham, MD: Scarecrow Press, 2009). There has also been a renewed interest in Dick's later work and his mystical epiphany of "2-3-74," as betokened by the recent release of *The Exegesis of Philip K. Dick,* eds. Jonathan Lethem, Pamela Jackson, Erik Davis, et al. (New York: Harcourt, 2011), and the essays by Erik Davis, Richard Doyle, and James Burton in *The World According to Philip K. Dick,* ed. Alexander Dunst (New York: Palgrave Macmillan, 2015). Both his humanism and his Christian-inflected religion can be seen in his pro-life views.

42. Hayles, *How We Became Posthuman*, 5.

43. Dick, "The Pre-Persons," 279.

44. Ibid., 286, 278, 285, 283.

45. Philip K. Dick, Note to "The Pre-Persons," 1978, reprinted in *Eye of the Sibyl*, 393.

46. Philip K. Dick, *The Man Whose Teeth Were All Exactly Alike* (New York: Tor Books, 1984), Kindle Edition.

47. Ibid.

48. Gregg Rickman, *To the High Castle: Philip K. Dick: A Life, 1928–1962* (Long Beach, CA: Fragments West, 1989), 359–361.

49. Lawrence Sutin, *Divine Invasions: A Life of Philip K. Dick* (New York: Carroll & Graf, 2009), 298.

50. Ibid., 108.

51. Philip K. Dick, *We Can Build You* ([1972] New York: Mariner Books, 2012), 207–208.

52. Ibid., 219.

53. Ibid., 208.

54. Ibid.

55. Ibid., 14.

56. Philip K. Dick, *Dr. Bloodmoney* ([1965] New York: Mariner Books, 2012).

57. Sara Dubow, *Ourselves Unborn: A History of the Fetus in Modern America* (New York: Oxford University Press, 2011), 64–65.

58. Mary Ziegler, *After Roe: The Lost History of the Abortion Debate* (Cambridge, MA: Harvard University Press, 2015), 74–76.

59. Philip K. Dick, *The Crack in Space* (New York: Ace Books, 1966), 37.

60. Sutin, *Divine Invasions*, 17–19.

61. Philip K. Dick, *Ubik* ([1969] Boston: Mariner Books, 2012), 217.

62. Hayles, *How We Became Posthuman*, 191.

63. Philip K. Dick, "The Android and the Human," in *The Shifting Realities of Philip K. Dick: Selected Literary and Philosophical Writings*, ed. Lawrence Sutin (New York: Vintage, 1996), 185.

64. Ibid., 205.

65. Rubenfeld, "The Right of Privacy," 782.

66. On blushing and race, see Ruth Bernard Yeazell, *Fictions of Modesty: Women and Courtship in the English Novel* (Chicago: University of Chicago Press, 1991), 72.

67. Michael Bérubé, "Disability, Democracy, and the New Genetics," in *The Disability Studies Reader*, ed. Leonard J. Davis (New York: Routledge, 2013), 74–87.

68. For pro-life activists who hold this view, see Luker, *Abortion and the Politics of Motherhood*, 207–209. As Karen Weingarten points out, the anti-abortion stance was historically connected to eugenics, as white women of the 20s and 30s were encouraged to bear more children. Weingarten, *Abortion in the American Imagination*, 66–95. More

recently, disability studies activist Ruth Hubbard compares abortion of the disabled to eugenics, although she insists that a woman should still have a right to choose. See Ruth Hubbard, "Abortion and Disability: Who Should and Should Not Inhabit the World?" in *The Disability Studies Reader*, 4th ed., ed. Leonard J. Davis (New York: Routledge, 2013), 74–87.

69. Simon Gikandi, *Slavery and the Culture of Taste* (Princeton: Princeton University Press, 2011), 237–238.

70. Dick, *Do Androids Dream of Electric Sheep?*, 138–139. Hereafter cited parenthetically in the text.

71. *American Heritage Dictionary*, s.v. "Rachel": https://www.ahdictionary.com/word/search.html?q=Rachel&submit.x=48&submit.y=15

72. See Sutin, *Divine Invasions*, 208–234.

73. Philip K. Dick, "The Exegesis" (unpublished manuscript) (October 25, 1980), 5. Original uncorrected text available at http://zebrapedia.psu.edu/, Folder 1, 92.

74. Vonnegut, "The Big Space Fuck."

75. Ellison, "Croatoan." For Vonnegut's pro-choice stance, see William Rodney Allen and Paul Smith, "An Interview with Kurt Vonnegut," in *Conversations with Kurt Vonnegut* (Jackson: University Press of Mississippi, 1988), 279.

76. Quoted in Julie Phillips, *James Tiptree, Jr.: The Double Life of Alice B. Sheldon* (New York: St. Martin's Press, 2015), 509.

77. Tiptree, "Morality Meat," 79.

78. MacKinnon, "Reflections on Sex Equality Under Law," 1314. This same observation, comparing feminist discourse treating the fetus as an invasive alien and SF/horror, is made with respect to film by A. Robin Hoffman. See Hoffman, "How to See the Horror," 150–172. As Hoffman points out, Adrienne Rich also compares the fetus to "an alien" in *Of Woman Born* (1976) (quotation on 153). See also Ernest Larsen, "The Fetal Monster," in *Fetal Subjects, Feminist Positions*, 236–251, which discusses "Bloodchild" and several popular films, but does not explore the legal context.

79. Octavia E. Butler, "Afterword," in *Bloodchild and Other Stories*, 30. Hereafter excerpts from "Bloodchild" and the afterword are cited parenthetically in the text.

80. Gerry Canavan, "The Octavia E. Butler Papers," *Eaton Journal of Archival Research in Science Fiction*, vol. 3 (November 2015): 52.

81. Octavia E. Butler, *Seed to Harvest* (New York: Open Road, 2012), see, e.g., 541–542.

82. An overwhelming majority of SF readers were male in the pulp era, and in polls between 1971 and 1977 conducted by *Locus Magazine*, only 17 to 20 percent of SF readers were female, though that percentage would grow with the rise of feminist SF in the 70s and 80s. See Brian M. Stableford, *The Sociology of Science Fiction* (Wilbraham, MA: Borgo Press, 1987), 65–66.

83. Randall Kenan, "An Interview with Octavia Butler," in *Conversations with Octavia Butler*, ed. Consuela Francis (Jackson: University Press of Mississippi), 30

84. Previous criticism about "Bloodchild" attempts to reconcile the stark narrative of domination with Butler's comments in the afterword that it is not "about slavery," that it is a "love story." For instance, Amanda Thibodeau focuses on the "love story," aspect, reading it as a narrative of queer intimacy, while Alys Eve Weinbaum thinks of it as illustrating the continuities between slavery and neoliberal capitalism. Kristen Lillvis argues that Gan inherits a tradition of Black motherhood as described by Hortense Spillers in which motherly love can destroy oppressive family hierarchies. My own suggestion is that thinking about it as an engagement with radical feminism, which viewed consent as impossible under patriarchy, explains how the story could be "[not] about slavery," a "love story," and a story about domination all at once. Amanda Thibodeau, "Alien Bodies and a Queer Future: Sexual Revision in Octavia Butler's 'Bloodchild' and James Tiptree, Jr.'s 'With Delicate Mad Hands,'" *Science Fiction Studies*, vol. 39 (2012): 262–282; Alys Eve Weinbaum, "The Afterlife of Slavery and the Problem of Reproductive Freedom," *Social Text*, vol. 31, no. 2 (115) (2013): 49–68; Kristen Lillvis, "Mama's Baby, Papa's Slavery? The Problem and Promise of Mothering in Octavia E. Butler's 'Bloodchild,'" *MELUS*, vol. 39, no. 4 (2014): 1–16.

85. For some of this history, see Dorothy Roberts, *Killing the Black Body* (New York: Pantheon, 1997). See also, on Butler, Aimee Armande Wilson, *Conceived in Modernism: The Aesthetics and Politics of Birth Control* (New York: Bloomsbury, 2016), 119–136.

86. For *Frankenstein* and female authorship, see Sandra Gilbert and Susan Gubar, *The Madwoman in the Attic: The Woman Writer and the Nineteenth Century Imagination*, 2nd ed. ([1979] New Haven and London: Yale University Press, 2000), 213–247.

87. Canavan, "Octavia E. Butler Papers," 49–50.

88. Gerry Canavan places it in the context of disability studies by comparing it to other narratives of Huntington's disease, arguing that "Evening" is unusual in narrating "a fully human life that can retain its own dignity and vitality despite hardship." See Gerry Canavan, "Life Without Hope?: Huntington's Disease and Genetic Futurity," in *Disability in Science Fiction: Representations of Technology as Cure*, ed. Kathryn Allan (New York: Palgrave Macmillan, 2013), 169–187. See also, for a penetrating comparison of DGD sufferers to African Americans, particularly in light of their controlled reproduction, Isiah Lavender III, "Digging Deep: Ailments of Difference in Octavia Butler's 'The Evening, the Morning, and the Night,'" in *Black and Brown Planets: The Politics of Race in Science Fiction*, ed. Isiah Lavender III (Jackson: University Press of Mississippi, 2014), 65–82.

89. Butler, "The Evening, the Morning and the Night," in *Bloodchild and Other Stories*, 46, 41.

90. Ibid., 47.

91. On the importance of California as a trailblazing state, see Luker, *Abortion and the Politics of Motherhood*, 66–125.

92. Annalee Newitz recognizes Shusterman as extending "The Pre-Persons." See Annalee Newitz, "What Does Science Fiction Tell Us About the Future of Reproductive Rights?" *io9* (February 22, 2012): http://io9.com/5887139/what-does-science-fiction-tell-us-about-the-future-of-reproductive-rights

93. On the first *Alien* film and abortion, see Hoffman, "How to See the Horror," 150–172. On *Star Trek* and abortion, see Robin Roberts, *Sexual Generations: Star Trek, the Next Generation and Gender* (Urbana: University of Illinois Press, 1999), 144–164.

94. Margaret Atwood, *MaddAddam* (New York: Doubleday, 2013).

95. *Planned Parenthood of Southeastern Pa. v. Casey* 505 U.S. 833 (1992), 861.

96. Sandra Day O'Connor noted this possibility in an earlier opinion: "As medical science becomes better able to provide for the separate existence of the fetus, the point of viability is moved further back toward conception." *Akron v. Akron Center for Reproductive Health, Inc.* 462 U.S. 416 (1983) (O'Connor, S. D., dissenting), 459.

97. *Planned Parenthood of Southeastern Pa. v. Casey* 505 U.S. 833 (1992), 852.

98. *2001. : A Space Odyssey*, dir. Stanley Kubrick (MGM, 1968).

99. This connection has been made before. See Karen Newman, *Fetal Positions: Individualism, Science, Visuality* (Stanford: Stanford University Press, 1996), 10–17; and Zoe Sofia, "Exterminating Fetuses: Abortion, Disarmament and the Sexo-Semiotics of Extraterrestrialism," *Diacritics*, vol. 14, no. 2 (Summer 1984): 47–59.

100. Ursula K. Le Guin, "Standing Ground," 86–87.

101. Patricia Lockwood, "A Childhood in the Pro-Life Movement," *New Yorker* (February 11, 2017): http://www.newyorker.com/books/page-turner/a-childhood-in-the-pro-life-movement

102. Drucilla Cornell, "Dismembered Selves and Wandering Wombs," in *Left Legalism/Left Critique*, eds. Wendy Brown and Janet Halley (Durham: Duke University Press, 2002), 348, 346.

103. Johnson, "Apostrophe, Animation, and Abortion," 34.

Chapter 4

1. *The Exorcist*, dir. William Friedkin (Warner Bros., 1973).

2. As liberal society carves out a space of private life that is shielded from public view, it may inevitably generate anxieties about what might be transpiring within that private space. See Karen Halttunen, *Murder Most Foul: The Killer and the American Gothic Imagination* (Cambridge, MA: Harvard University Press, 2000).

3. See, for instance, Stephen King, *Danse Macabre* (New York: Gallery Books, 1981), 180. See also Carol J. Clover, *Men, Women, and Chainsaws: Gender in the Modern Horror

Film (Princeton: Princeton University Press, 1992), which takes up the way horror invites predominantly male viewers to empathize with female protagonists.

4. "Child Abuse Prevention and Treatment Act," Public Law 93–247 (January 31, 1974): https://www.congress.gov/93/statute/STATUTE-88/STATUTE-88-Pg4.pdf

5. Linda Gordon, *Heroes of Their Own Lives: The Politics and History of Family Violence: Boston, 1880–1960* (New York: Viking, 1988), 28.

6. Ian Hacking, "Kind-making: The Case of Child Abuse," in *The Social Construction of What?* (Cambridge, MA: Harvard University Press, 1999), 135. See also Ian Hacking, "The Making and Molding of Child Abuse," *Critical Inquiry*, vol. 17, no. 2 (Winter 1991): 253–288.

7. See Gordon, *Heroes of their Own Lives*, 289–301; Linda Gordon, "The Politics of Child Sexual Abuse: Notes from American History," *Feminist Review*, vol. 28 (January 1988): 56–64; Elizabeth Pleck, *Domestic Tyranny: The Making of Social Policy Against Family Violence from Colonial Times to the Present* (New York: Oxford University Press, 1987), 145–164.

8. C. Henry Kempe, et al. "The Battered-Child Syndrome," *Journal of the American Medical Association (JAMA)* vol. 181 (1962): 17–24, reprinted in *JAMA*, vol. 241, no. 24 (June 1984): 3288–3294, quotation on 3289.

9. Ian Hacking, "Kind-making," 126, 133.

10. Barbara J. Nelson, *Making an Issue of Child Abuse: Political Agenda Setting for Social Problems* (Chicago: University of Chicago Press, 1984), 76–92.

11. Richard Nixon, "Veto of the Economic Opportunity Amendments of 1971" (December 9, 1971), in *The American Presidency Project*, eds. Gerhard Peters and John T. Woolley: https://www.presidency.ucsb.edu/documents/veto-the-economic-opportunity-amendments-1971

12. Quoted in Nelson, *Making an Issue of Child Abuse*, 102. Mondale's Child Abuse Prevention and Treatment Act (CAPTA) set aside $90 million for programs to prevent and treat child abuse and neglect; it created two federal agencies to study and report on incidences of child abuse; and it mandated various regulations on states—including one that would require states to give welfare authorities the ability to remove children from the home for three days. See Nelson, *Making an Issue of Child Abuse*, 104.

13. David Gil, "Violence Against Children," *Journal of Marriage and Family*, vol. 33, no. 4 (November 1971): 637–648.

14. Hearings Before the Subcommittee on Children and Youth of the Committee on Labor and Public Welfare, US Senate, Ninety-Third Congress, First Session, 17.

15. For the outline of this narrative, I draw mostly on Nelson, *Making an Issue of Child Abuse*, 92–126. See also Jill Lepore, "Baby Doe," *New Yorker* (February 1, 2016): 46–58.

16. See Leroy H. Pelton, "Child Abuse and Neglect: The Myth of Classlessness,"

American Journal of Orthopsychiatry, vol. 48, no. 4 (October 1978): 608–617. See also Senate Hearing, Ninety-Third Congress, 18.

17. Quoted in Susan Schecter, *Women and Male Violence: The Visions and Struggles of the Battered Women's Movement* (Boston: South End Press, 1982), 192.

18. Quoted in Pleck, *Domestic Tyranny*, 197.

19. Geraldo Rivera, "Devil Worship: Exposing Satan's Underground," *Geraldo Rivera Show* (October 22, 1988), NBC. Even though the now-infamous segment won its time slot, NBC may have lost money due to trouble finding advertisers. Some of the only advertisers willing to purchase commercials were horror films. See Jay Sharbutt, "Cauldron Boils over Geraldo's 'Devil Worship': 'Satan' Wins Ratings, Loses Advertisers," *Los Angeles Times* (October 27, 1988): https://www.latimes.com/archives/la-xpm-1988-10-27-ca-449-story.html

20. See Jay Sharbutt, "Steinberg Case Also Puts Live TV Coverage on Trial," *Los Angeles Times* (January 3, 1989): https://www.latimes.com/archives/la-xpm-1989-01-03-ca-116-story.html/; Patricia Volk, "The Steinberg Trial: Scenes from a Tragedy," *New York Times* (January 15, 1989): http://www.nytimes.com/1989/01/15/magazine/the-steinberg-trial-scenes-from-a-tragedy.html?pagewanted=all

21. The class and media aspects of the Steinberg case are discussed in Martha Minow, "Words and the Door to the Land of Change," *Vanderbilt Law Review*. vol. 43, no. 1665 (1990): 1678–1681.

22. Lawrence Schiller, *Perfect Murder, Perfect Town: The Uncensored Story of the JonBenet Murder and the Grand Jury's Search for the Final Truth* (New York: HarperCollins, 1999).

23. See Christopher Lasch, "The Socialization of Reproduction and the Collapse of Authority," in *The Culture of Narcissism: American Life in an Age of Diminishing Expectations* (New York: Norton, 1979), 154–187. See also David Riesman, *The Lonely Crowd: A Study of the Changing American Character* ([1950] New Haven: Yale University Press, 2001), 37–65.

24. See, in addition to Riesman, Annette Lareau, *Unequal Childhoods: Class, Race, and Family Life* (Berkeley: University of California Press, 2011).

25. See Franco Moretti, "Dialectic of Fear," *New Left Review*, vol. 1, no. 136 (November–December 1982): 67–85.

26. Annie McClanahan, *Dead Pledges: Debt, Crisis, and Twenty-First Century Culture* (Stanford: Stanford University Press, 2017), 143–185.

27. See, among others, Richard Beck, *We Believe the Children: A Moral Panic in the 1980s* (New York: PublicAffairs, 2015), which connects the scandal to concern about the decline in family values.

28. See Catharine A. MacKinnon, "Privacy v. Equality: Beyond *Roe v. Wade* (1983)," in *Feminism Unmodified: Discourses on Life and Law* (Cambridge, MA: Harvard University Press, 1988), 93–102.

29. Ira Levin, "'Stuck with Satan': Ira Levin on the Origins of *Rosemary's Baby*," *Criterion Collection* (November 25, 2012): https://www.criterion.com/current/posts/2541--stuck-with-satan-ira-levin-on-the-origins-of-rosemary-s-baby

30. *Griswold v. Connecticut* 381 U.S. 479 (1965), 486; *Roe v. Wade* 410 U.S. 113 (1973), 154.

31. See Lily Rothman, "When Spousal Rape First Became a Crime in the U.S.," *Time* (July 28, 2015): http://time.com/3975175/spousal-rape-case-history/

32. Ira Levin, *Rosemary's Baby* ([1967] New York: Pegasus Books, 2010), 99.

33. On suburban architecture and privacy in postwar America, see Sarah Igo, *The Known Citizen: A History of Privacy in Modern America* (Cambridge, MA: Harvard University Press, 2018), 108–122.

34. *Katz v. United States* 389 U.S. 347 (1967), 361.

35. Levin, *Rosemary's Baby*, 178.

36. Ibid., 26. Nearly identical lines about child abuse also appear in the film.

37. J. D. Connor, *Studios After the Studios: Neoclassical Hollywood, 1970–2010* (Stanford: Stanford University Press, 2015), 74–77. See also Kevin Heffernan, *Ghouls, Gimmicks, and Gold: Horror Films and the American Movie Business, 1953–1968* (Durham, NC: Duke University Press, 2004), 189–201. As Heffernan points out, the novel and the film were marketed in tandem, and certain cryptic scenes in the film (e.g., the dream sequence, the satanic orgy) seem to demand that the reader go out and purchase the book for an interpretation—which is why I read the two so closely in concert (see 196–197).

38. Stuart Elliot, "A TV Salute to the Designer of Some Memorable Movie Promotions," *New York Times* (April 28, 2005): https://www.nytimes.com/2005/04/28/business/media/a-tv-salute-to-the-designer-of-some-memorable-movie.html. See, for examples, the *Atlanta Constitution* (June 19, 1968): 26; or *The Sun* (June 11, 1964): C24.

39. *New York Times* (April 3, 1968): A1 (front page).

40. The combination of motifs from art-cinema and horror flick is discussed in Heffernan, *Ghouls, Gimmicks and Gold*, 189–201.

41. William Peter Blatty, *Which Way to Mecca, Jack?: From Brooklyn to Beirut: The Adventures of an American Sheik* ([1960] New York: Lancer Books, 2015), Kindle Edition.

42. A satirical account of Blatty's time in the Middle East can be found in Blatty's *Which Way to Mecca, Jack*. For the importance of the nuclear family to the USIA, see Laura Belmonte, *Selling the American Way: U.S. Propaganda and the Cold War* (Philadelphia: University of Pennsylvania Press, 2011), 136–158; as well as Elaine Tyler May, *Homeward Bound: American Families in the Cold War Era* (New York: Basic Books, 1988).

43. Insert for *News Review*, no. 47, *Family of Man* (November 21, 1958), Near East Regional Service Center Beirut, Records of the U.S. Information Agency, 6084628, National Archives, Washington, DC.

44. Blatty, *Which Way to Mecca, Jack?*

45. Abigail Van Buren, *Dear Teen-Ager* ([1959] New York: Pocket Books, 1960), 157. On his authorship of *Dear Teen-Ager*, see William Peter Blatty, *Finding Peter* (Washington, DC: Salem Media, 2015), 85–87.

46. Van Buren, *Dear Teen-Ager*, 44–46.

47. William Peter Blatty, *The Exorcist* ([1971] New York: HarperCollins, 2011), 345. Hereafter cited parenthetically in the text.

48. Ann Douglas, "The Dream of the Wise Child: Freud's 'Family Romance' Revisited in Contemporary Narratives of Horror," *Prospects*, vol. 9 (October 1984): 294–295.

49. While other critics have imagined that demon children like Regan and Niles represent anxieties about parenting—"How responsible must I be, can I be, do I want to be for 'that thing upstairs?'"—it is equally true that imagining demonic children makes it easier for viewers to imagine how parents might be tempted into abuse. See ibid., 295.

50. On the decision to remove Elvira from the screenplay, see William Peter Blatty, *If There Were Demons, Then Perhaps There Were Angels* (New York: Tom Doherty, 1998), Kindle Edition.

51. See Judy Klemesrud, "They Wait Hours—to Be Shocked," *New York Times* (January 27, 1974): D1, D13.

52. On *Psycho* as an event, see Linda Williams, "Discipline and Fun: *Psycho* and Postmodern Cinema," in *Reinventing Film Studies*, eds. Christine Gledhill and Linda Williams (New York: Oxford University Press, 2000), 351–379. Before *Psycho*, viewers would come and go in the middle of films, but Hitchcock refused to let anyone into the film late.

53. Klemesrud, "They Wait Hours—to Be Shocked."

54. Joyce Haber, "'Exorcist' Queues Get a Coffee Break," *Los Angeles Times* (January 9, 1974): E10.

55. See, for instance, Pauline Kael, "The Current Cinema: Back to the Ouija Board," *New Yorker* (January 7, 1974): 59–62.

56. Some of the context of production is discussed in William Paul, *Laughing, Screaming: Modern Hollywood Horror and Comedy* (New York: Columbia University Press, 1994), 287–292.

57. Rosemary Counter, "The Most Cursed Hit Movie Ever Made," *Vanity Fair* (June 1, 2017): https://www.vanityfair.com/hollywood/2017/06/the-most-cursed-hit-movie-ever-made-rosemarys-baby

58. Malachi Martin, *Hostage to the Devil: The Possession and Exorcism of Five Contemporary Americans* ([1976] San Francisco: HarperCollins, 1992); Michelle Smith and Lawrence Pazder, *Michelle Remembers* (New York: Pocket Books, 1980).

59. King, *Danse Macabre*, 426.

60. Stephen King, *On Writing: A Memoir of the Craft* (New York: Scribner, 2000), 26.

61. Ibid., 18–19.

62. Ibid., 21.

63. Stephen King, *Carrie* (New York: Doubleday, 1974), 302. Hereafter cited parenthetically in the text.

64. Carrie is not the only character to have thoughts narrated in this way, but she has by far the most of them—and they do correspond to the exercise of her powers. On King's use of modernist techniques and his imagination of himself in the literary field, see my "*The Shining* and the Media Conglomerate: Or, How All Work and No Play Made Jack a Creative Artist in the 1970s," *American Literature,* vol. 91, no. 1 (March 2019): 151–182.

65. Stephen King, *The Shining* ([1977] New York: Anchor Books, 2012), 269. Hereafter cited parenthetically in the text.

66. Andy Greene, "Stephen King: *The Rolling Stone* Interview," *Rolling Stone* (October 31, 2014): https://www.rollingstone.com/culture/culture-features/stephen-king-the-rolling-stone-interview-191529/

67. On King's relationship to adaptation and literary fiction, see my "*The Shining* and the Media Conglomerate."

68. *DeShaney v. Winnebago County Department of Social Services* 489 U.S. 189. The decision was reaffirmed in *Town of Castle Rock v. Gonzales* 545 U.S. 748 (2005). See Jeannie Suk, *At Home in the Law: How the Domestic Violence Revolution Is Transforming Privacy* (New Haven: Yale University Press, 2009), 106–131.

69. "Chapter One: The Vanishing of Will Byers," *Stranger Things*, dir. the Duffer Brothers (Netflix, 2016).

70. *The Sixth Sense*, dir. M. Night Shyamalan (Buena Vista Pictures, 1999).

71. On the rise of the VHS tape and its influence on horror, see Caetlin Benson-Allott, *Killer Tapes and Shattered Screens: Video Spectatorship from VHS to File Sharing* (Berkeley: University of California Press, 2013). And yet, Benson-Allott reads the VHS in *The Sixth Sense* as a "relatively simplistic use of video as a medium for the truth the dead know" and not as enabling the audience, like Cole, to see dead people. Of course, *The Sixth Sense* had significant box office sales—it was one of the highest grossing films of all time—and yet, studios could expect to make significantly more money from VHS sales and rentals than they could from box office releases. This is why the film's primary scene of self-dramatization would involve VHS.

72. Toni Morrison, *The Bluest Eye* ([1970] New York: Vintage, 2007), 126. Hereafter cited parenthetically in the text.

73. Toni Morrison, *God Help the Child* (New York: Knopf, 2015).

74. Mark Seltzer, *Serial Killers: Death and Life in America's Wound Culture* (New York: Routledge, 1998).

Chapter 5

1. Derek Humphry and Mary Clement, *Freedom to Die: People, Politics, and the Right-to-Die Movement* (New York: St. Martin's Press, 2000), 249.

2. *The Oregonian* (April 13, 1986): B4.

3. On the way that neoliberalism appropriates 1960s ideals of freedom and autonomy, see David Harvey, *A Brief History of Neoliberalism* (Oxford: Oxford University Press, 2005), 41–42.

4. Brief for Ronald Dworkin, Thomas Nagel, Robert Nozick, John Rawls, Thomas Scanlon, and Judith Jarvis Thomson as amicus curiae, *Washington v. Glucksberg* 521 U.S. 702 (1997) and *Vacco v. Quill* 521 U.S. 793 (1997), 4.

5. *Planned Parenthood of Southeastern Pa. v. Casey* 505 U.S. 833 (1992).

6. Ronald Dworkin, *Life's Dominion: An Argument About Abortion, Euthanasia, and Individual Freedom* (New York: Knopf, 1993), 209, 211, 199.

7. Shai J. Levi, *The Modern Art of Dying: A History of Euthanasia in the United States* (Princeton: Princeton University Press, 2005).

8. For histories of euthanasia that begin before 1970, see Ian Dowbiggin, *A Merciful End: The Euthanasia Movement in Modern America* (Oxford: Oxford University Press, 2003); Ezekiel J. Emanuel, "The History of Euthanasia Debates in the United States and Britain," *Annals of Internal Medicine*, vol. 121, no. 10 (November 1994): 793–802; and Stephen Louis Kuepper, "Euthanasia in America, 1890–1960: The Controversy, the Movement, and the Law" (PhD dissertation, Rutgers University, 1981), ProQuest Dissertations & Theses Global.

9. Amy Kaplan, *The Social Construction of American Realism* (Chicago: University of Chicago Press, 1988), 65–87; Mark McGurl, *The Novel Art* (Princeton: Princeton University Press, 2001), 85–91.

10. Kaplan, *Social Construction*, 66.

11. Charles Eliot Norton, "A Plea for Euthanasia," republished in *St. Louis Medical Review* (January 27, 1906): 73.

12. See James Turner, *The Liberal Education of Charles Eliot Norton* (Baltimore: Johns Hopkins University Press, 1999), xxi–xii.

13. Norton, "A Plea for Euthanasia," 73.

14. Edith Wharton to Sally Norton (September 15, 1905), Edith Wharton Papers, Box 29, Folder 899, Beinecke Library, Yale University, New Haven, CT. Irene Goldman-Price discovered this reference in an unpublished conference paper that she very kindly shared with me. Irene Goldwin-Price, "'Is It Ever Right to Speed the Departing Sick?': Euthanasia Circa 1906," conference paper, Edith Wharton at Newport, 2000.

15. Simeon Baldwin, "The Natural Right to a Natural Death," *St. Paul Medical Journal* (1899): 875–889, quotations on 879, 884.

16. Donna Campbell, introduction to Edith Wharton, *The Fruit of the Tree* (Boston: Northeastern University Press, 2000), xv.

17. G. Lowes Dickinson, "Euthanasia: From the Notebook of an Alpinist," *The Living Age* (February 17, 1906): 445–447.

18. Ibid.

19. Editorial, *New York Times* (April 10, 1910): 35.

20. "Is It Ever Right to Speed the Departing Sick?" *New York Tribune* (January 21, 1906): C2.

21. Ibid.

22. Wharton, *Fruit of the Tree*, 429. Hereafter cited parenthetically in the text. A commonplace or commonplace book is a type of diary or scrapbook in which individuals copy quotes or observations they want to remember.

23. *New York Medical Journal* (November 2, 1907): 840.

24. *New York Times*, review of *Fruit of the Tree* (October 19, 1907): BR649.

25. *New York Sun*, Edith Wharton Papers, Beinecke Library, Box 5, Folder 128, Yale University, New Haven, CT.

26. Dworkin, *Life's Dominion*, 192.

27. Quoted in Cynthia Davis, *Charlotte Perkins Gilman: A Biography* (Stanford: Stanford University Press, 2010), 397.

28. "Comment and Review," *The Forerunner*, vol. 1 (1909): 23–24.

29. Ibid.

30. "Euthanasia Again," *The Forerunner*, vol. 3 (1912): 262–263.

31. "Euthanasia for Incurables," Charlotte Perkins Gilman Papers, Schlesinger Library, Radcliffe Institute, Folder 226, Harvard University, Cambridge, MA, 13–14, available at: http://schlesinger.radcliffe.harvard.edu/onlinecollections/gilman/

32. Charlotte Perkins Gilman, "The Right to Die—I," *Forum and Century*, vol. 94 (November 1935): 297–307.

33. Charlotte Perkins Gilman, *With Her in Ourland*, published in *The Forerunner*, vol. 7 (1916): 320.

34. Quoted in Davis, *Charlotte Perkins Gilman*, 397.

35. Gilman, "Right to Die—I."

36. Neil Gorsuch, *The Future of Assisted Suicide and Euthanasia* (Princeton: Princeton University Press, 2006), 99.

37. "It's Over Debbie," *Journal of the American Medical Association (JAMA)*, vol. 259, no. 2 (January 1988): 272.

38. African Americans more often tend to oppose it, likely because of a suspicion of doctors' not having their best interest at heart; some have been concerned that women, whose complaints of pain are often downplayed by doctors, would not have the same

access to euthanasia—or, conversely, would be disproportionately compelled to sacrifice themselves for their family. See R. L. Lichtenstein et al., "Black/White Differences in Attitude Toward Physician-Assisted Suicide," *Journal of the National Medical Association*, vol. 89, no. 2 (February 1997): 125–133; Jennifer A. Parks, "Why Gender Matters to the Euthanasia Debate," *Hastings Center Report*, vol. 30, no. 1 (January–February 2000): 30–36; Susan M. Wolf, *Feminism and Bioethics: Beyond Reproduction* (New York: Oxford University Press, 1996), 282–317.

39. Larry McMurtry, *Lonesome Dove* (New York: Simon & Schuster, 1985), 826.

40. On the twentieth-century western, see Richard Slotkin, *Gunfighter Nation: Myth of the Frontier in the Twentieth Century* (Norman: University of Oklahoma Press, 1998), which shows how the myth of the frontier has been utilized for liberal and illiberal uses alike.

41. "Sold Under Sin," *Deadwood*, dir. Davis Guggenheim (HBO, 2011).

42. Wirt Williams, "Book Review: *Welcome to Hard Times*," *New York Times* (September 25, 1960): https://archive.nytimes.com/www.nytimes.com/specials/ragtime/hard1.html

43. See Fredric Jameson, *The Political Unconscious: Narrative as a Socially Symbolic Act* (Ithaca: Cornell University Press, 1981), 118–119.

44. Randy Roberts and James S. Olson, *John Wayne: American* (New York: Simon & Schuster, 1995), 614.

45. Ibid.

46. See Marcia Angell, "May Doctors Help You to Die?" *New York Review of Books* (October 11, 2012).

47. Glendon Swarthout, *The Shootist* ([1975] Lincoln: University of Nebraska Press, 2011), Kindle Edition.

48. Leon Kass, *Life, Liberty, and the Defense of Dignity: The Challenge for Bioethics* (San Francisco: Encounter Books, 2002), 273.

49. Roberts and Olson, *John Wayne*, 514.

50. McMurtry, *Lonesome Dove*, 875. Hereafter cited parenthetically in the text.

51. See *Cruzan v. Director, Missouri Department of Health* 497 U.S. 261 (1990).

52. Larry McMurtry, *Streets of Laredo* (New York: Simon & Schuster, 1993), 463. Hereafter cited parenthetically in the text.

53. Larry McMurtry, *Walter Benjamin at the Dairy Queen: Reflections at Sixty and Beyond* (New York: Simon & Schuster, 1999), 175.

54. In most of Larry McMurtry's fiction—whether *The Last Picture Show*, *Terms of Endearment*, or *Lonesome Dove*—someone dies of a terminal illness like cancer or contemplates euthanasia because of an accident. This trope appears in his first novel, *Horsemen, Pass By* (1961), which is narrated by a seventeen-year-old named Lonnie. The novel concludes when Lonnie's grandfather Homer is hit by a car and has fallen into a

ditch; Hud, his ne'er-do-well stepson, shoots him as a mercy killing. But it is not clear to Lonnie if Hud has done it "for kindness or for meanness." The sequence of events in the novel—sick cattle being euthanized, Lonnie's friend falling off a bull, Homer's mercy-killing—all serve to emphasize the bad luck in the milieu of the contemporary west. Like *No Country for Old Men*, the title alludes to a poem by Yeats, drawing on the poetic imagination as signifying the possibility of life after death. Larry McMurtry, *Horsemen, Pass By* (New York: Simon & Schuster, 1961), 160. McMurtry, like his contemporaries Annie Proulx and Cormac McCarthy, writes about a west that is no longer the frontier of imagination, but rather a post-agrarian wasteland of stymied possibility. To tell the story of a west that is no longer (at least for white Americans) a frontier of opportunity and promise, they turn to old age and euthanasia.

55. McMurtry, *Walter Benjamin at the Dairy Queen*, 105.

56. The addition of euthanasia/abortion does not appear in drafts marked June 2004, but first appears in Draft of *No Country for Old Men* (June 12, 2014), Cormac McCarthy Papers, the Witliff Collection, Box 83, Folder 2, Texas State University, San Marcos, TX.

57. Cormac McCarthy, *No Country for Old Men* (New York: Vintage, 2005), 197. Hereafter cited parenthetically in the text.

58. Draft of *No Country for Old Men* (1987), Cormac McCarthy Papers, the Witliff Collection, Box 79, Folder 2, Texas State University, San Marcos, TX.

59. Temple Grandin, "Euthanasia and Slaughter of Livestock," *Journal of the American Veterinary Medical Association,* vol. 204 (1994): 1354–1360.

60. W. B. Yeats, *Yeats's Poetry, Drama, and Prose*, ed. James Pethica (New York: Norton, 2000), 81, line 29.

61. Cormac McCarthy, "The Kekulé Problem: Where Did Language Come From?" *Nautilus* (April 20, 2017): http://nautil.us/issue/47/consciousness/the-kekul-problem

62. Mark Goble, "How the West Slows Down," conference paper, Post45 conference, University of North Carolina-Chapel Hill (October 25, 2014).

63. Jodi Picoult, *Mercy* (New York: G. P. Putnam's Sons, 1996), 477.

64. Ibid., 203.

65. Ibid., 379.

66. David T. Mitchell and Sharon L. Snyder, *Narrative Prosthesis: Disability and the Dependencies of Discourse* (Ann Arbor: University of Michigan Press, 2000), 1–15.

67. Ryan Gilbey, "'I'm Not a Thing to Be Pitied': The Disability Backlash Against *Me Before You*," *The Guardian* (June 2, 2016): https://www.theguardian.com/film/2016/jun/02/me-before-you-disabled-backlash-not-pitied

68. Felicia Ackerman, "Assisted Suicide, Terminal Illness, Severe Disability, and the Double Standard," *Physician Assisted Suicide: Expanding the Debate*, eds. M. Pabst Battin, Rosamond Rhodes, and Anita Silvers (New York: Routledge, 1998), 151.

Conclusion

1. For the observation that genre and literary fiction have converged, see Lev Grossman, "Literary Revolution in the Supermarket Aisle: Genre Fiction Is Disruptive Technology," *Time Magazine* (May 23, 2012): https://entertainment.time.com/2012/05/23/genre-fiction-is-disruptive-technology/. For critiques of the idea that the boundaries between genre and literary fiction are disappearing, see Günter Leypoldt, "Social Dimensions of the Turn to Genre: Junot Díaz's *Oscar Wao* and Kazuo Ishiguro's *The Buried Giant*," *Post 45* (March 31, 2018): https://post45.org/2018/03/social-dimensions-of-the-turn-to-genre-junot-diazs-oscar-wao-and-kazuo-ishiguros-the-buried-giant/; and Jeremy Rosen, "Literary Fiction and the Genres of Genre Fiction," *Post45* (August 7, 2018): https://post45.org/2018/08/literary-fiction-and-the-genres-of-genre-fiction/

2. For a version of this perspective, see Seo-Young Chu, *Do Metaphors Dream of Literal Sleep?: A Science Fictional Theory of Representation* (Cambridge, MA: Harvard University Press, 2011).

3. See, on the rise of conglomerates, Dan Sinykin, "The Conglomerate Era: Publishing, Authorship, and Literary Form, 1965–2007," *Contemporary Literature*, vol. 58, no. 4 (Winter 2017): 462–491. As Sinykin points out, an interesting exception is the rise of nonprofits like Graywolf, which nonetheless seek symbolic capital that is convertible into financial capital. Thus we could read a book like Carmen Maria Machado's *Her Body* as drawing on generic forms like the Grimm fairy tale and *Law and Order* in order to channel disgust at abusive patriarchal values. The horror and disgust provide some market potential, but the political point the book makes give it the symbolic cultural capital Sinykin describes. For an argument that liberal reading still persists in some form, see Rachel Greenwald Smith, *Affect and American Literature in the Age of Neoliberalism* (Cambridge, UK: Cambridge University Press, 2015).

4. Mark McGurl, "Unspeakable Conventionality: The Perversity of the Kindle," *American Literary History*, vol. 33, no. 2 (Summer 2021): 394–415.

5. Shoshana Zuboff, *The Age of Surveillance Capitalism: The Fight for a Human Future at the New Frontier of Power* (New York: Hachette, 2019), 7.

6. Mark McGurl, *The Program Era: Postwar Fiction and the Rise of Creative Writing* (Cambridge, MA: Harvard University Press, 2011).

7. Gish Jen, Interview with the author (May 28, 2021), telephone, quotation used with permission of Gish Jen.

8. Ibid.; Gish Jen, *The Girl at the Baggage Claim: Explaining the East-West Culture Gap* (New York: Penguin, 2017), 21.

9. Jen, *Girl at the Baggage Claim*, 224–225; Jen, Interview with the author (May 28, 2021).

10. Gish Jen, *The Resisters* (New York: Knopf, 2020), cover.

11. Gish Jen, "The Resisters," book talk at American Academy of Arts & Sciences (March 6, 2020), Cambridge, MA, used with permission of Gish Jen.

12. Jen, *The Resisters*, 6.

13. Jen, *The Girl at the Baggage Claim*, 59–147.

14. Meredith Maran, Interview with Gish Jen, "Horror Has Become Normal," *Los Angeles Review of Books* (July 8, 2020): https://lareviewofbooks.org/article/horror-has-become-normal-an-interview-with-gish-jen/

15. Jen, *The Resisters*, 3.

16. See Laura McGrath, "Comping White," *LA Review of Books* (January 21, 2019): https://lareviewofbooks.org/article/comping-white/

17. Raffi Khatchadourian, "N. K. Jemisin's Dream Worlds," *New Yorker* (January 20, 2020): https://www.newyorker.com/magazine/2020/01/27/nk-jemisins-dream-worlds

18. N. K. Jemisin, Hugo Award acceptance speech (August 19, 2018): https://www.youtube.com/watch?v=8lFybhRxoVM

19. N. K. Jemisin, *The Fifth Season* (New York: Orbit Books, 2015), 422.

20. Khatchadourian, "Jemisin's Dream Worlds."

21. N. K. Jemisin, "Growing Your Iceberg," lecture for the Writers' Digest Online Workshop and Annual Conference (August 2015), available at N. K. Jemisin, "Worldbuilding 101": https://nkjemisin.com/2015/08/worldbuilding-101/

22. *Lawrence v. Texas* 539 U.S. 558 (2003) (Thomas, C., dissenting), 606. Thomas quoted from Justice Potter Stewart.

23. Ruth Bader Ginsburg, "Some Thoughts on Autonomy and Equality in Relation to *Roe v. Wade*," *North Carolina Law Review*, vol. 63 (1984): 375–386, quotation on 386.

24. *United States v. Krueger*, No. 14–3035, 16 (10th Cir. 2015) (Gorsuch, N., concurring). See my "Privacy Cultures," *Public Books* (July 25, 2018): https://www.publicbooks.org/privacy-cultures/

Index

Page numbers in *italics* refer to illustrations.

abortion, 1–2, 4–5, 16, 75–100, 114, 156–57, 169
"Abortion and the Conscience of the Nation" (Reagan), 75
Ackerman, Felicia, 162
Adorno, Theodor, 8–9, 41
Again, Dangerous Visions (Vonnegut), 93
Alien 3 (film), 98
Allison, Hughes, 50, 53
Als, Hilton, 51
alterity, 24–25, 34
alternative medicine, 4
Amazon, 165
The Ambassadors (James), 39, 41, 45
American Civil Liberties Union (ACLU), 4, 6
"The Android and the Human" (Dick), 88–89
Angle of Repose (Stegner), 148
"Apostrophe, Animation, and Abortion" (Johnson), 77
Arnold, Matthew, 25
"Art and Fortune" (Trilling), 35
"The Art of Fiction" (James), 26, 45
Atonement (McEwan), 127
Atwood, Margaret, 1–2, 76–77, 98
Austen, Jane, 166

Bacall, Lauren, 150
background checks, 22

The Bad Seed (film), 101
Baldwin, Simeon E., 136
Ball, John, 50
Barth, John, 78–79
"The Battered-Child Syndrome" (Kempe et al.), 104–5
Beast in View (Millar), 31–34, 45
"Beast in View" (Rukeyser), 33
Becker, Ernest, 147
Beloved (Morrison), 127
Berlant, Lauren, 77
Bérubé, Michael, 89
"Bewilderment" (Hughes), 28
Bierce, Ambrose, 103
"The Big Space Fuck" (Vonnegut), 93
Bill of Rights, 3–4
Black Power movement, 73
Blade Runner (film), 92
Blatty, William Peter, 16, 108, 112
Blind Man with a Pistol (Himes), 64, 72
Blood and Guts in High School (Acker), 127
"Bloodchild" (Butler), 13, 94–95, 97
The Bluest Eye (Morrison), 65, 126–27
The Blunderer (Highsmith), 40
Boone, Daniel, 148
Booth, Wayne, 24–25, 45
Boucher, Anthony, 72
Brandeis, Louis, 3, 6, 22
Broady, Charles, 49, 62
The Broken Earth (Jemisin), 168–69

213

Broome, Homer, 62
Brown, Charles Brockden, 101, 103
Brown, Claude, 65
Brown, Lloyd L., 54
Brown, Nicholas, 9
Brown, Sterling, 49
"Brown Doughboy" (Kimbrough), 63
"Bury Me Not on the Lone Prairie" (song), 148
Bush Mama (film), 51
Butler, Octavia, 2, 11–15, 77, 79, 94–98, 108

California, 98
California Eagle (newspaper), 60
Canavan, Gerry, 96
The Canterbury Tales (Chaucer), 1
Capote, Truman, 35, 43–44
Carrie (De Palma), 107, 125
Carrie (King), 103, 104, 107, 118, 119–21, 123
Carson, Ben, 75
Castle, William, 103, 109, 112
The Castle of Otranto (Walpole), 10
Cast the First Stone (Himes), 48
Chabon, Michael, 164
Chaucer, Geoffrey, 1
Chiang, Ted, 164
child abuse, 14, 16, 101, 104–8, 110, 112, 114–28
Child Abuse and Prevention and Treatment Act (CAPTA, 1974), 14, 104, 105
chivalric romance, 131, 132
The Cider House Rules (Irving), 127
civil liberties, 3
Civil Rights Act (1965), 3
civil rights movement, 73
Clark, Walter Van Tilburg, 149
Cocteau, Jean, 72
Cohen, Kathryn, 18
Cohen, Larry, 101, 112
Coleridge, Samuel Taylor, 151, 152
collectivism, 143, 145, 146, 147
Collins, Suzanne, 171

Collins, Willkie, 103
The Color Purple (Walker), 127
communism, 7, 20, 21
The Confessions of Nat Turner (Styron), 65
The Conjure-Man Dies (Fisher), 50
contraception, 22, 81, 82
Cooper, James Fenimore, 10, 131, 148
Cornell, Drucilla, 100
"Corollary" (Allison), 50, 53
Cotton Comes to Harlem (Himes), 73
Coward-McCann (publisher), 35, 39
The Crack in Space (Dick), 87
Cram, Ethel, 135–36
The Crazy Kill (Himes), 61
credit bureaus, 22
crime fiction, 2, 11, 14, 26–47, 53
"Croatoan" (Ellison), 93
Cronin, Mary Jane, 106
Crouching Tiger, Hidden Dragon (Lee), 166
The Cry of the Owl (Highsmith), 40
The Curse of the Cat People (film), 103

Dark Certainty (Hughes), 28
Deadwood (television series), 148
Dear Teen-Ager (Van Buren), 114, 115
Death with Dignity Act (Oregon, 1997), 14, 16, 129
Debs, Eugene V., 59
Defender of the Angels (Kimbrough), 65–69
Denial of Death (Becker), 147
DeShaney v. Winnebago County (1989), 124
Díaz, Junot, 164
Dick, Anne, 85
Dick, Philip K., 2, 9, 12, 13, 15, 75–79, 83–92, 97–98
Dickinson, G. Lowes, 136–37, 138
Didion, Joan, 78–79
"The Dilemma of the Negro Novelist in the U.S." (Himes), 71
dime novels, 147, 148
disability studies, 13, 96, 161

Do Androids Dream of Electric Sheep? (Dick), 75, 76, 77, 86, 89–92, 96
Dr. Bloodmoney (Dick), 86–87
Doctorow, E. L., 149
Donne, John, 194n14
Don Quixote (Cervantes), 155
Double Indemnity (Wilder), 26
Douglas, William O., 4
Doyle, Arthur Conan, 20
Dragnet (radio and television program), 50
Duden, Barbara, 77
due process, 4, 124
Duhamel, Marcel, 48, 54, 72
Dunphy, Jack, 43
Dworkin, Ronald, 131, 136, 142, 149, 153, 158

Eburne, Jonathan, 69–70
Ehrlich, Paul, 87
Eisenstadt v. Baird (1972), 4
11/22/63 (King), 118
Eliot, T. S., 194–95n15
Ellenborough's Act (1803), 80
Ellison, Harlan, 15, 77, 93
Ellison, Ralph, 52–53, 73
The End of a Primitive (Himes), 54, 72
The End of the Affair (Greene), 25
The End of the Road (Barth), 78–79
Enoch Dawson (Kimbrough), 65
Ethan Frome (Wharton), 141
eugenics, 16, 89, 96
euthanasia, 4; legalization of, 129; in realist fiction, 13, 16, 132, 133–43, 146; in romance novels, 16, 160–62; in science fiction, 143–46; in westerns, 16, 130–31, 146–60
"Euthanasia Again" (Gilman), 144
"Euthanasia for Incurables" (Gilman), 144–45
"The Evening, the Morning, and the Night" (Butler), 96–97
The Exorcist (Blatty), 112–16
The Exorcist (Friedkin), 101, 103–4, 107, 108, 116, 119, 123, 126

Fall River textile strike, 59
Farrow, Mia, 101, 110
Faulkner, William: Highsmith influenced by, 35–36, 46; Himes influenced by, 48, 51, 56–57, 58, 61, 69; King's allusion to, 121, 123; liberal personhood embraced by, 165; on privacy, 8
federalism, 3
"Female Gothic" (Moers), 79
The Feminine Mystique (Friedan), 23
feminism, 13, 108
Fiedler, Leslie, 26–27
The Fifth Season (Jemisin), 169
Finkbine, Sherri, 87
First Amendment, 4
"First-Person Novel" (Highsmith), 18–19, 37
Fisher, Rudolph, 50
The Fixed Period (Trollope), 146–47
Flash (magazine), 63
flat characters, 10, 13, 20, 51–52, 58, 69, 73, 74, 103
Fletcher, Ben, 59
Ford, John, 149
Forerunner (magazine), 143–44
For Love of Imabelle / *A Rage in Harlem* (Himes), 55, 61, 69–70, 72
Forman, James, Jr., 50
Forster, E. M., 10, 25
Fourteenth Amendment, 4
Fourth Amendment, 4
Frankenstein (Shelley), 10, 77, 79–80, 96
Frankfurt, Steve, 110
Franzen, Jonathan, 8
freedom of assembly, 4
freedom of association, 22
The French Connection (Friedkin), 116
Freud, Sigmund, 104
Friday the Thirteenth (film), 124
Friedan, Betty, 6, 23
Friedkin, William, 117
The Fruit of the Tree (Wharton), 13, 16, 132, 133–43

Gaddis, William, 42
Gardiner, Harold C., 25
gay and lesbian rights, 4, 5, 6
Gay Liberation Front, 6
Georgia Sundown (Kimbrough), 64
Gibbs, Matthew, 60
Gibson, William, 164
Gikandi, Simon, 89
Gil, David, 105
Gilman, Charlotte Perkins, 13, 16, 132, 143–46
Ginsburg, Ruth Bader, 170
Giono, Jean, 72
The Girl at the Baggage Claim (Jen), 165
Glendon, Mary Ann, 7
Goble, Mark, 160
God Help the Child (Morrison), 127
Goines, Donald, 51
Goldberg, Arthur, 22
Goodin, David, 27
Gordon, Hugh, 59
Gorsuch, Neil, 147, 170–71
The Great Gatsby (Fitzgerald), 39, 41
The Green Mile (King), 118
Greene, Graham, 25
Greenlee, Sam, 50–51
Griffin, Melvin, 60–61
Grisham, John, 164
Griswold v. Connecticut (1965), 2, 4, 5, 14, 15, 22, 49, 108

Habermas, Jürgen, 7, 8–9, 25
Hacking, Ian, 104
Halloween (film), 124
Halperin, David, 40
Hamilton, James H., 137
The Handmaid's Tale (Atwood), 1–2, 98
Harper & Co., 35
Harris v. McRae (1980), 96
Hartouni, Valerie, 77
Hauck, Christina, 77
Hayles, N. Katherine, 83, 88
Haywood, Bill, 59
Heard, Nathan, 51
The Heat's On (Himes), 64, 70

"He Knew" (Himes), 58, 69
Hemlock Society, 129
Herland (Gilman), 145
Hernandez, Kelly Lytle, 50, 66
The Hidden Persuaders (Packard), 110
Highsmith, Patricia, 2, 9, 12, 15, 18–21, 27, 28, 34–46
Hill, Anna, 135, 137
Hill, Ellen, 18
Hilton, James, 161
Himes, Chester, 2, 12, 15, 48–61, 64, 66, 69–74
Himes, Joe, 70
Hitchcock, Alfred, 103
Hobbs, Ronald, 65
Hoberek, Andrew, 9
Horseman, Pass By (McMurtry), 129
Hostage to the Devil (Martin), 117
Housekeeping (Robinson), 127
The House of Mirth (Wharton), 141
Howe, Irving, 26
Hughes, Dorothy, 15, 19–21, 27, 28–31, 46
Hughes, Langston, 49
The Hulk (Lee), 166
Humphrey, Gordon, 106
Humphries, Laud, 23
Humphry, Derek, 129, 160
"Humpy" (Kimbrough), 64
The Hundred Thousand Kingdoms (Jemisin), 168
The Hunger Games (Collins), 7
Hunt, Lynn, 7
Hunter, Evan, 48
Huntington's disease, 97
Hurston, Zora Neale, 49
Hyde Amendment (1976), 50

I, AutoHouse (Jen), 168
Iceberg Slim, 51
identity theft, 13, 15, 47
If He Hollers Let Him Go (Himes), 53
Igo, Sarah, 7
Imperial Valley lettuce strike (1930), 59
"Imposture" (Allison), 50, 53

In a Lonely Place (Hughes), 29–30, 31
In Cold Blood (Capote), 43–44
Industrial Workers of the World (IWW), 59, 60
In re Quinlan (1976), 14
International Literature (magazine), 59, 63
interracial marriage, 81
In the Heat of the Night (Ball), 50, 65
Ishiguro, Kazuo, 164
It (film), 125
It (King), 118
It Lives Again (Cohen), 112
It's Alive (Cohen), 101, 112, *113*

Jackson, Delphinia, 61
James, Henry, 13, 25, 26, 39, 45–46, 135, 143
James, Marlon, 164
Jameson, Fredric, 83, 185n96
Jefferson, Thomas, 89
Jemisin, N. K., 164, 168–70
Jen, Gish, 164, 165–68, 170
Jean's Way (Humphry), 160
Johnson, Barbara, 77, 78, 100
Johnson, Samuel, 41
Jonson, Ben, 194n14
Joyce, James, 46, 121, 123

Kant, Immanuel, 158
Kaplan, Amy, 134
Kass, Leon, 150
Katz v. United States (1967), 4, 15, 33, 50, 109
Kempe, C. Henry, 104
Ketchum, Jack, 118
Kevorkian, Jack, 147
Kimbrough, Jess, 15, 49, 50–52, 58–69, 74
King, Stephen, 2, 9, 12, 16, 104, 118–24, 166
Kinsey, Alfred, 23, 26
A Kitchen in Sandton (Kimbrough), 65
"Kubla Khan" (Coleridge), 151, 152
Kubrick, Stanley, 99
Ku Klux Klan, 60

L'Amour, Louis, 149
Lapsley, Gaillard, 136
Latimer, Heather, 77
League of American Writers, 49
Lee, Ang, 166
Lee, Chang-rae, 164
Le Guin, Ursula K., 15, 77, 99–100
Lem, Stanislaw, 88
Leone, Sergio, 149, 160
Lesch-Nyhan syndrome, 97
Lethem, Jonathan, 164
Levin, Ira, 16, 108
The Liberal Imagination (Trilling), 26
liberalism: classical formulation of, 7, 10, 12, 25, 107; complexity and fragility of, 164; empathy linked to, 15, 31, 42–43, 143; family life and, 161; genre fiction vs., 9, 12, 13, 27, 46, 163, 164; posthumanist rejection of, 83, 92; postwar vision of, 4, 5, 6, 8, 12, 14, 15, 20, 21, 23, 36, 38, 47, 165; rationality linked to, 8, 27, 107, 118, 135, 143; Trilling's view of, 24, 38; westerns and, 148, 149, 150, 152–53, 160
lie detectors, 22
Life (magazine), 77, 81, 99
Lincoln, Abraham, 75
Link, Kelly, 164
Llewellyn Iron Works strike (1916), 59
Lockwood, Patricia, 100
Logan's Run (film), 147
Lolita (Nabokov), 26, 27
The Lonely Crowd (Riesman), 21
The Lonely Crusade (Himes), 48, 53–54, 66
Lonesome Dove (McMurtry), 16, 129, 147, 148, 153–54, 155–56
Lovecraft, H. P., 103
"The Lure of the Black Belt" (Kimbrough), 63

Ma, Ling, 164
Macbeth (Shakespeare), 41
Macdonald, Dwight, 8–9, 26, 41, 76
Machado, Carmen Maria, 164

MacKinnon, Catharine, 94, 95
MaddAddam (Atwood), 98
The Magic Flute (Mozart), 90
Maher v. Roe (1977), 96
Make Room! Make Room! (Harrison), 147
Manchild in the Promised Land (Brown), 65
"Manners, Morals, and the Novel" (Trilling), 23–24
Manson, Charles, 117
The Man Whose Teeth Were All Exactly Alike (Dick), 83–84
The Man Who Shot Liberty Valance (Ford), 148
marital rape, 5, 23
Marnie (Hitchcock), 103
Marsten, Richard (pseud. of Evan Hunter), 48, 55, 69
Martin, Gertrude, 55
Martin, Malachi, 117
Martin, Theodore, 10, 52
Marxism, 13
"The Masque of the Red Death" (Poe), 123
Mass Culture (anthology), 26
Massood, Paula J., 187–88n18
McBain, Ed (pseud. of Evan Hunter), 48, 50
McCann, Sean, 27, 51
McCarthy, Cormac, 2, 132, 149, 156–60
McClanahan, Annie, 108
McEwan, Ian, 164
McGurl, Mark, 8, 40–41, 76, 134, 165
McMurtry, Larry, 9, 16, 147–49, 153–56, 160
Me Before You (film), 162
Medicaid, 96
mental illness, 4
Mercy (Picoult), 16, 132, 160–61, 162
Methodism, 133
Michelle Remembers (Smith and Pazder), 108, 117
Mill, John Stuart, 25
Millar, Margaret, 15, 19–21, 27, 28, 31–34, 46

Miller Act (1948), 23, 36
Mills, C. Wright, 21
Mitchell, David, 161–62
modernism, 40–41, 45
Moers, Ellen, 77, 79
Mondale, Walter, 16, 105–6, 119, 124
"Morality Meat" (Sheldon), 93–94
morphine, 133
Morrison, Toni, 126–27
Muhammad, Khalil Gibran, 52
Murakami, Haruki, 164
Myrdal, Gunnar, 52, 53
The Mysteries of Udolpho (Radcliffe), 101

Nagel, Thomas, 131
The Naked Society (Packard), 21, 110
National Center on Child Abuse and Neglect, 104
National Organization for Women, 6
Native Son (Wright), 52, 53
Nazis, 146
The Negro Caravan (Brown), 49
Nelson, Deborah, 78
Neoplatonism, 136, 138
New Ethicists, 12–13
News Review (magazine), 112
New Yorker, 34, 35, 43
New York Sun, 141–42
New York Times, 137, 141
Nguyen, Viet Thanh, 164
Nightmare on Elm Street (film), 124
Nineteen Eighty-Four (Orwell), 7
Nixon, Richard M., 105
No Country for Old Men (Coen brothers), 148
No Country for Old Men (McCarthy), 14, 129, 156–60
Norton, Charles Eliot, 135, 137, 142
Norton, Sally, 136
"Notes from a Respectable Cockroach" (Highsmith), 45
Nozick, Robert, 131
Nussbaum, Hedda, 106
Nussbaum, Martha, 7

O'Connor, Sandra Day, 99
Of Woman Born (Rich), 82
Oliver Twist (Dickens), 104
Olmstead v. United States (1927), 22
The Omen (film), 117, 119, 125
"On Privacy" (Faulkner), 8
On Writing (King), 118
The Organization Man (Whyte), 21
The Other (film), 101, *102*, 119, 125
Our Town (Wilder), 39
overpopulation, 87, 93
The Ox-Bow Incident (Clark), 148

Packard, Vance, 21, 110
Pamela (Richardson), 10
Partisan Review, 35
"A Path Upward" (Kimbrough), 63
Patternist series (Butler), 94
Patterson, James, 164
Pazder, Lawrence, 108
Perrin, Tom, 36
personality tests, 22
Petchesky, Rosalind Pollack, 77, 78
phenylketonuria, 97
Picoult, Jodi, 16, 118, 132, 160–61
Pike, James, 92
Pinchev, Julius, 64
Pinktoes (Himes), 72
Planned Parenthood v. Casey (1992), 5, 99, 131
Play It as It Lays (Didion), 78–79
Poe, Edgar Allan, 10, 20, 123
point of view, 45–46
Polanski, Roman, 112
police procedurals, 2, 12, 47, 50
policing, 22
polygraph tests, 22
The Population Bomb (Ehrlich), 87
Portis, Charles, 150
posthumanism, 83, 88, 92, 98
Powers, Richard, 8
"The Pre-Persons" (Dick), 76, 83–84, 92, 98
The Price of Salt (Highsmith), 19, 35, 36–37, 38, 40

privacy torts, 3
private investigators, 21–22
Prometheus (film), 98
Proulx, Annie, 148, 149
Psycho (Hitchcock), 103, 116, 120, 125
"The Psychology of the Negro Criminal" (Kimbrough), 62–63
Puberty (Munch), 90
"Purity" (Hughes), 28

The Quality of Hurt (Himes), 70–71
queer theory, 13
Quinlan, Karen Ann, 150

A Rage in Harlem / For Love of Imabelle (Himes), 55, 61, 69–70, 72
Rabbit Run (Updike), 78–79
Ramsey, JonBenét, 75, 112
Rawls, John, 5–6, 131
The Real Cool Killers (Himes), 58, 70
The Recognitions (Gaddis), 42
Rehnquist, William, 124
The Resisters (Jen), 165–68
Revolutionary Road (Yates), 78–79, 83
Rich, Adrienne, 82
Richardson, Samuel, 10
Riesman, David, 21
"rights revolution," 3
"The Right to Die" (Gilman), 145–46
"The Right to Privacy" (Warren and Brandeis), 3, 6
Rinzler, Alan, 65–66
Ripley novels (Highsmith), 9, 10, 12, 18–19, 20, 35, 38–47
Rivera, Geraldo, 106
Roberts, Dorothy, 6
Robinson, Kim Stanley, 164
Roe v. Wade (1973), 2, 14, 77, 79, 82, 108, 109; criticisms of, 5, 76, 84, 170; expanded privacy rights linked to, 4, 5, 6, 15, 49, 75, 76; limited effect of, 49–50, 95–96; outlook for, 17; trimester framework of, 81
Rokotov, Timofei, 191n74
romance novels, 16, 160–62

Romanticism, 42, 151, 152
Room (Donoghue), 127
Rosemary's Baby (Polanski), 101, 103, 107, 108–12, 119, 124
Roth, Philip, 131
Rubenfeld, Jed, 82
Rukeyser, Muriel, 33
Runaway Black (Marsten), 48, 51, 54–56
Run Man Run (Himes), 55–56

"Sailing to Byzantium" (Yeats), 158–59
Salem's Lot (King), 118
Sanctuary (Faulkner), 48, 51, 56–57
Scanlon, Thomas, 131
Schenkar, Joan, 42
science fiction, 1, 2, 10, 11, 15, 75–100, 132, 146
Scott, Daryl Michael, 52
Sedgwick, Eve Kosofsky, 40, 45–46
search and seizure, 4
Seltzer, Mark, 127
Sense and Sensibility (Austen), 166
sex work, 4
The Shadow of the Glen (Synge), 30–31
Shaft (Tidyman), 65, 66
Shakespeare, William, 41, 131
Sheldon, Alice (James Tiptree, Jr.), 15, 77, 93–94
Shelley, Mary, 10, 77, 79
Shelley, Percy Bysshe, 80
The Shining (King), 118, 121–24
The Shining (Kubrick), 103, 107, 125, 126
The Shootist (Portis), 150–53
The Shootist (Swarthout), 16, 129, 149, 150, 153
Shusterman, Neal, 98
Shyamalan, M. Night, 125
The Sixth Sense (Shyamalan), 125–26
The Silent Scream (film), 78
Sinykin, Dan, 164
Skattebol, Kate "Kingsley," 36
slavery, 15, 55, 67, 75–76, 78, 82, 89, 95
Smith, Adam, 12, 25
Smith, Michelle, 108
"The Snail-Watcher" (Highsmith), 37–38
Snyder, Sharon, 161–62
The Sociological Imagination (Mills), 21
Solove, Daniel, 5
Sontag, Susan, 39
Soylent Green (film), 147
The Spook Who Sat by the Door (Greenlee), 50–51
spousal rape, 5, 23
stalking, 13, 15, 47
"Standing Ground" (Le Guin), 99–100
Star Trek: Enterprise, 98
Stearns, Henry S., 137
Stegner, Wallace, 148, 149
Steichen, Edward, 114
Steinberg, Joel, 106
Steinberg, Lisa, 106
The Stepford Wives (Levin), 108
sterilization, 81
Stevens, John Paul, 5
Stewart, Jimmy, 150
The Stone Sky (Jemisin), 169
stop and frisk, 50
Strangers on a Train (Highsmith), 40–42, 46
Strangers on a Train (Hitchcock), 40
Stranger Things (television series), 124
Straub, Peter, 118
stream of consciousness, 45, 46, 119, 121, 123
A Streetcar Named Desire (Kazan), 37
Streets of Laredo (McMurtry), 129, 154–55
"Streets of Laredo" (song), 148
Student Nonviolent Coordinating Committee (SNCC), 66
Styron, William, 65
subliminal advertising, 22, 110
Superfly (film), 51
surveillance, 4, 5, 13, 15, 21–22, 165
Sutin, Lawrence, 85
Swarthout, Glendon, 16, 150–51, 156, 160

Sweet Sweetback's Baadasssss Song (film), 51
Synge, J. M., 30

The Talented Mr. Ripley (Highsmith), 35, 38–47
Targ, William, 56
Tate, Sharon, 117
Tearoom Trade (Humphries), 23
Terry v. Ohio (1968), 50
thalidomide, 80, 86–87, 96, 97
A Theory of Justice (Rawls), 5–6
The Theory of Moral Sentiments (Smith), 12
Thomas, Clarence, 170
Thompson, Jim, 27
Thomson, Judith Jarvis, 81, 131
Thornburgh v. American College of Obstetricians and Gynecologists (1986), 5, 82
Tidyman, Ernest, 65
Timon of Athens (Shakespeare), 161
Tiptree, James, Jr. (Alice Sheldon), 15, 77, 93–94
"Tits-Up in a Ditch" (Proulx), 148
Tolstoy, Leo, 131
totalitarianism, 7, 20, 21
Trask, Michael, 39, 45
The Tremor of Forgery (Highsmith), 40
Tribe, Laurence, 82
Trilling, Lionel, 7, 23–27, 35–36, 38, 39, 45, 163
Tristram Shandy (Sterne), 34
Trollope, Anthony, 146–47
True Grit (film), 148, 150
Trumbo, Dalton, 64
The Turn of the Screw (James), 45
2001: A Space Odyssey (Kubrick), 7, 99

Ubik (Dick), 88
Ulysses (Joyce), 40
unenumerated rights, 4
Unforgiven (Eastwood), 148

U.S. Information Agency (USIA), 112, 114
Unwind (Shusterman), 98
Updike, John, 78–79
utilitarianism, 135

Vacco v. Quill (1997), 14, 131
Van Buren, Abigail, 114
VanderMeer, Jeff, 164
Van Vechten, Carl, 72
Vonnegut, Kurt, 15, 77, 93

Wallace, David Foster, 8, 163
Walpole, Horace, 10
Walter Benjamin at the Dairy Queen (McMurtry), 155
War on Crime, 14, 15
War on Drugs, 50
War on Poverty, 14, 15, 49, 50
Warren, Earl, 4
Warren, Samuel, 2–3, 6
Washington v. Glucksberg (1997), 131
The Waste Land (Eliot), 194–95n15
Watt, Ian, 7, 25
Watts riots (1965), 50, 60, 68, 73
Wayne, John, 147, 148, 150, 153
The Wealth of Nations (Smith), 12
We Can Build You (Dick), 85–86, 91
Weingarten, Karen, 77
Welcome to Hard Times (Doctorow), 149
westerns, 16, 129–31, 146–60
Wharton, Edith, 16, 132, 133–35, 138–43, 146, 149
Whitehead, Colson, 164
Whyte, William H., 21
Wieland (Brown), 103
Wilder, Thornton, 39
Williams, John, 149
Williamson, Adina, 66
Wilson, Edmund, 8, 26
Wilt, Judith, 79
Wimsatt, W. K., 24

wiretapping, 21, 109
With Her in Ourland (Gilman), 145
The Woman in White (Collins), 103
The Woman Warrior (Kingston), 127
Woods, Gerald, 62
Woolrich, Cornell, 27
Wordsworth, William, 178n46
World and Town (Jen), 166
Wright, Richard, 52, 53, 73

Xenogenesis trilogy (Butler), 94, 96

Yates, Richard, 78–79, 83
Yeats, William Butler, 158–59
Yesterday Will Make You Cry (Himes), 48
Yu, Charles, 164

Ziegler, Mary, 4
Zuboff, Shoshana, 165

Joseph Darda, *The Strange Career of Racial Liberalism*

Jordan S. Carroll, *Reading the Obscene: Transgressive Editors and the Class Politics of US Literature*

Michael Dango, *Crisis Style: The Aesthetics of Repair*

Mary Esteve, *Incremental Realism: Postwar American Fiction, Happiness, and Welfare-State Liberalism*

Dorothy J. Hale, *The Novel and the New Ethics*

Christine Hong, *A Violent Peace: Race, U.S. Militarism, and Cultures of Democratization in Cold War Asia and the Pacific*

Sarah Brouillette, *UNESCO and the Fate of the Literary*

Sophie Seita, *Provisional Avant-Gardes: Little Magazine Communities from Dada to Digital*

Guy Davidson, *Categorically Famous: Literary Celebrity and Sexual Liberation in 1960s America*

Joseph Jonghyun Jeon, *Vicious Circuits: Korea's IMF Cinema and the End of the American Century*

Lytle Shaw, *Narrowcast: Poetry and Audio Research*

Stephen Schryer, *Maximum Feasible Participation: American Literature and the War on Poverty*

Margaret Ronda, *Remainders: American Poetry at Nature's End*

Jasper Bernes, *The Work of Art in the Age of Deindustrialization*

Annie McClanahan, *Dead Pledges: Debt, Crisis, and Twenty-First-Century Culture*

Amy Hungerford, *Making Literature Now*

J. D. Connor, *The Studios After the Studios: Neoclassical Hollywood (1970–2010)*

Michael Trask, *Camp Sites: Sex, Politics, and Academic Style in Postwar America*

Loren Glass, *Counterculture Colophon: Grove Press, the Evergreen Review, and the Incorporation of the Avant-Garde*

Michael Szalay, *Hip Figures: A Literary History of the Democratic Party*

Jared Gardner, *Projections: Comics and the History of Twenty-First-Century Storytelling*

Jerome Christensen, *America's Corporate Art: The Studio Authorship of Hollywood Motion Pictures*

The authorized representative in the EU for product safety and compliance is:
Mare Nostrum Group
B.V Doelen 72
4831 GR Breda
The Netherlands

www.ingramcontent.com/pod-product-compliance
Lightning Source LLC
Chambersburg PA
CBHW030620230426
43661CB00053B/2083